The Freud Wars

GW00836252

The Freud Wars offers a comprehensive introduction to the crucial question of the justification of psychoanalysis.

Part I examines three powerful critiques of psychoanalysis in the context of a recent controversy about its nature and legitimacy: is it a bankrupt science, an innovative science, or not a science at all but a system of interpretation? The discussion makes sense of the entrenched disagreement about the validity of psychoanalysis, and demonstrates how the disagreement is rooted in the theoretical ambiguity of the central concept of psychoanalysis, the unconscious. This ambiguity is then presented as the pathway to a new way of understanding psychoanalysis, based on a mode of thinking that precedes division into mental and physical. The reader is drawn into a lively and thought-provoking analysis of the central issues:

- What would it mean for psychoanalysis to count as a science?
- Is psychoanalysis a form of hermeneutics?
- How can mental and physical explanations coincide?

Part II contains the source material for Part I: the influential critiques of psychoanalysis by Adolf Grünbaum, Thomas Nagel and Jürgen Habermas.

No specialized knowledge is assumed, and the book is clear and accessible while still conveying the complexity and richness of the subject. It provides a fascinating introduction to philosophical thinking on psychoanalysis for students and practitioners of psychoanalysis, psychotherapy and philosophy.

Lavinia Gomez is a psychotherapist in private practice in London.

The Freud Wars

Robert J. Elliott
81 Purley Vale
Purley
Surrey CR8 2DW
020 8660 2634

An introduction to the philosophy of psychoanalysis

Lavinia Gomez

Routledge
Taylor & Francis Group

LONDON AND NEW YORK

First published 2005 by Routledge
27 Church Road, Hove, East Sussex, BN3 2FA

Simultaneously published in the USA and Canada
by Routledge
270 Madison Avenue, New York, NY 10016

Routledge is an imprint of the Taylor & Francis Group

© 2005 Lavinia Gomez

Typeset in Times by Keystroke, Jacaranda Lodge, Wolverhampton
Printed and bound in Great Britain by Biddles Ltd, Guildford and King's Lynn
Paperback cover design by Sandra Heath

This publication has been produced with paper manufactured to strict
environmental standards and with pulp derived from sustainable forests.

British Library Cataloguing in Publication Data
A catalogue record for this book is available from the British Library

Library of Congress Cataloging in Publication Data
Gomez, Lavinia.
   The Freud wars : an introduction to the philosophy of psychoanalysis /
Lavinia Gomez.
       p. cm.
   Includes bibliographical references (p.   ) and index.
   ISBN 1-58391-710-1 (hbk) — ISBN 1-58391-711-X (pbk) 1. Psychoanalysis
—Philosophy. I. Title.

   BF175.G649 2005
   150.19'5—dc22

                                              2004025924

ISBN 1-58391-710-1 (hbk)
ISBN 1-58391-711-X (pbk)

Contents

Preface

My earlier book, *An Introduction to Object Relations* (1997), ends with a question. What does it mean to hold to the principles of Object Relations? What ideas are we signing up to when we endorse or participate in object-relational psychotherapy or counselling, or see ourselves and others as the deeply relational creatures that Object Relations describes? Like other branches of psychoanalysis, Object Relations embraces a series of paradoxes: between the individual and the group as the basic human unit, and between the physical concept of instinct and the mental construct of relationship as our fundamental motivation. The book left me pondering these conundrums.

The premises of Object Relations led to the premises of psychoanalysis itself. After too many wrong turnings and blind alleys, the focus of this book emerged: how can psychoanalytic thinking be justified? There can hardly be a more central question for psychotherapists, counsellors and others who make use of the idea of unconscious motivation in their work. Without a solid sense of what underwrites this fundamental concept, we can bring no more than a surface accountability to our practice; and with different approaches proceeding on different philosophical foundations, the field as a whole is confined to piecemeal and fragmented development.

For philosophers, psychoanalysis represents a particular challenge. Its focal concept, the 'unconscious', constitutes a radical critique to traditional perspectives on the mind while eluding any definitive classification. Psychoanalysis stands at the crossroads between the different philosophical programmes to which it has been annexed, allowing their basic principles to be examined together rather than in isolation from each other. The disputed ground of psychoanalysis allows an unusual insight into the junctions and intersections of the divergent philosophical approaches on which psychoanalysis divides, as well as into the grounds of psychoanalysis itself.

Thus the foundation and legitimation of psychoanalytic thinking are far from resolved; but this is more than a professional or academic concern. It speaks to all of us who assume as private individuals that understanding ourselves and others means going deeper than ordinary consciousness can show. In grappling with the implications of this belief we come to know our own minds better. Encountering what lies behind our habitual ways of thinking reveals the tensions, contradictions and potential insights they contain.

As with my previous book, the intention is to make a specialized field accessible, without oversimplification and without denuding it of its complexity and depth. The philosophy of psychoanalysis is not a dull and abstruse specialism. It is a way of taking further the kind of questions that those who would not consider themselves philosophically or psychoanalytically experienced probably already ask. How do we know what we know? Can science explain everything? And that enduring enigma, whatever is a person? Psychoanalysis has its own distinctive slant on these fundamental philosophical concerns. I hope to communicate the excitement and illumination of bringing these two powerful modes of enquiry together to enhance and extend our professional and everyday thinking and understanding.

Acknowledgements

The original version of this book was a dissertation for a little-used MA by dissertation (official acronym: MAD), under the auspices of the innovative philosophy department at the University of Essex. My deepest thanks go to Katrin Flikschuh, without whose steadfast encouragement, unerring critical eye and skilled induction into philosophical thinking this project would certainly not have seen the light of day. I am also grateful to Karl Figlio, Director of the University's Centre for Psychoanalytic Studies, for his interested involvement and invaluable psychoanalytic knowledge; and to Mark Sacks, Director of Graduate Studies, for support and guidance at a crucial time.

I would like to thank the editorial staff of Brunner-Routledge for their help and advice in the rather complicated preparation of this book, particularly Kate Hawes, Claire Lipscomb and Helen Pritt. The book owes much to the publishers who gave permission for the papers in Part II to be reproduced. Particular thanks are due to Professor Grünbaum for drawing his 'Critique of Psychoanalysis' to my attention. I am very grateful to my friends and colleagues Catherine Leder and Kristiane Preisinger, who generously volunteered to act as 'test readers' as I was rewriting the academic version for a wider readership. Their steady interest was a welcome source of encouragement, and their forthright comments led to considerable improvements in clarity and structure. My continuing appreciation, finally, to David, Cathy and Chris, as well as other family members, for the personal involvement which keeps the writing and everything else going.

Part I

How can psychoanalytic thinking be justified?

Dialogue between Socrates and Alcibiades

Soc: The user and the thing he uses are different, are they not?

Alc: How do you mean?

Soc: For instance, I suppose a shoemaker uses a round tool, and a square one, and others, when he cuts.

Alc: Yes.

Soc: And the cutter and user is quite different from what he uses in cutting?

Alc: Of course.

Soc: And in the same way what the harper uses in harping will be different from the harper himself?

Alc: Yes.

Soc: Well, then, that is what I was asking just now – whether the user and what he uses are always, in your opinion, two different things.

Alc: They are.

Soc: Then what are we to say of the shoemaker? Does he cut with his tools only, or with his hands as well?

Alc: With his hands as well.

Soc: So he uses these also?

Alc: Yes.

Soc: Does he use his eyes, too, in his shoe-making?

Alc: Yes.

Soc: And we admit that the user and what he uses are different things?

Alc: Yes.

Soc: Then the shoemaker and the harper are different from the hands and eyes that they use for their work?

Alc: Apparently.

Soc: And man uses his whole body too?

Alc: To be sure.

Soc: And we said that the user and what he uses are different?

Alc: Yes.

Soc: So man is different from his own body?

Alc: It seems so.

Soc: Then whatever is man?

(Alcibiades I, quoted in Taylor 1979, p. 67)

Chapter 1

Introduction

What sort of subject might psychoanalysis be?

This book is an introduction to the philosophy of psychoanalysis, for those with an interest or engagement in philosophy, psychotherapy, or both, as well as anyone wanting to explore this profound and overlapping field. Although this is a complex subject, no prior knowledge or experience of either philosophy or psychoanalysis is required. When specialized terms are introduced, they are explained and expressed in ordinary language, with a glossary for instant reference. Nevertheless, this is not an introduction which avoids the big questions, or leaves them to the 'advanced' stage. The subject matter of the book is more fundamental than either psychoanalysis itself or any particular branch of philosophy. Our concern is with the common ground of all psychoanalytic approaches, and the focus is on the divergent principles which different philosophers have used to justify or to reject psychoanalytic thinking. The aim is to work towards an understanding of psychoanalysis through its central concept, the unconscious, which recognizes and makes sense of the entrenched disagreement about what its foundational principles are.

Part I is built around a recent controversy on the nature and legitimation of psychoanalysis. It is designed to be a free-standing introduction to our subject, without the need to refer to the critiques which it discusses. However, versions of these critiques are reprinted in Part II, so that those who wish can engage directly with them and come to their own conclusions. The two appendices address details of the overall argument which do not fit within the main body of the text.

This introductory chapter is divided into three sections. The first sets the context for the enquiry as a whole. The second provides theoretical background with a brief outline of psychoanalytic theory. The third highlights the theme of the enquiry and gives an idea of its general direction and outcome.

The context of the enquiry

'The Freud Wars'

In the mid-1990s, the *New York Review of Books* (NYRB) published an acrimonious exchange of reviews, responses and counter-charges on the nature and validity of psychoanalysis.[1] 'The Freud Wars' was launched by an uncompromising personal and theoretical attack by a professor of literature and formerly sympathetic proponent of psychoanalysis who has gone on to become its unremitting critic.[2] Frederick Crews' 'The Unknown Freud' (Crews 1993) condemns the whole edifice of psychoanalysis as a vast confidence trick played on suggestible patients and an unwary public by an unscrupulous and self-seeking psychoanalytic establishment. The documentary evidence makes clear, he maintains, that the observations on which psychoanalysis is based are mostly fabrications, cynically constructed out of Freud's insatiable craving for recognition as a scientific celebrity. Psychoanalysis, as Crews sees it, is at best a bankrupt science and at worst a counterfeit science, peddling uncorroborated and often ludicrous propositions which fail to meet the standards of rational discourse, let alone scientific reasoning. He concludes, in the 'Afterword' to his compilation of the dispute, that 'Freud has been the most overrated figure in the entire history of science and medicine' (Crews 1995, p. 298).[3]

Crews is happy to credit the details of his various criticisms to the authors whose books form a minor topic in his review. One of the most significant of these is Adolf Grünbaum's critical study *The Foundations of Psychoanalysis* (Grünbaum 1984). This is widely recognized as a scholarly and influential negative assessment of psychoanalysis from the point of view of a traditionally-minded philosopher of science. Grünbaum argues that psychoanalysis is not a 'pseudo-science' but a genuinely scientific body of theory, which can and must be assessed on standard scientific criteria. But having built up the scientific case for psychoanalysis, Grünbaum then proceeds to knock it down, constructing ingenious tests which psychoanalysis, as he describes it, must fail. His final verdict is that psychoanalysis is scientific, but unsuccessfully so.[4]

Crews' objections to psychoanalysis' claim to scientific status are drawn largely from Grünbaum's work. It is consequently Grünbaum's views that the philosopher Thomas Nagel takes issue with, in a review published a few months later as the NYRB's response to Crews' accusations and the ensuing correspondence.[5] Nagel is one of North America's leading philosophers, a flexible and witty thinker whose philosophical writings range over the subjects of ethics and politics, science and subjectivity, knowledge and the mind. 'Freud's Permanent Revolution' (Nagel 1994a) is a relaxed and sympathetic portrayal of psychoanalysis, in the form of a review of two recent defences of psychoanalysis against some of its foremost contemporary critics, including Grünbaum (Robinson 1993; Wollheim 1993). Nagel rejoins that Grünbaum takes too narrow a view of his subject matter. Psychoanalysis, he argues, introduces a new way of thinking which has triumphantly succeeded in transforming our views of what a person is, within a broader conception of empirical science.

The two philosophers' opposing views form the centrepiece of an eighteen-month debate, with philosophers, psychoanalysts, academic psychologists and others all joining in. Grünbaum's and Nagel's respective judgements jostle for position as psychoanalysis is in turn dismissed as a bogus science and supported as a pioneering and fruitful science. The two critiques give us a solid platform from which to assess the scientific credentials of psychoanalysis. By considering their arguments for and against, we can begin to clarify what it would take to justify psychoanalytic thinking on scientific grounds. The critiques are discussed in detail in the next two chapters, and are represented in the first two papers of Part II. Grünbaum's views are represented by his 'Critique of Psychoanalysis' (in Erwin 2002), which includes the main points of his book and of his response to Nagel. Nagel's review is included in full, together with an 'Addendum' written in answer to Grünbaum's reply (Nagel 1994b).

One question which is never considered throughout the erupting debate is whether psychoanalysis should be categorized as a science in the first place. The possibility of classing it with the humanities is not even entertained. This is the one point on which Nagel and Grünbaum are in hearty unanimity; but it is not a foregone conclusion, nor is the scientistic bias it reflects typical of psychoanalysis as a whole.[6] This enquiry would be incomplete without a critique which puts psychoanalysis forward as an interpretative or 'hermeneutic' subject. The inaugural hermeneutic critique by Jürgen Habermas (1971) seems a particularly appropriate example, as a reading which Grünbaum explicitly and Nagel implicitly rejects.

Habermas' critique of psychoanalysis is Grünbaum's first target. His strategy is to set up a version of Habermas' account as a kind of sitting duck, which he then mows down, in the words of an admiring colleague, 'with a sort of argumentative tank' (Caws, in Grünbaum et al. 1986, p. 230). Grünbaum argues that any interpretative reconstruction of psychoanalysis is misguided. Its validity would depend entirely on scientific considerations, since interpretative forms of validation are parasitic on scientific methods. For Nagel, equally, the justification of psychoanalysis as a system of interpretation can be no substitute for scientific validation: 'if all Freud succeeded in doing was to develop a new way of talking or seeing things, he failed' (1994a: see p. 150 below). He would surely include Habermas' approach to psychoanalysis as a prime example of what he sees as 'the facile subjectivism that now blights many of the humanities and social sciences' (ibid.: see p. 150 below).

Habermas, however, is not so easily defeated. He is probably the foremost social philosopher of recent times, a creative and resourceful critic of everything from practical political philosophy to traditional approaches to knowledge. His influence on psychoanalysis is out of all proportion to the brief attention he pays it, in the last three chapters of his general critique of knowledge, *Knowledge and Human Interests* (1971). Its wordy style, coupled with awkward translation from the original German, makes Habermas' views less accessible than Nagel's or Grünbaum's. But Habermas' reading continues to exert its influence as a landmark text for the flourishing hermeneutic schools of psychoanalysis. Chapter 4, 'Self-Reflection as Science',[7] discusses Habermas' hermeneutic reconception of psychoanalysis. The crucial chapter from his critique is reproduced as the final paper of Part II.

Empirical and hermeneutic principles

It will come as no surprise to hear that 'The Freud Wars' were neither won nor lost. Inside and outside the psychoanalytic world, psychoanalysis continues to be viewed in line with the different verdicts reached, with little discussion and scarcely a hint of resolution. Essential psychoanalytic concepts from the 'unconscious' to the 'ego' have entered into ordinary language, suggesting an informal endorsement; but adjacent disciplines such as psychiatry and psychology typically treat it as little more than old-fashioned conjecture. Even within psychoanalysis itself, where its validity is not disputed, there is no consensus on where its authority lies: practitioners and theorists are divided as to whether its ideas are scientific or interpretative by nature. There are thus two questions for this enquiry to consider. Can psychoanalysis be justified at all? And should its acceptance or rejection depend on scientific or hermeneutic principles of knowledge? In the first case, its concepts and theories would be evaluated on the 'empirical' standards and principles which developed through studying the measurable world of nature. In the second, they would be tested through the 'hermeneutic' or interpretative principles through which we further our understanding of the unquantifiable world of language, symbol and culture.

The empirical–hermeneutic distinction is a dichotomy which goes back to the very root of Western thought. It is the matter–mind divide transposed to the theoretical level. The differences between the two approaches will grow clearer as we examine the work of our three philosophers. Meanwhile, the etymology brings out their essential meaning. 'Empirical' derives from 'empeiria' – experience – referring to the sensory experience by which we come to know a world outside ourselves; 'hermeneutics' is related to Hermes, messenger of the gods and symbol of communication. Thus empirical science looks at phenomena from the outside. It uses the language of mechanics, going back to the physical laws and concepts through which we understand the material world. Hermeneutic approaches explain phenomena – sometimes the same phenomena – from the inside. Their explanations are couched in the subjective language of desire and belief, value and intention, emotion and experience. These terms reflect the background of personal meaning and purpose which differentiates the action of a person from the output of a system, or a state of mind from a state of matter.

A terminological note might be helpful at this point. 'Science', in itself, means nothing more than an organized body of theory. However, it has become overwhelmingly identified with 'empirical science', often with the implication that this kind of knowledge is more 'real' than any other kind. Hermeneutic theorists such as Habermas challenge these assumptions. They claim that the knowledge represented by developed interpretational systems is just as legitimate as that of empirical systems, and should therefore be called 'hermeneutic science'. Although they have a valid point, qualifying the term 'science' whenever it is used would make for unnecessarily clumsy reading. When 'science' appears alone in this book, it means 'empirical science' in its everyday sense. 'Hermeneutic science' is used in full when it is intended. There is no implication, however, that either kind of knowledge is intrinsically superior to the other.

Like other investigations into 'human' subject matter, psychoanalysis addresses a domain which can be approached in either way: empirically, as a 'human science', or hermeneutically, as a humanities subject. In most disciplines it is clear from the context and purpose of the enquiry which framework should apply. In psychoanalysis, intriguingly, this remains a matter of dispute. To find out why, we must turn to psychoanalysis itself.

The theoretical background

The 'mental', the 'physical' and the 'psychical'

The sources of the confusion in psychoanalysis go back to its point of departure. Freud developed psychoanalysis as one of a number of contemporaneous attempts to solve the most frustrating puzzle of nineteenth-century psychiatry.[8] Some bodily symptoms seemed only to be explicable by assuming a mental rather than a physical cause. Even in cases of full-blown paralysis, they appeared to be manifestations not of any organic abnormalities but of an 'excessively intense idea' (Freud 1895, *Standard Edition* (S.E.) 1, p. 347). The symptomology matched patients' own notions of how their bodies were constructed, in defiance of their actual anatomy. How a mere idea could have such direct and dramatic physical effects was a scientific mystery, and formulating a framework for causal chains which cross between the mental and physical categories was conceptually baffling. A physiological theory could not incorporate ideas, but it was difficult to see how ideas could be treated scientifically. Freud presents psychoanalysis as the beginnings of a response to this conundrum, in a rudimentary science of the 'psychical' as the zone where mental and physical explanations converge.

Freud uses the term 'psychical' for the special form of existence manifested in the psyche and its functioning, which he sees as the unconscious ground of mental life. In common parlance, 'psychical' denotes either the disregard of the physical ground of phenomena, by describing them in non-physical terms, or its suspension, as in events which appear to defy the laws of physics. In the Freudian sense, however, it refers to a ground which is both subjective and embodied. His use of the term 'psychical' denotes a contrast with reality conceived in either purely mental or purely physical terms. In Western modes of thought, the usual understanding of mental reality is that it is unmediated: we experience thoughts, feelings and sensations immediately rather than at one remove. Physical reality, by contrast, is mediated. It cannot be known directly, but only through its impact on our sensory system or its mechanical extensions. 'Psychical reality' is Freud's third area, lying between the physical and the mental realms, but conceivable only in mental or physical terms.

This means the psychical has no language of its own. It cannot be broken down into mental and physical components, yet it can only be thought of as though it were mental, or as though it were physical. Seen in this light, the disagreement as to how psychoanalytic thinking should be vindicated comes as no surprise. Its 'mentalistic' side suggests it must be grounded in hermeneutic principles, while its 'physicalistic' side implies grounding in the empirical principles of physics, the overarching science of the physical. It is not easy to envisage theoretical terms on which these two frameworks could meet.

The double-sided nature of the psychical is the thread which runs throughout our enquiry. It is at once a crucial and a strangely neglected feature of Freud's thought. A brief review of psychoanalysis enables us to place it in the architecture of Freud's theories for the purposes of general orientation. We shall be going into closer detail as this becomes necessary.

The three levels of psychoanalytic theory

Freud's psychoanalysis is a multilayered system of concepts and theories which range from the immediate to the obscure. There are three main levels: the clinical theories, the metapsychological models and theories, and the metapsychological foundations. Each level of psychoanalytic theory treats the concept of the 'psychical' in its own way. The clinical theories approach it through the framework of mental reality; the metapsychological models and theories, through the framework of physical reality. The metapsychological foundations state formally that there must be a point of meeting between the two.

The clinical theory

The clinical or practical theories are the familiar face of psychoanalysis. They are set in the first-person perspective, and cover all psychoanalytic concepts that can be expressed in the language of experience. At their centre are the basic psychoanalytic concepts of the unconscious, resistance and repression. According to this triangle of ideas, ordinary conscious experience, neurotic and otherwise, has an unconscious substratum. This includes an unwillingness to allow into consciousness the thoughts and wishes we find most disturbing ('resistance'), and a method by which we may try to keep them under wraps ('repression'). The workings of resistance and repression remain out of ordinary awareness. Unless they break through into consciousness, all we can know directly is their results.

The clinical theories are 'mentalistic'. The processes they refer to are unconscious, but they use the framework and terminology that we apply to conscious mental life. Freud explains:

> if, for instance, we say: 'At this point an unconscious memory intervened', what that means is: 'At this point something occurred of which we are totally unable to form a conception, but which, if it had entered our consciousness, could only have been described in such and such a way.'
>
> (Freud 1938a, S.E. 23, p. 197)

Because there is no direct access to unconscious mental processes, we cannot conceive them with perfect clarity. The closest we can get is to express them by analogy with conscious mental processes.

The metapsychological models and theories

The clinical theories name and to some extent describe the psychical phenomena that Freud's observations lead him to postulate, but they cannot explain them. They do not say what it is about the psyche that makes processes such as 'transference', 'resistance' or 'repression' occur, just that they do. Thus the clinical theories are themselves something to be explained. Freud's way of explaining them is termed the 'metapsychology', a word Freud coins as a direct counterpart to 'metaphysics'. 'Metaphysics' and 'metapsychology' refer to the 'first principles' of the sciences of physics and psychology respectively. They give the initial picture of reality that has to be assumed before any theoretical programme can get going at all; for example, that the natural world is made up of matter and energy, and that perceptions are organized spatially (see below). Metaphysical and metapsychological theories and principles are unprovable, since by definition there can be no deeper theoretical level on which 'first principles' can rest. They must also be linked, since both exist in the same world.

The metapsychology is divided into two parts: the metapsychological models and theories, and their underlying foundations. The metapsychological foundations are not always included as part of the metapsychology, but since they fall within the boundary of psychoanalytic theorizing, it seems reasonable to do so. In this enquiry, 'metapsychology' is treated as a category which includes both these levels. When any particular element is intended, it is specified. Otherwise, the term refers to the common ground and essential feature of all aspects of the metapsychology: the conception of the psychical as the primary psychophysical reality.

The uppermost level of the metapsychology consists of a loose association of models and theories set in an external perspective. They represent the conclusions Freud draws from the clinical theory about the structure and workings of the psyche. Where the clinical theories are mentalistic, the metapsychological models and theories are 'physicalistic': their relation with physical concepts is also one of analogy. The structures and processes they refer to are not ordinary physical objects, but they are formulated in the spatial and quantitative terms used to express physical reality.

Freud's main metapsychological proposition is that psychical phenomena can be thought of in three different ways: 'when we have succeeded in describing a psychical process in its dynamic, topographical and economic aspects, we should speak of it as a metapsychological presentation' (Freud 1915a, S.E. 14, p. 181). Each of these metapsychological principles, or forms of organization, is reflected in particular models or theories.

The 'economic' or quantitative aspect of the psychical is expressed in the theory of the drives or instincts,[9] as the psychobiological substratum of mental life. They allow psychical processes to be viewed in terms of their directional force, or combination of forces. Psychical 'topography' or structure is expressed in the three-part model of id, ego and super-ego, and the division into unconscious and conscious-preconscious modes of psychical functioning.[10] These enable psychical processes to be located in different parts of a composite psychical 'system'.[11] The 'dynamic' regulation of the psyche is formulated in the principle of defence by which it protects itself against the over-accumulation of psychical 'energy', prototypically, but not exclusively, through repression.[12] This formulation explains psychological defences as the manifestation of the psyche's intrinsic capacity for active self-regulation.

Thus the clinical theories form the ground of explanation for Freud's psychoanalytic observations, and the metapsychological models and theories form the ground of explanation of the clinical theories. They are primary in that they cannot be proved or disproved, but they are still not the absolute foundation of psychoanalysis. This is to be found in the presuppositions they carry, which set out the unconditional starting-point for psychoanalytic theorization.

The metapsychological foundations

The foundational level of the metapsychology consists of the 'fundamental hypotheses' and the 'basic assumption' of psychoanalysis. The two 'fundamental hypotheses' lie immediately 'beneath' the metapsychological models and theories, and take up the mentalistic and physicalistic aspects of the psychical in turn. The first hypothesis sets out its physicalistic side – the side that can be expressed only by comparing it to physical reality. It proposes that the psyche has to be conceived as a complex 'apparatus', with mental activity as its output. 'We assume that mental life is the function of an apparatus to which we ascribe the characteristics of being extended in space and of being made up of several portions' (Freud 1938a, S.E. 23, p. 145). Freud is asserting that we can only think about the psyche as the objective source of mental processes through the spatial terms in which physical reality is conceived. We can indeed see that the metapsychological models and theories presuppose this hypothesis. Their topographical, economic and dynamic 'forms of organization' all assume a quasi-physical base.

The second 'fundamental hypothesis' is presupposed by the clinical theories. It takes up the mentalistic aspect of the psychical in the once controversial proposal that what is 'mental' can also be 'unconscious'. In passages such as the following, Freud is using the term 'psychical' to mean mental processes as such, rather than just their unconscious underlay. 'The majority of philosophers . . . declare that the idea of something psychical being unconscious is self-contradictory. But this is precisely what psycho-analysis is obliged to assert, and this is its second fundamental hypothesis' (ibid., p. 158). If unconscious mental processes are not to be left stranded in a purely abstract space, this second hypothesis must also carry the connection between the psychical and the physical. 'It explains the *supposedly* somatic [bodily] concomitant phenomena [of mental processes] as being what is truly psychical, and thus in the first instance disregards the quality of consciousness' (ibid., added emphasis).

Freud is saying that the essential hallmark of the mental or the psychical is not consciousness but unconsciousness. Our conscious experience is not rooted in itself, but in something underlying. Before psychoanalysis, this underlying level was usually thought of as being physical in nature, with what is 'mental' viewed as synonymous with what is conscious. Freud is claiming that on the contrary, it is the '*supposedly* somatic' (added emphasis) processes which are assumed to accompany conscious processes that are what is 'truly psychical'. Conscious mental processes are simply the way we perceive a particular kind of psychical process which, like all psychical processes, is 'unconscious in itself'. Thus Freud's description of the psyche is of a quasi-physical 'apparatus' churning out a continuous stream of quasi-mental 'processes'. Like ordinary physical processes, psychical processes are unconscious, and cannot be accessed directly; but like conscious mental processes, they have to be explained through a psychological framework.

These two hypotheses are still not the most fundamental level of psychoanalysis. This is to be found in the 'basic assumption' and ultimate bedrock of Freud's psychoanalysis: that a theory of mental life must begin with the unified conception of processes which are usually cast in either physical or mental terms.

> We know two kinds of things about what we call our psyche (or mental life): firstly, its bodily organ and scene of action, the brain (or nervous system) and, on the other hand, our acts of consciousness, which are immediate data and cannot be further explained by any sort of description . . . Our two hypotheses start from these ends or beginnings of our knowledge.
>
> (Freud 1938a, S.E. 23, pp. 144–145)

Freud is saying that an adequate explanation of mental life cannot ignore either our direct experience of mental phenomena on the one hand or the fact of their bodily environment on the other. The task of psychoanalysis is to '[act] as an intermediary between biology and psychology' (Freud 1913, S.E. 13, p. 182). Both physical and mental ways of thinking must be taken into account to describe whatever 'lies between'.

The problem and the promise of psychoanalysis

What sets psychoanalysis apart from other theoretical enquiries is that neither the mental nor the physical conception of reality is allotted priority. Freud does not define the mental as merely an 'epiphenomenon' or offshoot of the physical, nor the physical as no more than an 'idea' within the mind. He treats 'psychical reality' as a sphere in itself, with its own characteristics, categories and laws. But this is an approach which comes with problems attached. With no tangible or measurable evidence for any of the models or theories which make these attributes specific, Freud's fundamental proposition begins to look more like an article of faith than the basis of a science. The metapsychological models and theories themselves constitute a reason *not* to depart from the tried and tested ways of dealing with psychological subject matter scientifically, as a part of physical reality, or hermeneutically, as an aspect of mental reality.

Freud observes that the metapsychological models and theories which make up the upper level of the metapsychology are not essential to psychoanalysis. He is acutely aware of their speculative and wide-ranging nature, the difficulties of establishing empirical links, and their special susceptibility to change and replacement (see Freud 1924c, S.E. 20, pp. 32–33). If nothing in the metapsychology went further than these dubious attributes, there would be no reason for him or for us to treat it as anything other than a kind of theoretical folly. Its main significance, however, lies in the deeper metapsychological level: in the 'fundamental hypotheses' and especially the 'basic assumption' of psychoanalysis. It is here that Freud's concept of the psychical as a primary psychophysical reality is made explicit. Whatever the problems of the metapsychological models and theories, Freud's theories point towards, although they do not reach, a conception of psychological subject matter in which the mental and the physical are no longer set against each other but are demonstrably at one. It is this that holds the key to justifying psychoanalytic thinking. The 'basic assumption' of psychoanalysis is also its ground of validation.

The outcome of the enquiry

The psychophysical basis of psychoanalysis presents a unique theoretical challenge; and this enquiry argues that unless it is placed in the centre, psychoanalysis cannot be fully vindicated. The authors of our three critiques treat psychoanalysis in the traditional theoretical terms of empirical science or hermeneutic theory. They depend on principles which uphold the theories of matter and the body on the one hand, or theories of culture and the mind on the other. The hub of their disagreement is the conceptual model they attribute to psychoanalysis; the root of their difficulties is their common presumption that it must fall into one category or the other. The problems and limitations thrown up by each approach bring us to an impasse. If neither is fully satisfactory, where then should psychoanalysis look for its legitimation?

Chapters 2, 3 and 4 examine the cases made by Grünbaum, Nagel and Habermas respectively. The aim is to establish that any authority that psychoanalysis can lay claim to must depend on Freud's concept of the psychical, and the principles on which the theories built upon it are to be appraised. Chapter 5 turns away from conventional frameworks to the thinking behind Freud's theories, in a search for the roots of their strange theoretical ambiguity. We find that this goes back to the very beginnings of his thought. His underlying philosophy is neither wholly scientific nor purely interpretative. He seems to hold a picture of reality which pre-empts the division into the mental and physical modes on which empirical and hermeneutic approaches rest.

Only fragments of this unusual orientation can be found within Freud's writings; but two very different studies of everyday 'pre-theoretical' thought help develop a way of beginning to fill in the gaps. Together with Freud's thinking, the work of the philosophers Sebastian Gardner (1993) and Peter Strawson (1959) suggest the basis for a new foundational approach which seems to come from within psychoanalysis itself. Instead of the empirical basis in the body, or the hermeneutic basis in the mind, psychoanalysis goes back to the psychophysical basis of the person, as the source from which all thinking must arise. From this nascent conceptual foundation, psychoanalysis appears neither as inadequate science nor as overblown hermeneutics. It is revealed, instead, as a form of enquiry which potentially challenges the empirical–hermeneutic divide, by pointing to the unity beneath the scientific ground of matter and the interpretational sphere of mind.

This way of looking at psychoanalysis is not intended as the 'answer' to the vexed question of the 'right way' to understand and justify psychoanalytic thought. All that can be done in this relatively brief enquiry is to consider the basic principles on which the dominant scientific and hermeneutic psychoanalytic groupings divide, and what might immediately follow from this. Each of the established approaches is embedded in its own philosophical traditions; each has developed to a high degree its own theoretical account of psychoanalysis and its own contributions to practice; each has its own committed adherents. But neither side has managed to win over the other. In this investigation, we begin to find out why.

Chapter 2

The Foundations of Psychoanalysis

What would it mean for psychoanalysis to count as a science?

Introduction

Our first critique sets out to evaluate psychoanalysis as a normal empirical science. This means that it must demonstrate that psychoanalytic concepts and explanations can be justified by 'experience', typically through the measurable data which sensory experience can access. This kind of data is usually gained through observation and experiment, methods which are systematic, replicable and open to public scrutiny. The claims of empirical science are judged as valid to the extent that they are supported by the evidence yielded by these methods, and invalid to the degree that such evidence falls short.

Adolf Grünbaum's *The Foundations of Psychoanalysis* (Grünbaum 1984) provoked reactions ranging from acclamation to animosity through the worlds of psychoanalysis, psychotherapy, and the philosophy of science and the mind. He presents his study as a 'philosophical critique of the foundations of Sigmund Freud's psychoanalysis' (Grünbaum 1984, p. 1), which he takes to be unequivocally those of a 'natural science'. Grünbaum sets out to demolish the previously accepted scientific view that psychoanalysis cannot meet the standards of normal empirical science. He argues that psychoanalysis does succeed in meeting one of its main criteria: scientific procedures can be devised to test its central propositions. But since, in his opinion, it has not passed any of these tests, he concludes that although it is scientific in its structure, psychoanalysis must be judged a failed or failing science.

In order to defend his claim, Grünbaum must meet two minimal conditions. He has to present an accurate account of psychoanalysis, so that what he goes on to evaluate is not in danger of being rejected as a misrepresentation of psychoanalysis or as only a peripheral part of it. In addition, he must demonstrate that the criterion of science he puts forward acts as a clear dividing line between scientific and non-scientific theoretical systems in general, and is applicable to psychoanalysis in particular. If these requirements are satisfied, he will have shown that psychoanalysis can indeed be evaluated through the principles of empirical science.

Grünbaum sets himself a further condition, which he deals with at the outset. He hopes to establish not only that psychoanalysis *may* be treated as an empirical science, but also that it *must*. Unless he can show that there is no valid alternative, any empirical-scientific account of psychoanalysis would simply take its place as one among a number of rival accounts. His first task is therefore to combat the main opposition, in the form of hermeneutic readings of psychoanalysis such as that of Habermas.[1] The hermeneutic reworking of psychoanalysis follows from an explicit rejection of the metapsychology, *in toto* or insofar as it embodies Freud's aspiration to connect the mental and the physical realms. Relieved of its physicalistic foundations, its proponents argue, psychoanalysis stands revealed as an interpretative discipline, founded in structures of communication and the mind rather than those of physics and the body.

Grünbaum takes a different position. Instead of rejecting the metapsychology outright, he dismisses it as irrelevant. He suggests that Freud himself was far too aware of the uncertain status of the metapsychological models and theories to set any scientific store by them. In all but his earliest work, he continues, Freud rightly attributes scientific status to psychoanalysis on the basis of methodology rather than the ontology (the constitution) of its subject matter. Grünbaum argues that the metapsychology as a whole can be ignored because the scientific nature of psychoanalysis is assured on methodological grounds alone; and that both the content and the form of his appraisal are beyond dispute, since they correspond to Freud's own views.

Grünbaum puts his case with energy and rigour. I shall argue, however, that without the metapsychological foundations – the 'fundamental hypotheses' and 'basic assumption' which express the psychophysical basis of psychoanalysis – he cannot fully satisfy the three conditions. His attempt to circumvent the metapsychology falls through, and whether he likes it or not, he is confronted with the ontological status of psychoanalytic subject matter and its implications for scientific standing. Yet the mental-physical ambiguity of psychoanalytic concepts is not enough to eject psychoanalysis from the sphere of science. We cannot safely conclude that Grünbaum's critique has at least established that psychoanalysis is *not* an empirical science. His overall approach betrays a physicalistic bias, leading him to present a one-sided picture of psychoanalysis which he goes on to subject to an inappropriate form of testing. We are left with the question of whether a more faithful reading might come up with an alternative criterion which recognizes the special nature of psychoanalytic subject matter, avoids the metapsychological pitfalls, yet still acts as a convincing benchmark of empirical science.

Background

Grünbaum's conception of science

Grünbaum's scientific thinking is based on the traditional model of the mainstream empirical sciences set by the influential post-war philosopher, Karl Popper. Popper describes the essential scientific method as 'conjecture and refutation' (Popper 1962). This involves coming up with a possible explanation of an observable event which can then be tested out in practice, or 'experience'. To fit in with this model, propositions must be open to empirical refutation: they must be constructed in such a way as to lend themselves to publicly observable attempts to show that they are false.

Explanations within this model are known as 'hypothetico-deductive' explanations, because they consist of deduction from a hypothesis, or logical reasoning on the basis of an appropriately structured proposition. The hypothetico-deductive formula, *Law + Conditions → Event*, makes sense of phenomena by presenting them as the logical outcome of universal natural laws operating under specific conditions. Newton's 'conjecture', for example, can be expressed as follows: Gravity (hypothesized universal law) plus Apple detaching from tree (conditions) leads to Apple falling to ground (event to be explained). The 'event' of the falling apple can be deduced from the hypothesis of a universal law of gravity operating under the right conditions (apple detaching from tree, no counter-force, etc.). The formulaic structure enables hypotheses to be treated as predictions and submitted to experimental tests designed to detect possible loopholes. If the prediction is borne out and the event does indeed follow from the specified conditions, the hypothesis is supported. If not, it is refuted, in whole or in part.

Popper excludes psychoanalysis from empirical science because of the difficulties of devising predictive tests of this kind for psychoanalytic propositions. Grünbaum aims to get round this problem by using an 'inductivist' modification of the normal hypothetico-deductive structure.[2] Rather than deriving (or de-ducing) a particular phenomenon from a general law and specific causal circumstances, the investigator starts with the phenomenon to be explained and goes on to infer (in-duce) conclusions about its possible causes. For example, instead of deducing the fall of the apple from the specified causal condition on the assumption of a general law of gravity, a range of similar 'events' might be considered. If an instance can be found in which the hypothesized causal conditions have not occurred – if an apple detaching from a tree in a spaceship still fell to the floor, for instance – the explanation as a whole is proved false: the law, the conditions, or both must be wrong. It is on this methodological principle of 'refutation by induction' that Grünbaum builds his case.

Discussion

Grünbaum's main task is to explain the grounds on which he judges psychoanalysis to be scientific in its structure. Only methodological grounds will do, since his claim depends on excluding the ambiguous psychophysical foundation represented by the metapsychology. At the same time, he risks the accusation that what he is assessing is not psychoanalysis, or is only marginal to it. He is therefore at pains to establish that his views coincide with Freud's on two counts: that the metapsychology is irrelevant to the scientific standing of psychoanalysis, and that the principle of refutation by induction is central. The first part of the discussion section is confined to Freud's estimation of psychoanalysis and the place of the metapsychology within it. This leaves his methodological criterion itself to the next part, where we examine its viability as a general demarcation line between science and non-science, using psychoanalysis as an example.

Does Freud see the metapsychology as scientifically superfluous?

Grünbaum's strategy is to set out his stand on the seemingly unassailable rostrum of Freud's own words; but his approach is too selective to succeed. At the start of the book, Grünbaum stresses that 'throughout his long career, Freud insisted that the psychoanalytic enterprise has the status of a natural science' (1984, p. 2). Grünbaum refers to a number of passages in which Freud does indeed insist just this. But professing to know what Freud 'really' thinks is notoriously hazardous. The extensiveness, variety and intermittent inconsistency of his writings mean that quotations can be found to support diametrically opposing claims.

Investigation shows that Freud is not always as whole-hearted in his presentation of psychoanalysis as an ordinary 'natural science' as Grünbaum makes out. He points out the differences as well as the similarities between psychoanalysis and the physical sciences:

> Every science is based on observations and experiences [NB: not 'experiments'] arrived at through the medium of our psychical [not sensory] apparatus. But since our science has as its subject that apparatus itself, the analogy [between psychoanalysis and physics] ends there.
>
> (Freud 1938a, S.E. 23, p. 159)

'Strictly speaking there are only two sciences: psychology, pure and applied, and natural science' (Freud 1932, S.E. 22, p. 179). These remarks, and others like them, indicate that Grünbaum's initial premise cannot be upheld as categorically as he proposes. It seems fair to say that Freud does not waver from casting psychoanalysis as a science in general terms, although this does not stop him bringing in further definitions at times.[3] Overall, however, his writings leave more leeway for it to diverge from the scientific norm than Grünbaum allows.

Proceeding to his main contention, Grünbaum states that for all but a short initial period, Freud attributes the scientific status of psychoanalysis not to how its material is classified, but to how it is treated: 'Freud forsook his initial, ontologically reductive notion of scientific status in favor of a methodological, epistemic one' (Grünbaum 1984, p. 5). That is, Freud began by linking the scientific status of psychoanalysis to the ultimately physical constitution of its subject matter, but soon dropped this condition in favour of a solely methodological condition of knowledge ('epistemic' refers to epistemology, the theory of knowledge). On the first view, psychological phenomena can be included within empirical science only if they can be expressed in purely physical terms. This reduction to the physical enables psychology (or psychoanalysis) to take its place as an ordinary science of the physical. On the second view, any theoretical proposition whatsoever can count as potential scientific knowledge, just so long as it can be treated in accordance with what is recognized as scientific methodology.

Grünbaum assumes that in relinquishing his early aim of physical reduction, Freud is also dropping the metapsychology from whatever might count as essential psychoanalytic 'knowledge': 'Freud explicitly deemed the metapsychology *epistemologically expendable* as compared to the clinical theory' (1984, p. 84, original emphasis). It is the specifically clinical theory of repression, he observes, that Freud designates as '"the cornerstone on which the whole structure of psychoanalysis rests", and "the most essential part of it"' (Freud 1914b, S.E. 14, p. 16, quoted Grünbaum 1984, p. 84). He goes on to cite Freud's endorsement of the concept of repression as 'a theoretical inference legitimately drawn from innumerable observations' (Freud 1914b, S.E. 14, p. 17, quoted Grünbaum 1984, p. 6) – not as a logical deduction drawn from prior theory. His final appeal is to Freud's declaration that 'the foundation of science . . . is observation alone' (Freud 1914b, S.E. 14, p. 77, quoted Grünbaum 1984, p. 5). Grünbaum feels justified in concluding that Freud rules out ontological considerations from the foundations of science in general and psychoanalysis in particular.

Grünbaum's references are perfectly accurate, but they do not conclusively uphold his case. In his main supporting quotation, Freud describes the metapsychology as 'a speculative superstructure of psycho-analysis, any portion of which can be abandoned or changed without loss or regret the moment its inadequacy has been proved' (1924c, S.E. 20, pp. 32–33, quoted Grünbaum 1984, p. 5). Grünbaum takes this to mean that if any single portion of the metapsychology is expendable, then all of them must be, making the metapsychology redundant in its entirety. If Freud was in fact basing the scientific nature of psychoanalysis on methodology alone, this would surely be the case. But abandoning the metapsychology altogether would mean severing the theoretical link between the mental and the physical aspects of his proposed psychical processes. Plenty of further quotations can be found which indicate that this was never Freud's intention.[4]

In one of his most detailed and self-conscious final statements, Freud designates not method but the postulation of unconscious mental processes as the factor which makes psychoanalysis a science: the 'view . . . that the psychical is unconscious in itself, enabled psychology to take its place as a natural science like any other' (Freud 1938a, S.E. 23, p. 158). His reason is that it is only this hypothesis that ties conscious mental processes to an underlying psychophysical continuum. This enables psychoanalysis, like any other 'natural science', to claim to be investigating a 'reality' which exists independently of its perception. It is the unconscious nature of the psychical that makes the 'processes with which it [psychoanalysis] is concerned . . . in themselves just as unknowable as those dealt with by other sciences, by chemistry or physics, for example' (ibid.). In the same way that we hypothesize that the frequency of light waves underlies what we perceive as colour, so Freud hypothesizes that a stream of psychical processes underlies the experiences which appear to us in consciousness.

Freud goes on to speak directly about the metapsychology, describing the 'fresh hypotheses and . . . concepts' by which psychoanalysis theorizes its findings as the rudiments of a new science:

> They can lay claim to the same value as approximations that belong to the corresponding intellectual scaffolding found in other natural sciences, and we look forward to their being modified, corrected and more precisely determined as further experience is accumulated and sifted.
>
> (Freud 1938a, S.E. 23, pp. 158–159)

This makes it clear that Freud sees the content of the metapsychology as provisional, but not its very existence. Without scaffolding, any building in progress would very soon fall down.[5]

> So too it will be entirely in accordance with our expectations if the basic concepts and principles of the new science (instinct, nervous energy, etc.) remain for a considerable time no less indeterminate than those of the older sciences (force, mass, attraction, etc.).
>
> (ibid., p. 159)

The basic concepts of a science are bound to change, but this does not make them redundant as general expressions of its organizing principles.

These further references are not in accord with Grünbaum's interpretation of Freud's views. Far from treating the metapsychology as wholly 'epistemologically expendable', Freud appears to see it as a symbol of the mental-physical connectedness on which he bases the scientific status of psychoanalysis at least in part. This means that he cannot be said to locate the scientific authority of psychoanalytic knowledge, and the scientific nature of psychoanalysis itself, consistently and unequivocally in methodology alone. Thus Grünbaum fails to establish that on Freud's own views, psychoanalysis must be treated as an orthodox empirical science to which the metapsychology is irrelevant.

Is Grünbaum's methodological criterion applicable to all kinds of subject matter?

Grünbaum's argument could still partially succeed if he can show that methodology without ontology is a valid scientific criterion for all kinds of subject matter. He could then propose that although Freud holds on to his metapsychological inclinations well past their sell-by date, psychoanalysis can still be judged as scientific on methodological grounds alone. The chief strength of Grünbaum's inductive method is that it represents a distillation of 'scientific method' as it is usually understood. Despite problems in the 'small print',[6] propositions that can be tested by his method count as 'scientific' in the normal sense, and passing such tests reinforces their scientific credentials. But the hidden ontological baggage means that it is not the same in reverse. The main weakness of his criterion is that ineligibility for this kind of test may not be enough to make a theory non-scientific, and failing such tests does not necessarily mean that it is false. This leaves a gap of uncertainty between a theory which fails empirical tests through negative results, and one which apparently falls short because it cannot be tested in this way. Psychoanalysis is an example of a subject falling into this gap.

This problem arises because Grünbaum's model is not ontologically neutral but entirely physicalistic. It can be used to check the external signs of psychoanalytic phenomena where these are consistent and measurable, but it cannot encompass psychoanalytic phenomena themselves. This does not mean that psychoanalytic concepts and propositions are simply unevaluable. There is a hermeneutic alternative, but this is usually seen as a non-scientific form of justification. Grünbaum intends his initial foray against hermeneutic validation to close off this possibility. However, he inadvertently undercuts his own claim by reverting to a 'common-sense' interpretative form of evaluation in relation to a particular class of 'slips of the tongue'. In doing so, he is tacitly conceding that the hypothetico-deductive method is not the only way of justifying subjectively conceived phenomena. Thus he himself supplies the final piece of the argument against his own case.

Refutation by induction

The hypothetico-deductive model was developed in the physical sciences, with physics as the paradigm science. It fits the human sciences less well, since human actions cannot be investigated in the same way as other happenings. The more they are seen as the expression of individual decisions rather than the effects of external causes, the more inevitable it is that staged experiments or theoretical predictions must degenerate into self-fulfilling or self-defeating prophecies.[7] It was this that led Mill to advocate the inductive method for 'human' subject matter. This approach treats human actions as no different in principle from other natural events, but only as more complicated. 'Free will' is seen as a first-person illusion, making actions, thoughts and feelings as precisely predetermined as anything else. It is only their numerous partial 'causes' and the intricacy of their interaction that prevent the causal conditions from being identified fully and clearly; and this, in turn, is why predictions in this sphere lack reliability.

Inferring causal conditions from a given event avoids the pitfalls of prediction, but induction can be a far more chancy business than deduction. Grünbaum notes that Popper's dismissal of psychoanalysis as an empirical science takes place in the context of his rejection of inductivism. Popper rates the inductive method as 'too permissive' a criterion for confirming explanatory hypotheses, making it unsuitable as a demarcation line between science and non-science. Grünbaum agrees that confirmation by induction is entirely unreliable. Almost any hypothesis can be 'confirmed' by finding instances in which it is apparently borne out, without this meaning that a genuine causal link has been identified. Refutation by induction, however, is another matter. Any causally constructed hypothesis can be refuted if a single disconfirming instance can be found; and Freud's theories, Grünbaum points out, are 'replete with causal hypotheses' (1984, p. 104). We can investigate the problems of applying this model to a certain kind of subject matter through Grünbaum's reconstruction of a hypothesis which he sees as central to psychoanalysis.

Grünbaum extracts the following basic 'testable hypothesis' from Freud's writings: 'Repression of traumatic experiences is essential for neurosis to develop' (Grünbaum et al. 1986, p. 266).[8] Grünbaum has since elaborated on this hypothesis (see Grünbaum 2002, pp. 122–123 below), and in addition, it is not an accurate reflection of Freud's position. Freud sees the concept of repression as a way of understanding or explaining neurosis, but does not claim that eradicating repression is the causal condition of 'cure'.[9] However, neither of these points affects the present argument. Grünbaum's original formulation serves to illustrate the pitfalls of employing the hypothetico-deductive model to a certain kind of subject matter. As a first step towards clarifying the problem, we can express the hypothesis in ways which fit the hypothetico-deductive structure:[10]

- If repression causes neurosis, then the lifting of repression must cure neurosis
- Neurosis caused and maintained by repression (law) + lifting of repression through correct interpretation (condition) → cure of neurosis through correct insight (event to be explained)
- R(epression) + L(ifting of repression) → C(ure)[11]

Each version can be inferred from the others, and in each explanation, any two terms sets up the third to be adduced. Reducing them to mathematical terms makes this self-evident:

- $R + (-R) = No\ R$

Refutation by induction means that a single disconfirming instance of a hypothetico-deductive formulation proves that the hypothesized cause cannot be a necessary condition of the event to be explained, and/or the law cannot hold universally. If 'C' can be shown to occur in the absence of 'L', then either 'R' or 'L' cannot be true. This feature of the hypothetico-deductive structure rests on further empirical assumptions, two of which will be examined here. The first assumption is that the components of the hypothesis or formula are publicly identifiable, so that there can be no argument about whether or not particular phenomena are examples of them. The second is that the phenomena in question reflect a conceptual organization which allows them to be reduced to mathematical terms. The subjective dimension of psychoanalytic subject matter brings Grünbaum's criterion into difficulty on both these counts.

Are the elements of psychoanalytic hypotheses publicly identifiable?

Grünbaum's model is supposed to capture the common causal structure linking all kinds of phenomena; but if there is no reliable way of agreeing what constitutes the elements of his hypothesis, his criterion is weakened. Popper argues that it is impossible to know for sure whether events such as repression or the lifting of repression have actually occurred. If he is right, the majority of psychoanalytic propositions could only be provisionally evaluated through empirical 'tests'. Neither confirmations nor refutations could be upheld with certainty, and Grünbaum's formula would be of limited use in assessing their validity.

Popper initially suggests that psychoanalytic propositions are untestable because it is impossible to specify causal conditions that enable all actions except the one predicted to be ruled out: 'There was no conceivable human behaviour which could contradict them' (Popper 1962, p. 37). Grünbaum hopes to circumvent this problem by starting with the behaviour and working back to its causal conditions. But Popper elaborates:

> (A) If people do not repress traumatic experiences, then they will not become victims of neurosis. (B) If in childhood people are protected from traumatic experiences, then they are not expected to become neurotic . . . (A) and (B) are if-then sentences, but it is impossible to test them, for this would demand that we make sure that the 'if' part (the antecedent) is true (which is hardly ever possible) even if the 'then' part is false rather than true (which psychoanalysts are likely to assert anyway).
>
> (Popper, in Grünbaum et al. 1986, p. 254)

Popper is saying that whether someone is neurotic or merely anxious or eccentric, whether they have suffered a trauma or just a mishap, and whether repression or simple forgetting has occurred, is all a matter of opinion. There are no definitive external signs, particularly in the negative: 'who has ever met a prospective patient who was told by his prospective psychoanalyst that he was not neurotic?' Snide remarks aside, Popper's argument is persuasive. If there is no clear way of identifying the absence of neurosis or repression, there can be no exact way of knowing what constitutes their presence, either. He seems to be right in saying that

> scientific testability . . . cannot be achieved by speaking of alleged or hidden states, such as 'repression' or 'trauma' or 'neurosis', states whose hypothetical presence or absence cannot be tested (and of which it even remains questionable whether they are ever absent).
>
> (ibid., pp. 254–255)

Grünbaum, of course, considers that both he and Freud have found a way of testing his hypothesis:

the nub of their [Freud's and Breuer's] inductive argument for inferring a repression etiology can be formulated as follows: the *removal* of a hysterical symptom S *by means of lifting* a repression R is *cogent evidence* that the repression R was causally necessary for the formation of the symptom S . . . For if an ongoing repression R is *causally necessary* for the pathogenesis *and* persistence of a neurosis N, then the removal of R must issue in the eradication of N. Hence the inferred etiology yielded a deductive explanation of the supposed remedial efficacy of undoing repressions.

(Grünbaum 1984, p. 179; emphasis original)

Grünbaum is saying that if neurotic symptoms consistently disappear with the lifting of repression, Freud would be justified in concluding that repression is a necessary causal condition of neurotic symptomology. The formula would be confirmed; or rather, it would not be refuted. Although he goes on to argue against this outcome, he does not dispute that repression and neurosis are empirically identifiable. Either the symptom disappears following a psychoanalytic interpretation, or it does not. In practice, however, things would not be so simple. There would be no way of telling from the external signs whether a 'symptom' has disappeared, gone into abeyance, changed its form, changed its meaning, or remained as a behavioural shell that no longer merits being called a 'symptom'. Only subjective (and intersubjective) forms of understanding could tell us that. The validity of the explanation and all its terms depend on internal rather than external grounds.

The disagreement between Popper and Grünbaum leads back to their divergent views of the distinction between phenomena which are subjectively conceived and those which are objectively conceived. Popper's argument is that scientifically speaking, we can only guess at the causal link between the observable signs of an action or state of mind and their subjective underlay. Any behaviour from which the signs are inferred could also be explained by a different subjective state; but 'scientific testability is a question of overt behaviour' (Popper, in Grünbaum et al. 1986, p. 255). Even without challenging the hypothetico-deductive principle of full determination, Grünbaum's claim looks in doubt. The difficulty of deducing subjective states from external phenomena seems to rule out a common mode of explanation precise enough to meet scientific as against merely practical standards.

Grünbaum replies that this problem is not peculiar to psychoanalysis: 'Even in physics, empirical evidence underdetermines theoretical states, indicating their presence only more or less probabilistically' (ibid., p. 267). In all arenas, including that of the most exemplary of natural sciences, there are theoretical states that cannot be categorically inferred from the data: 'even a circular array of iron filings does not deductively guarantee the presence of a magnet' (ibid.). He is of course right;[12] no physical evidence can ever totally justify any theoretical concept. But this is an argument against the reliability of scientific knowledge as such, rather than a vindication of knowledge authorized by Grünbaum's criterion. One reason why physics is more scientifically secure than psychoanalysis is that the external signs of a hidden physical state are far less variable than those of a mental state. But another reason is that it can be as questionable to transport the physical framework of the natural sciences to the mental sphere as it would be to assimilate the physical sphere to a mental framework. This raises doubts about using Grünbaum's criterion to evaluate psychoanalysis not just in practice, but in principle. To investigate this issue, we need to move away from the debate between Grünbaum and Popper to the underlying philosophical issues.

Physical organization and mental organization

The clinical level of psychoanalysis inhabits the arena of practical subjectivity. Dreams, slips and symptoms are conceived as intentional or purposive structures built around what they mean to the individual rather than on any general or physical property. Almost from the start, Freud's explanations of psychological symptoms follow this thread of meaning and intention, in contrast to the physiological explanations of his colleague Josef Breuer: 'I had taken the matter less scientifically [than Breuer]; everywhere I seemed to discern motives and tendencies analogous to those of everyday life [only unconscious]' (Freud 1914b, S.E. 14, p. 11). Freud's comment reminds us that 'human' phenomena can be approached in more than one way. Practical psychological explanations adopt the immediate, first-person perspective which makes them subject to validation through inner recognition. Scientific explanations hold the external and impersonal perspective which enables them to be supported or refuted by publicly observable signs.

The clinical tier of psychoanalysis is set at the practical psychological level, with the metapsychology representing the external perspective demanded by empirical science. In excluding the metapsychology, Grünbaum is locating psychoanalysis entirely at the practical or clinical level. Like Freud, he is confronted with the task of reconciling a subjective, psychological account of psychoanalytic phenomena with an objective, scientific account. His criterion assumes that a scientific account 'from the outside' can be used to check a practical account 'from the inside'. This implies, in turn, that there is no actual disjuncture between external and internal forms of knowing. We can accept that scientific reasoning is likely to be more reliable than practical intuition, but it can act as its guarantor only if they carry the same presuppositions and conceptual framework. Otherwise, they must be different kinds of knowing, giving different knowledge.

Hypothetico-deductive formulation views its field of application through a mechanical template which assumes that reality consists of distinct and identical units in constant interaction. Because these primary constituents are interchangeable, their interactions follow arithmetical rules: it is only because 'R' is completely cancelled out by '–R' that any exception adds up to a watertight refutation. The regularity of the constitution and activity of these units is realized in the causal order that the material world appears to manifest, and underwritten by its expression in formulaic terms. According to the principle of full determination, everything that happens is both a necessary cause and an inevitable effect of other states and happenings, with each cause being conceptually distinct from each effect. This gives an unbreakable network of linear causal chains which are entirely predictable in principle, though not always in practice.[13] It is reflected in the symmetry between explanation, prediction and retrodiction (the deduction of prior causal conditions) which hypothetico-deductive formulation expresses, and on which refutation by induction depends.

This tells us that Grünbaum's criterion of science is not ontologically 'neutral' but wholly physicalistic. It transfers the atomistic conception of physical reality directly to the mental realm. Applying his inductive criterion to subjective phenomena means treating them as though they too are composed of interchangeable units in regular causal interaction, making emotions, thoughts and actions as logically predetermined as any other natural event. There is only one philosophical approach in which this picture makes sense, and that is a thorough-going 'eliminative materialism'. This approach 'eliminates' mental phenomena from the scene by reducing them to epiphenomena or by-products of a particular kind of physical phenomenon:[14] the very existence of a mental domain is denied. It is a convenient approach for empirical science to take because it facilitates a purely external vantage point on all kinds of phenomenon. But it is not compatible with the practical standpoint taken in everyday life, or clinical psychoanalysis.[15]

Eliminative materialism holds that because mental and physical phenomena arise within the same 'reality', they are therefore explainable in the same way. While this is arguable at a theoretical level, it does not do away with the need for two distinct domains. The reason for dividing our perceptions into separate realms in the first place is because their respective phenomena appear to us in such very different ways. A mental occurrence, or experience, cannot be wholly conveyed in purely physical terms. No physical facts can explain what it is like to see the colour orange, grasp a hypothetico-deductive formula, or experience a moment of emotion. The disparities between mental and physical conceptions of reality are many and various. They include the viewpoint from which phenomena are perceived, the structure attributed to their background and context, and the ways in which we link them with other phenomena. The underlying difference is that if phenomena are conceived in physical terms, they are reducible to mathematical formulation; if they are conceived in mental terms, they are not.[16]

This divergence does not stem from 'reality' itself, but from the different organizations we accord to our conceptions of 'physical' and 'mental' reality. It may be that from a wholly abstract viewpoint (a 'God's-eye view') eliminative materialism is right, and the external conditions of each and every mental occurrence are pre-programmed as precisely as those of a chemical reaction.[17] This is not something that can ever be determined; but whether or not it is so, practical living starts from a conviction that mental phenomena are not the automatic outcome of prior events but can to some degree be chosen. Otherwise, our actions could not be planned, intended, or reflected on, and our thoughts and emotions would amount to no more than the whirring of mindless robots.[18] Subjectively, we exempt our own and other people's subjectivity from full determination. Even those who uphold it in theory necessarily deny it in practice. The clinical theory of psychoanalysis is 'mentalistic'. It is concerned with practical 'mental life', albeit at an unconscious level, and its concepts and frame of reference are 'analogous to those of everyday life'. Since they reflect the mental rather than the physical conception of reality, they cannot be reduced to mathematical formulation.

The difference is not solely one of degree. Subjective accounts are not simply erratic versions of objective or physical accounts; they involve a different conceptual scheme. There is nothing to prevent us from assuming a 'skeleton' of physical determinism, but in seeing ourselves and others as bearers of mental states – as 'I's – we are expressly pointing up a *non*-mechanical conception of our being. A 'person' is not an object, a robot, or a machine; the adjudicating 'ego' is set apart from the biologically-driven 'id'. The dimension of subjectivity introduces into our idea of ourselves a layer of organization which is not just predictively weaker but qualitatively different from physical organization. It illuminates another way of patterning the perceptual field, with lateral associations rather than linear chains, and shifting gestalts rather than summable units.

The fundamental categories of subjective phenomena are meaning and intention rather than matter and physical determinism. In physical reality, the same causes always give the same effects; but in 'mental' reality we expect the same circumstances to give rise to different actions and states of mind, depending on what the situation 'means' to the individual concerned. In this conceptual sphere there is no single 'right answer' to be inferred or deduced by logical reasoning, but a potentially infinite range of credible accounts which can be reached only through personal insight or empathic imagination.

The contrasting conceptions of physical and mental reality are reflected in their respective forms of explanation. A sufficient scientific explanation treats an action, a thought or a state of mind as an objective and therefore generalizable event. A sufficient practical explanation makes it comprehensible as a phenomenon which is personal, and therefore unique. Its source of evaluation is not the hypothetico-deductive ideal of perfect correspondence between prediction, retrodiction and explanation, but the inner resonance which makes a practical explanation ring true or false to those who are in a position to participate in that particular world of meaning. The more deeply subjective a phenomenon is, the less systematically it can be correlated with the external signs on which scientific evaluation and explanation rely. Unconscious mental processes are the most empirically opaque of all.

This line of thinking would be anathema to Grünbaum. For him, a theoretical explanation which does not aim to give the only possible outcome of the causal conditions is a contradiction in terms: 'if a theory *does not exclude* any behaviour at all, no matter what the initial conditions, how then can it deductively *explain* any *particular* behaviour? To explain deductively is to exclude' (Grünbaum 1984, p. 115, original emphases). All of which is true, but Grünbaum does not pause to consider whether there might be any different model or standard of explanation where subjective subject matter is involved.

This is not to rule out the contribution that hypothetico-deductive explanation can make to the understanding, especially the predictive understanding of 'human' phenomena. Since human behaviour cannot be calculated in the way that other events can, predictions in the social sciences are deductive but probabilistic. Provided all the elements are empirically identifiable, then with causal conditions x, and the propensity (or weak 'law') of a certain group of people to act in way y, the overall probability of outcome z is calculable within specifiable margins of error. Explanations of this kind depend on observable signs; they are oriented towards the 'what' rather than the 'why' of human actions, and their formulations apply to groups far better than to individuals. These factors severely limit the extent to which such explanations can be used to evaluate psychoanalytic propositions.

Grünbaum's two examples

Grünbaum includes two examples which illustrate the different ways of explaining psychological phenomena. The first is intended to establish that despite Popper's arguments to the contrary, psychoanalysis is open to hypothetico-deductive explanation and evaluation. His official view is that this is the only legitimate form of validation. However, his second, unintended example endorses a separate, interpretational form of explanation which effectively undermines his case.

Grünbaum's first example is an ingenious inductive test which he proposes for Freud's linking of paranoia, repression and homosexuality (Grünbaum 1984, p. 38).[19] He observes that Freud's proposition that 'repressed homosexual love is causally necessary for being afflicted by paranoid delusions' is open to statistical testing. If the proposition were true, the incidence of paranoid delusion should have decreased as homosexuality has become more accepted and therefore less liable to be repressed (ibid.). Since this is most unlikely to have happened, as it stands it probably cannot be considered a psychological 'law'. It would be difficult to screen out extraneous factors; but it would be quite feasible to measure, over time, the changes in any (negative) correlation between the observable signs of paranoia and homosexuality, provided it could be agreed what these might be. To that degree, Grünbaum's test could provide confirmation or disconfirmation for the proposition that they do not generally exist together, particularly if this is understood as a universal law which says that they can never exist together.

Psychoanalysis, however, does not stand or fall on its causal propositions, but on the validity of its clinical concepts; and these cannot be evaluated in this way. Whatever this test might establish about the incompatibility of paranoia and open homosexuality, it could not appraise the primary psychoanalytic concept of repression presupposed within it. The observable signs from which repression could be 'diagnosed', or which are merely consistent with the idea of repression, would always be explainable in other ways. Conversely, if enough people feel inwardly convinced that a memory, thought or impulse has emerged from a state which the concept of repression describes best, it is difficult to see on what basis this should be rejected as a practical rather than a scientific idea. The primary psychoanalytic concepts of transference and repression, resistance and the Oedipus complex are not physicalistic but mentalistic. This means they cannot be calculated from any given condition, or inferred with logical certainty from any empirical action or particular set of words. They reflect the non-mechanical organization of practical subjectivity, rather than the mathematical organization of physical objectivity.

For all these reasons, the inductive or deductive explanations of empirical science cannot be described as more accurate versions of the interpretative explanations of clinical psychoanalysis. They cannot be used to check the validity of interpretative explanations, because they are a different genre. Instead of seeking inner meaning, hypothetico-deductive explanations look for the manifest pattern of events. They only track the sequence of external signs which can be treated as ordinary physical phenomena, linked by physical causality. The materialist presuppositions of hypothetico-deductive explanations prevent them from picking up on mental processes themselves, or on the explanatory potential of meaning as such. Only interpretative explanations can do that.

Grünbaum, of course, will not hear of an independent interpretational form of explanation. He objects that far from being set against them, interpretative explanations trade on probabilistic causal explanations which, as we know, he sees as consistent with determinism. Accordingly he thinks it does not matter what the elements of hypothetico-deductive explanations are 'made' of:

> The *causal relevance* of an antecedent state X to an occurrence Y is *not* at all a matter of the *physicality* of X; instead, the causal relevance is a matter of whether X – be it physical, mental, or psycho-physical – MAKES A DIFFERENCE to the occurrence of Y, or AFFECTS THE INCIDENCE of Y.
>
> (Grünbaum 1984, p. 72; emphasis original)

Grünbaum is arguing that 'meaning' is significant only through being causally efficacious:[20]

> the very quest for the veiled 'meaning', which psychoanalytic investigation is expected to disclose, cannot redeem its avowed promise [to explain the phenomenon in question] without prior reliance on . . . exactly those cognitive procedures that they are wont to categorize as endemic to the natural sciences.
>
> (Grünbaum 1984, p. 57)

If the meaning of an experience is explanatory only to the extent that it facilitates generalizable predictions, it can then be treated like any other 'causal condition', and can take its place in a refutable hypothetico-deductive formula.

This only follows, however, if we accept that there is a single model of explanation for subjective processes: the 'eliminative' model which reduces them to objectifiable events. 'Explanation' would then be synonymous with 'empirical explanation', and the category of practical or interpretative explanation would drop away. In essence, this is what Grünbaum is implying, but in practice, even he cannot go this far. Theoretically and practically, the cost of abandoning a separate subjective dimension is too high.

This brings us to the second example. At the close of his book Grünbaum concedes, despite himself, that 'it may perhaps still turn out that Freud's brilliant theoretical imagination was actually quite serendipitous for psychopathology or the understanding of some subclass of slips' (Grünbaum 1984, p. 278). He is suggesting that by a fluke of the imagination, Freud may have come up with valid explanations of some subjective phenomena. But Grünbaum's concession does not stem from scientific considerations. There is no weighing of empirically identifiable evidence, or deductive or inductive reasoning. He is using the 'commonsense credibility' of practical explanation as an alternative criterion of evaluation for his chosen group of psychoanalytic concepts and explanations.[21]

Grünbaum notes that the structure of 'Freudian slips' seems also to apply to slips which he considers transparent to the point of being self-evident. He quotes the case of 'the man who turns from the exciting view of a lady's exposed bosom muttering, "Excuse me, I have got to get a *breast* of *flesh* air!"' (Grünbaum 1984, p. 200; also discussed in Sachs 1989, p. 373; Nagel 1994a, p. 149 below). Grünbaum presents this as an 'action' with so recognizable a 'cause' that he does not even bother to spell it out. In the same way, he allows that some dreams are clearly instigated by a wish. Grünbaum's example turns on such unquantifiable factors as meaning and perceived similarity of sound and rhythm, within uniquely personal associations. In endorsing such 'obvious' cases, he is tacitly acknowledging that 'causal conditions' can be explanatory without being generally predictive, and that immediate recognition can take the place of step-by-step induction or deduction. Grünbaum himself illustrates the differences between interpretative and hypothetico-deductive explanation.

Of course, this is not what he intends. What he means to establish is that scientific explanation is redundant for processes that are accessible to consciousness, whether or not they are not at its forefront. Only where the distinctively psychoanalytic explanation of 'repression' is postulated must the hypothetico-deductive apparatus be wheeled out. But this proviso is not enough to safeguard the exclusivity of his criterion. By allowing even an iota of credibility to 'commonsense' explanation, Grünbaum is acknowledging that subjective subject matter is open to an alternative kind of explanation. This does not mean that practical explanations are unrevisable or universally justified, nor that scientific explanations are redundant or inferior, nor that psychoanalytic explanations are valid; just that the idea of interpretative explanation cannot be automatically dismissed, although such explanations reflect a very different conceptual organization from that assumed by normal empirical science. On Grünbaum's own account, explanations are not rendered worthless if they hold an interpretative rather than a predictive form, and reflect the mental rather than the physical organization of reality.[22]

Thus Grünbaum undermines his own claim that there is only one model for explaining psychological subject matter. At the same time, his methodological criterion falls short of being universally applicable. It cannot be divorced from ontological considerations because a physical ontology is assumed within it. Hypothetico-deductive formulation can be used to chart the external signs of subjective subject matter, but cannot take up the 'inner track' of meaning. On practical and theoretical grounds, Grünbaum's criterion cannot stand as the primary tool of evaluation for clinical psychoanalysis, or for any concepts or explanations which turn on the interpretation of meaning rather than on scientific credibility. He therefore does not achieve his objective of providing a level scientific ground for physical and non-physical subject matter alike.

Conclusion

If Grünbaum's analysis is unsatisfactory, must we then conclude that subjectively-conceived phenomena are not open to scientific treatment? Are we compelled to return to Popper's view that psychoanalysis is not even a candidate for scientific status? It is here that the metapsychology is significant. Freud seems to have realized that psychoanalysis involves the linking of the mental and physical realms; and even if he did not, one might argue that this is entailed in his project. Whatever its substantive weaknesses and shortcomings, the metapsychology can be seen as standing for a commitment to a unified metaphysics, as yet undeveloped, in which the physical and mental conceptions of reality are conceived in harmony with each other. Freud appears to be envisaging a new ontological category in which the practical dimension of psychoanalytic conceptualization finds a meeting place with the theoretical dimension of empirical science.

The arguments which throw doubt on Grünbaum's reading of psychoanalysis are not sufficient to establish this picture as the only possible alternative. Freud's fluid and multilayered writings probably support an irreducible plurality of interpretations. It is clear, however, that there is more than one way of understanding psychoanalysis. The root of Grünbaum's problem is that Freud's project looks to be an altogether more ambitious undertaking than he imagines. For Grünbaum, the aim of psychoanalysis can be no more than the causal explanation of observable behaviour and whatever can be inferred from it. He is tied to a conception of subjective states which relies on their consistent identifiability by external signs. Grünbaum may be treating a body of interpretative theory, governed by meaning and personal intention, as though it were an empirical-scientific theory, governed by physical cause and effect.

In trying to force psychoanalysis into the hypothetico-deductive mould, Grünbaum is treating the clinical theory of psychoanalysis as though it were no more than the sum of its causal propositions. Since Freud designates repression as a 'cornerstone' of psychoanalysis, Grünbaum concludes that casting doubt on its causal role strikes a blow to the heart of the psychoanalytic corpus. But it is at least as arguable that Freud's clinical theory reflects a theoretical organization which, like the subjective phenomena it sets out to explain, is more than the sum of its parts. Repression is not the only or even the main 'cornerstone'. The list of basic theories Freud cites as '*The Corner-Stones* [plural] *of Psychoanalysis*' is headed by '[the] assumption that there are unconscious mental processes' (Freud 1922a, S.E. 18, p. 247). The remainder are the 'theory of resistance and repression, the . . . importance of sexuality and of the Oedipus complex' (ibid.). To Freud, these are the subjectively (and intersubjectively) perceptible signs of unconscious mental processes, which are meaningful, like conscious mental processes, yet unconscious, like physiological processes.[23] Since the clinical theories reflect the mental rather than the physical conception of reality, no single 'cornerstone' need bear the whole evidential weight of psychoanalysis. Together, they can indeed be seen as mutually supporting scaffolding for its one essential concept.

Against his best intentions, Grünbaum's critique makes clear that psychoanalysis cannot fit comfortably into the contours of an orthodox natural science, but in attempting to force it into such a structure he distorts it to such an extent that his conclusions are undermined. A non-ontological criterion of science would appear to be tailor-made for psychoanalysis; but Grünbaum's demarcation line depends ultimately on a physical ontology, so the clinical concepts of psychoanalysis have no chance of meeting it.

Like a repressed motive, the question of the metapsychology returns to haunt him. The challenge he makes to the purely physicalistic view of science falls by the wayside, but the questions it poses remain. Is it possible for truly 'mental' subject matter to be treated scientifically, or must it be shorn of its most subjective elements before it becomes fit for scientific treatment? Can empirical science find a ground from which to articulate that phenomena which live in the mind also exist in the physical world? As an aspiring science of subjectivity, Freud's psychoanalysis confronts us with these questions in their most extreme form. Even if Grünbaum's approach does not succeed in answering them, might there be another way in which the psychoanalytic domain can be recognized as subjective yet also objective? Nagel's riposte to Grünbaum attempts to do just this.

Chapter 3

'Freud's Permanent Revolution'

Could psychoanalysis be a new kind of science?

Introduction

Officially, 'Freud's Permanent Revolution' (Nagel 1994a) is a measured endorsement of two recent defences of psychoanalysis within a wide-ranging reflection on
its nature and significance. Within the NYRB debate, however, its effect is to
throw Crews' and Grünbaum's conceptions of psychoanalysis and of empirical
science itself into disarray. This is the angle from which I shall approach Nagel's
review. Again, the aim is not yet to evaluate Freud's metapsychology as such, but
to show that without it, Nagel's case fares little better than Grünbaum's.

Grünbaum believes that there is only one way of vindicating theoretical systems:
the experimental approach and the hypothetico-deductive form of explanation
that goes with it. Together, these make up a well-honed tool for extracting what
the world can tell us about itself. Empirical science starts from the principle
that external reality impresses itself on the mind in an orderly, if not direct,
fashion, which the standard scientific method can then decode. Like Grünbaum,
Nagel takes science to be seeking 'objective' knowledge about the world: 'some
questions have right and wrong answers' (Nagel 1994a, p. 150 below). Unlike
Grünbaum, however, he holds that objective knowledge can be sought even about
phenomena which cannot be confined within the explanatory structures traditionally applied to physical states and events. He thinks there can be right and
wrong answers about subjective phenomena, just as there are about the material
world.

Where Grünbaum's thinking is centred on the hypothetico-deductive model,
Nagel's is impelled by a different conceptual ideal. His philosophical aim is to
work towards an 'ultimately incompletable' picture of reality in which subjective
and material phenomena would have an equal place.

> The subjectivity of consciousness is an irreducible feature of reality – without
> which we would be unable to do physics or anything else – and it must occupy
> as fundamental a place in any credible world view as matter, energy, space,
> time and numbers.
>
> (Nagel 1986, pp. 7–8)

In normal empirical science, thoughts and feelings, values and actions, are represented by their physical manifestations. In Nagel's ideal map, their essential subjectivity would appear in its own right.

Nagel's more inclusive mindset leads him to a different understanding of Freud's legacy. For Grünbaum, psychoanalysis is an ordinary science which has yet to vindicate its claims. For Nagel, its distinctive subject matter demands an exceptional form of scientific explanation and testing. He does not contest Grünbaum's verdict that psychoanalytic hypotheses have not received validation through the experimental method routinely applied in the natural sciences. Any faulty reasoning that Grünbaum may have unearthed leaves him unperturbed. His message is that Freud is not just another empirical scientist, and psychoanalysis is not simply an attempt to take forward an existing scientific programme. He sees it as a new perspective on a part of reality hitherto untouched by science, which enables questions to be asked and answers given that the framework of the mainstream sciences cannot accommodate. Nor, therefore, is their methodology adequate to its special requirements.

In the heat of the NYRB debate, Nagel's challenge is to demonstrate not only that psychoanalysis is scientific, but also that it is worthwhile; but how far he succeeds in this seems to depend on whether or not one was convinced in the first place. I shall argue that he does enough to defend his claim that psychoanalysis is of value, but not enough to demonstrate that this value is scientific. Nagel's review is an eloquent portrayal of psychoanalysis as a cultural development of great significance which demands evaluation by standards appropriate to its unique subject matter. But although the criteria he puts forward do not rule out regarding psychoanalysis as a science, neither do they rule it in. To establish that psychoanalysis is actually rather than provisionally scientific, he would need to show not just how it is different from other empirical sciences, but also more of the ways in which it is the same.

However, Nagel's case does not have to end here. A more persuasive argument can be put together by bringing in thoughts which he relegates to the margins of his review, but elaborates elsewhere. In an earlier paper (1974) Nagel discusses Freud's metapsychological conception of the psychical domain as the theoretical linchpin which holds subjective and objective 'reality' together.[1] Given the problems attached to the metapsychology, making it the focus of his case is not enough to establish psychoanalysis as an empirical science. But without it, psychoanalysis as Nagel describes it is more readily taken as a hermeneutic discipline in which the interpretation of meaning is the key. This is a conclusion he would thoroughly deplore.

Background

Nagel's individualistic approach makes his case more complex than Grünbaum's. After outlining his approach to science, this section goes on to explain more thoroughly the details of his claim and the main objection to it, identified by

Grünbaum. This prepares the ground for their closer examination in the discussion section.

Nagel's approach to science

Having started out a physicist, Nagel has a high regard for science. He attributes the scientific enterprise to the same impulse which gives rise to morality: the urge to gain a conceptual purchase on reality beyond one's own perspective.[2] Science, he believes, has given us real and concrete knowledge about reality: 'there is . . . an enormous body of incontestable discoveries, which make the rejection of realism in these domains nothing but a philosophical fantasy' (Nagel 1995, p. 182). As far as the basic elements of reality are concerned, he is saying, it is simply not rational to dispute that the scientific picture is a true reflection of what is really there.

On the other hand, Nagel's commitment to science is not unthinking or uncritical. Having moved from physics to philosophy, he is equally alert to the dangers of 'scientism' – the belief that knowledge produced by normal scientific means is superior to any other kind. In arguing that scientific methodology could go beyond the methodology of the natural sciences, he opens up a possibility closed to Grünbaum. Mental phenomena, he suggests, might be investigated scientifically without subjecting them to the terms and methods of the physical sciences.

> Objectivity in any area of thought requires some method of confirming or disconfirming the observations or judgements of one individual by reference to those of another. But the particular way we do this for physical data is determined by the nature of those data and should not be identified with objectivity in general.
>
> (Nagel 1995, p. 88)

He is saying that while the methodology of the physical sciences may give objective knowledge about their particular field, there must be other ways of achieving objective knowledge of mental phenomena.

Nagel declares these philosophical commitments to be among his most consistent. Over the twenty-five-year span of his collection of reviews, '[my] basic sympathies and antipathies – antireductionist and more or less realist – haven't changed much' (ibid., p. 3). As a realist, he assumes that 'reality' exists independently of our perception of it, and that it is possible for science to gain a reasonably accurate picture of it. As an antireductionist, he holds the view that the mental conception of reality cannot be reduced to the physical conception of reality. He believes that they are governed by different principles and different forms of explanation.

Nagel's position has specific implications for his current task. To reinstate psychoanalysis as an empirical science, he must demonstrate that it meets his own conditions of realism and antireductionism. This means establishing the objectivity of psychoanalytic subject matter while distinguishing it from reality physically conceived. He has to show that the psychoanalytic field of study exists independently of any particular point of view, is as real as the material world, and must be conceived, explained and corroborated equally but differently from it.

Nagel's claim

Nagel's claim begins where Grünbaum's leaves off. He agrees with Richard Wollheim, the author of the main book he reviews (Wollheim 1993), that psychoanalytic explanations are closer to the ordinary ways in which people seek to understand themselves and each other than they are to the propositions of the sciences that preceded them. It is 'commonsense psychology' that they build on, rather than nineteenth-century psychiatry or neurophysiology. Therefore, Nagel argues, the evidence on which psychoanalysis might be vindicated must be more like the evidence of common sense than the data which go to validate these other sciences and their modern counterparts. 'The main problem about the unconscious is not metaphysical', he blithely declares. 'The problem, rather, is whether the evidence supports such a vast extension, by analogy, of mental concepts to the unconscious' (1994a, p. 139 below). Nagel is saying that the main sticking-point for psychoanalysis is methodological rather than ontological. It is not the constitution of psychical processes which is problematic, but the question of whether the evidence of 'common sense' is enough to justify treating the psychical domain as a continuation of ordinary consciousness.

Both the traditional natural sciences and the newer social sciences deal with phenomena which are observable from the outside; this is why the supporting evidence must also be externally checkable. Psychoanalysis and 'commonsense psychology' work differently. They seek an 'understanding of human beings "from within", so that we could put ourselves in their shoes and make sense of their symptoms and responses' (ibid., p. 140 below). In the previous chapter, it became clear that the 'first-person' perspective assumes a mental rather than a physical conception of subjective phenomena. This effectively blocks the evaluation of psychoanalytic concepts by normal empirical means, but Nagel denies that this prevents psychoanalysis from being accorded scientific status. He suggests, with Wollheim, that by adding foundations in a dimension beyond consciousness, and organizing a pre-scientific body of knowledge into a coherent theoretical system, psychoanalysis raises 'commonsense psychology' to the level of an empirical science. Since it can only be a science of a very unusual kind, Nagel concludes that to evaluate psychoanalysis by the criteria of the traditional empirical sciences is to misconceive its nature.

Nagel argues nevertheless that in its broadest outlines, though not in its narrower specificities, psychoanalysis has already received empirical validation. It consists in the direct recognition of the psychoanalytic mode of explanation both inside and outside the psychoanalytic setting. The myriad individual endorsements that make up its general acceptance into the Western sense of human nature take the place of confirmation through experiment and prediction. Nagel sees this personal and professional 'evidence' as preceding and accompanying, rather than displacing, the formal testing through behavioural signs which Grünbaum advocates. Since the evidence of behaviour alone cannot touch the subjectivity of psychoanalytic subject matter, conventional scientific evidence will always fall short, and 'first-person' evidence will always be central.

Grünbaum's objection

Its faithfulness to actual psychoanalytic thinking gives Nagel's account of psycho-analysis a striking advantage over Grünbaum's. By placing what makes practical sense to individuals at the centre, he captures the immediacy of psychoanalytic illumination. Whether evidence that appears to be wholly subjective is compatible with a scientific approach, however, is another matter; and it is here that Grünbaum takes issue with Nagel. Crews discards Nagel's 'oversubtle arguments' as a case of 'special pleading' (in NYRB April 20, 1995, p. 73); but Grünbaum objects more cogently that 'this epistemological recipe of intuitive credibility . . . degenerates into subjectivity' (in NYRB August 11, 1994, p. 54).[3] He is remonstrating that subjective corroboration is not enough to validate theoretical knowledge. If psychoanalysis is to be accepted as an empirical science, more objective evidence must be brought to bear. Grünbaum has identified the central challenge con-fronting Nagel's case.

In contrast to Grünbaum's external perspective, Nagel's approach is distinc-tively internal. He is suggesting that far from being a conventional science, psychoanalysis introduces a fundamental change into how psychological reality is treated: 'Grünbaum identifies it with a set of general psychological principles; I identify it with a [new] form of understanding' (Nagel 1994b, p. 151 below). Grünbaum's underlying materialist foundations tether him to the traditional scientific conception of psychological subject matter as observable behaviour. Nagel, by contrast, takes what Freud is seeking to explain to be subjectivity itself. He sees Freud's genius in his reconception of the psychological in terms of the substructure rather than the superstructure of experience. Psychoanalysis, he argues, illuminates the unconscious yet subjective processes which give rise to experience, rather than the behavioural and physical signs to which experience itself gives rise. The 'core of his [Freud's] contribution lies . . . in a form of insight that depends not on the application of specifically psychoanalytic laws but on the extension of the familiar forms of psychological explanation beyond their tradi-tional, rational domain' (ibid., p. 151 below). Nagel does not see psychoanalytic explanations as the psychological equivalent of the universal laws of the physical sciences, as Grünbaum assumes. In Nagel's view, they depend not on specific causal propositions, but on extending the interpretative structures of 'common-sense psychology' beyond their normal reach.

If psychoanalysis is concerned with conscious and unconscious experience, there can be no means of direct external measurement. The immediate evidence, as Nagel remarks, must be more akin to first-person judgement. But this involves a form of explanation that appears to be at odds with the hypothetico-deductive model. Scientific validation rests on the hypothetico-deductive formula and the degree to which the data bear it out. The mathematical basis of the formula and the outwardly observable evidence applied give an objective measure of justification. Practical psychological explanations are validated differently. They depend less on outwardly observable evidence and deductive or inductive reasoning than on the extent to which they fit into 'a rationally coherent interpretation of the whole person as an intentional subject' (ibid., p. 151 below). A human action is not explained by analysing the observable movements of the body, but by understanding what the individual is trying to do. There is no wholly objective measure on which the justifiability of a practical explanation can be decided. It depends on the degree to which it makes subjective (or intersubjective) sense.

Grünbaum is quite aware that psychoanalysis seeks to explain experience as well as behaviour. What he cannot countenance is that the principles underlying psychoanalytic propositions are based not on objectively observable data, but on something he considers far more nebulous. Nagel himself describes the justifying principle of psychoanalytic concepts as the 'intuitive plausibility' of the explanations they engender. On the face of it, this looks like a retreat from his scientific defence of psychoanalysis; but he then goes on to explain why it bears comparison with the hypothetico-deductive process. The evidential base of psychoanalytic theory is constituted, he says, by the 'endless simple cases, in which . . . [the principle which makes the interpretation rationally coherent] can be confirmed by possibilities [not guarantees] of prediction and control . . . That's what I mean by intuitive plausibility', he states (ibid., p. 152 below). And that is also why he sees interpretative explanation as a form of causal explanation, and therefore defensible as a species of scientific explanation. Nagel's point is that even practical explanations, based on subjective forms of evidence, are like hypothetico-deductive explanations in that they too are directed in part towards gaining knowledge and control of what might happen in the future; it is just that they go about this in a different way.

At first sight, Nagel's claim looks farfetched. Interpretation is generally taken to be an alternative to scientific explanation rather than a version of it. While 'intuitive plausibility' and 'rational coherence' are the obvious ways of evaluating interpretative explanations, they say nothing about the 'factual' truth that science sets itself to attain. Nagel has to show that sweeping away established scientific goalposts in favour of apparently subjective factors is not, as Crews suggests, a resort to 'special pleading'. How can it be justifiable to suspend the normal scientific requirements of objectively definable subject matter and publicly observable testing? And how can his new criteria of 'rational coherence' and 'intuitive plausibility' be appropriately scientific? Both issues have to be resolved if psychoanalysis is to meet Nagel's own conditions for objectivity of realism on the one hand and antireductionism on the other.

Discussion

The first part of this section examines these two questions through the explicit case that Nagel makes in his review. The second part builds up and investigates the hidden case that emerges when his earlier discussion of the metapsychology is brought in.

Scientific status without the metapsychology

There are two grounds on which Nagel could justify the introduction of new scientific criteria: if psychoanalysis is so unlike other sciences that it can be evaluated only by radically different criteria; or if psychoanalysis is fundamentally continuous with other sciences but has special features which demand an adjustment to the normal criteria. The first puts psychoanalysis forward as a new kind of science; the second presents it as a conventional science investigating a new kind of subject matter.

Psychoanalysis as paradigm shift

Nagel opens his review with the transformation Freud's theories have wrought on the Western sense of personhood. For him, this takes the significance of Freud's work beyond any part of it. 'Great intellectual revolutionaries change the way we think. They pose new questions and devise new methods of answering them – and we cannot unlearn those forms of thought simply by discovering errors of reasoning on the part of their creators' (Nagel 1994a, p. 138 below). If we accept this, then Grünbaum's unpicking of individual propositions misses the point: 'Such thinkers have an effect much deeper than can be captured by a set of particular hypotheses' (ibid.).

What Nagel is describing sounds very much like what the philosopher Thomas Kuhn calls a 'paradigm change' (Kuhn 1996). This is a radical shift of perspective within a particular scientific field, instigated by the pressure to resolve a critical accumulation of anomalies, or failed predictions. In this context of impasse and frustration a new picture of the field's phenomena may emerge, gradually or suddenly, opening up new lines of enquiry which call for different methods of investigation and fresh standards of evidence. The accompanying upheavals in the science concerned are therefore normative (to do with rules, tests and standards) as well as cognitive (to do with theoretical content). They amount to a 'reconstruction of the field from new fundamentals . . . that changes some of the field's most elementary theoretical generalizations as well as many of its paradigm methods and applications' (Kuhn 1996, p. 85). Newton's gravitational laws, Darwin's natural selection and Einstein's relativity theory are all examples of paradigm shifts. Each brings in a new vision of reality involving not simply additional theoretical content but new *kinds* of concepts, principles and methodologies.

Seen in this light, the whole NYRB debate appears to fall into place as an episode in the struggle between the established paradigm of empirical science and the new Freudian paradigm. If this were accepted, a number of consequences would follow. Grünbaum's protestations that Freud himself insists on psychoanalysis being a normal science would cease to be relevant, since Freud would be in no position to assess and argue for the new ways in which his work might be scientific. Kuhn describes scientific revolutions as typically 'invisible', and changes of paradigm as often identifiable only in retrospect (ibid., ch. 11). Nagel would find himself free to evaluate psychoanalysis independently from Freud's documented views where necessary, as well as those of the traditional empirical sciences.

Finally, the obduracy of the disagreement between Nagel and Grünbaum would come as no surprise. Kuhn describes how the competing world views of different 'paradigms' prevent the settling of differences through an appeal to shared higher principles. The 'facts' to be explained can emerge fully only in the terms brought in by the new paradigm, and these are necessarily irreconcilable with those of the old paradigm. If there were a higher principle that could be agreed on and which could lead towards a resolution, the theory being introduced would be by definition not a new paradigm but a modification of an existing paradigm. This means there can be no supreme rules which all valid paradigms must meet and against which new paradigms can be judged. 'As in political revolutions, so in paradigm choice there is no standard higher than the assent of the relevant community' (ibid., p. 94).[4]

All these factors are borne out in the NYRB dispute. Grünbaum and Nagel both start from the premise that as a causal system, psychoanalysis needs empirical confirmation of its hypotheses; but this does not help them resolve their differences, nor even take them very much further. They seem to be talking about different subjects, set in different frames of reference, with different rules and standards, in just the manner that Kuhn describes. Where Grünbaum is concerned with externally identifiable signs, Nagel is looking at subjective experience. Grünbaum assumes a universal scientific model of conjecture and refutation, operated by prediction and experiment, based on evidence which must be there for all to see. Nagel is entertaining a broader conception of science which includes the practical vindication of modes of explanation which begin with personal meaning rather than a publicly identifiable event. Where 'evidence' is only privately observable, the causal links are inevitably less absolute and less clear cut.

These divergent assumptions culminate in Nagel's acceptance, and Grünbaum's rejection, of the idea of an unconscious realm of experience which is ordered, affective and dynamic, the force behind behaviour and consciousness. Grünbaum sees a bizarre speculation which is being introduced into an existing scientific paradigm and therefore requires unequivocal corroboration. Nagel sees the 'first principle' of psychoanalysis, the assumption that makes psychoanalytic explanations possible. As such, it can receive 'intuitive' support, but nothing like empirical 'proof'.

Apart from the ontological question, the foundational status of the psychoanalytic unconscious precludes empirical testing. Attempting to do so would mean assuming an even more basic principle, which would then itself require testing, until an initial assumption is finally made. Foundational principles, as Nagel remarks, can be confirmed only backwards: 'intuitive plausibility . . . necessarily applies in the first instance to specific explanations' (Nagel 1994b, p. 152 below). The ideas on which theoretical systems are built have first to be drawn from particular phenomena: 'confirmation goes from the particular to the general: the general theory of repression and psychosexual development has to be supported by its individual instances, rather than the reverse' (ibid.). These ideas can be used as actual theoretical resources only when enough individual instances have been gathered and (subjectively) confirmed to give confidence in their explanatory potential. Even then, they can be drawn on in individual instances but cannot be applied across the board.

Nagel's view is clearly the closer to Freud's, based as it is on the 'fundamental hypothesis' of unconscious mental processes; so at this point, it looks as though Nagel's case may be gaining ground. Accepting psychoanalysis as a new scientific paradigm, moreover, would make its mere survival *de facto* evidence for its validity as an empirical science. By Kuhn's definition, paradigms are only subject to evaluation during the process of acceptance. The testing of a new paradigm concludes either with its disappearance from the scientific scene, or with the 'assent of the relevant community' and the absorption of its theoretical structures into a new scientific orthodoxy. The intellectual and practical currency retained by psychoanalysis is evidence that it has passed some such test.

It may even be possible to lay to rest Grünbaum's objection that Nagel's criteria represent a '[degeneration] into subjectivity' (see p. 38 above). The Kuhnian passport to scientific status is very like the 'intuitive plausibility' that Nagel puts forward as the ultimate guarantor of all theoretical foundations. Kuhn's argument is in effect that all theories are interpretations of events. In the last resort, every theoretical system relies on the 'plausibility' of its fundamental principles and the overall 'rational coherence' of its explanations to those for whom they are important. While further conditions may also be entailed, his bare claim seems incontestable. If there were a higher authority for any form of knowledge than its considered acceptance by those who make use of it, no genuinely new developments could ever take place.

This subjective form of evaluation is not the soft option dismissed by Grünbaum. The testing undergone by a challenger paradigm must be more searching and less predictable than any applied to the developments of existing paradigms. A new paradigm must at least potentially offer a better 'fit' than its predecessor paradigm with the reality which confronts all attempts at explanation. As Kuhn points out, the upheaval of conceptual and methodological 'retooling' is only undergone when scientists are convinced that there is no other way forward. And as Nagel makes clear in his 'Addendum' (1994b, pp. 151–153 below), though not in the review itself, the 'relevant community' for psychoanalysis does not amount to Grünbaum's gullible mass. It includes not only psychoanalysts, psychotherapists and counsellors, whom Grünbaum would of course discount, but also the artistic world, big business,[5] and philosophers like Nagel and Wollheim, as well as at least some physical scientists. Nagel quotes Einstein's commendatory letter to Freud as an example (Nagel 1994a, p. 285 below).

Psychoanalysis as a new branch of psychology

For many reasons, then, it is enlightening to see Grünbaum's and Nagel's conflicting conceptions of psychoanalysis as the encounter of incompatible paradigms. It even looks as though the problematic metapsychology might be bypassed in favour of Nagel's first-person criteria. There is, however, a stumbling block. Psychoanalysis has neither displaced nor significantly influenced any scientific theory or paradigm, past or present, and certainly not the traditional hypothetico-deductive approach to psychological subject matter sanctioned by Grünbaum. With even the psychoanalytic world divided about its status, it is simply not tenable to maintain that psychoanalysis has proved its credentials by its survival *as a science*. Freud's influence is undeniable, but that in itself does nothing to underwrite the scientific standing of his theories. Science has no monopoly on intellectual revolution, particularly since its dislocation from philosophy began two centuries before Freud. As Nagel's review makes clear, the arena in which Freud's ideas have endured and in which their influence has spread is not scientific psychology but the practical psychology of everyday life. But this, together with its psychoanalytic extension, can more readily be seen as hermeneutic or interpretative in nature than as scientific. The bedrock on which these practical psychologies are built appears to be subjective rather than objective reality.

Nagel, however, is too careful a thinker to be too easily dismissed. He is writing a review, not a polemic, so he assumes a sympathetic readership, and even in the 'Addendum' answering Grünbaum's response, he goes into only a little more detail. What might he come up with if pressed further?

Grünbaum demands to know why the 'pervasive cultural influence' of psychoanalytic theory should count for any more than the 'intuitive plausibility' of superstitions, for example.[6] 'Does Nagel apply his cultural criterion to them? If not, why not?' (in NYRB August 11, 1994, pp. 54–55). Nagel replies that the difference lies in the continuity between psychoanalytic principles and established scientific principles and knowledge. He points out that while it would be inconsistent to subscribe both to modern science and, for example, to a belief in supernatural forces, psychoanalysis is 'not in any way incompatible with the rest of our scientific understanding of how things work. It is part of our idea of the natural order that people's behaviour is influenced by their mental condition'

(1994b, p. 153 below). Psychoanalysis simply proposes that this influence runs deeper than was previously thought.

Nagel's answer indicates that he is resting his claim not just on the differences between psychoanalysis and other empirical sciences, but also on their similarity; and there is no reason why psychoanalysis' most innovatory features should also be its most scientific. If the scientific standing of Freud's theories cannot be established by presenting them as a new kind of science, perhaps casting them as a new and rather eccentric branch of the established science of psychology might do the same job. Rather than being treated as a new scientific paradigm, psychoanalysis might then be vindicated on principles which it would share with other empirical sciences.

This way of understanding psychoanalysis seems to accord with Freud's own views. He refers to psychoanalysis as a 'young' science, and a 'new' psychology, describing the existing academic psychology as not really psychology at all, but 'belonging rather to the physiology of the sense organs' (Freud 1926, S.E. 20, p. 191); he means that this kind of psychology defines the human organism as a physical rather than an experiencing system, and so has no need for more than physical concepts. These remarks suggest that it is through the subjectivity of its subject matter that Freud sees psychoanalysis as marking a break with the existing experimental psychology, and thereby with the other sciences. Without psychoanalysis, he points out, there is no actual 'science of mental life'. There is only an unsystematic and fragmented field, 'with no respect and no authority', occupied by a motley assortment of novelists, philosophers, biographers and other amateurs; a field in which 'everyone can "run wild"', since 'everyone regards himself as a psychologist' (ibid., p. 192).

'Rational coherence' and 'intuitive plausibility' are the natural evaluators of the practical interpretations through which we make sense of this domain. But organizing 'commonsense psychology' into a coherent theoretical system is not enough to make it into the empirical science that Freud, for one, is convinced that it is. He refers to psychoanalysis as 'a branch of psychology' (Freud 1932, S.E. 22, p. 158), which he goes on to distinguish from biology and the physical sciences (ibid., p. 159). But he also calls psychology itself a 'natural science',[7] because it is the study of a 'natural' object, the psyche. Again, he seems to be portraying psychoanalysis as an enquiry into a new kind of scientific subject matter, rather than as a new way of looking at established scientific subject matter.[8] Just as Freud's view of psychoanalysis may not be so tightly bound to the normal criteria of the physical sciences as under Grünbaum's definition, so it may not be able to be cut loose from them to the degree that a paradigm shift would allow.

There is no overriding need to abide by Freud's own sense of the kind of subject psychoanalysis is. At the same time, there is no obvious reason to disagree with his apparent estimation that it is a branch of psychology made special by its subject matter. But provisionally accepting Freud's judgement means provisionally accepting its implications for psychoanalysis's mode of validation. A new paradigm is validated through its acceptance as a normal science, in the process setting new standards and methods by which scientific normality is judged. A theoretical system seeking acceptance on the basis of its similarity to other sciences, however, must show its continuity with them. While it need not be reducible to another science, it would have to meet criteria which are also applicable to other sciences within the same paradigm.

It is here that the absence of a focus on the metapsychology makes itself felt. Nagel's review gives it no more than the briefest of glances, to justify his comment that the 'main problem about the unconscious is not metaphysical' (see p. 37 above). This throwaway remark is suggesting that in psychoanalytic and practical psychology alike, the assumption that mental phenomena have a physical aspect prevents 'unconscious mental life' from being a contradiction in terms. Unless 'mental life' is taken to include an unconscious dimension, it would be like saying 'unconscious conscious life'; and unless mental processes have a physical realization as such, unconscious mental processes could have no actual existence. Nagel presumes that this assumption disposes of the metaphysical question. Since no new ideas are involved beyond what is already accepted in ordinary life, the normal picture of reality can remain undisturbed. The only *scientific* issue which remains is one of methodology: can first-person judgement legitimately stretch beyond its normal conscious scope to endorse unconscious processes?

Immediately, this begs the question of what the evidence of first-person judgement amounts to. As a realist, Nagel assumes that ordinary perception reveals a certain amount about the reality which science is interested in – the reality that exists independently of any particular person and any particular mind. To that extent, first-person evidence is at least not *anti*-scientific. But even if this is accepted, it still does not tell us which aspects of reality are reflected, and which distorted. This makes it difficult to use first-person evidence to construct a picture of reality that both science and psychoanalysis can share. All too easily, the same problems arise as with Grünbaum's hypothetico-deductive model. If the picture is of physical reality, 'intuitive plausibility' is no more to be trusted than first-person evidence in an identification parade, while the 'rational coherence' it affords could be as undependable as that provided by the ancient theory of the humours. If the picture is of 'mental reality', then the metaphysical question of the constitution of psychoanalytic processes returns with full force. Grünbaum's criticism of Nagel seems to be borne out: since first-person evidence is bounded by subjectivity, it cannot explain it in the objective sense that Nagel requires.

Nagel's remarks conceal as much as they reveal. His case is much improved when the metapsychological dimension is brought in, by considering the additional conditions for scientific status which are either implicit in his review or which can be drawn out from some of his earlier writings (Nagel 1974, 1986).

Bringing in the metapsychology

The resounding silence with which mainstream science has greeted Freud's theories means, then, that however innovative and insightful they may be, they do not amount to a *scientific* revolution. Nor, to be fair, does Nagel promote them as such. He takes for granted that the scientific worth of psychoanalysis, like any other science, must finally depend not on how coherent its theories are, but on how true they are: how accurately they represent the reality about the mind that exists independently of all interpretations and all frameworks. He has defended his 'antireductionist' belief that psychoanalytic concepts cannot be evaluated in the same way as physical concepts, but only by subjective endorsement. But it is not clear on what criteria he can defend his 'realist' principle that they represent processes and structures which are as objective as physical processes and structures.

Nagel's explicit criteria of 'intuitive plausibility' and 'rational coherence' are potentially misleading, because they could be playing either of two roles. On the one hand, they are the only possible criteria on which the 'first principles' of new scientific paradigms can be judged. On the other, they are the normal criteria for judging interpretative explanations. Since psychoanalysis does not stand up as a new scientific paradigm, Nagel's criteria cannot be accepted as sufficient for evaluating psychoanalysis as an empirical science. They would be enough to validate psychoanalysis as a system of interpretation, but this is very different from accepting it as an empirical science. Interpretative theories are founded on the multiple, person-centred 'truths' of relativism, rather than on the single objective 'truth' of empirical science. This is not a position that Nagel could ever entertain; hence his scorn for the 'facile subjectivism' he denounces as commonplace in the humanities today (1994a, p. 150 below).

If Nagel cannot accord scientific validity to psychoanalysis on his explicit criteria, perhaps he could do so by presenting it as a new theoretical system which is also scientific. Its 'pervasive cultural influence' can stand as evidence of its theoretical viability, on the basis of the 'intuitive plausibility' of its central concept and the 'rational coherence' of its general form of explanation. So all he needs to do is demonstrate how psychoanalysis meets the minimal conditions of empirical science. Since his review is not an academic paper he does not actually do this, but he indicates three ways in which he thinks it can be done. He suggests that Freud's apparently subjective subject matter is really objective; he records a vote of confidence in the method by which theoretical data are derived from the psychoanalytic setting; and he endorses the systematic nature of psychoanalytic theory and its essential congruence with established scientific knowledge.

Of these three conditions, the second and third can be set aside. While Grünbaum, for one, contests the reliability of psychoanalytic data, this comes down to his lack of trust in psychoanalytic thinking and training. He assumes that psychoanalytic theorists and practitioners will not have developed the capacity for dispassionate observation which would allow them to avoid contaminating their own data. But he provides no evidence for this accusation, and even if such evidence were forthcoming, it would not apply to the 'first principle' of psychoanalysis, the Freudian unconscious, which is our direct concern. The third criterion, the systematic structure of Freud's theories, is not generally disputed, and their compatibility with accepted scientific knowledge depends on how they are understood.

The first condition, the objectivity of psychoanalytic subject matter, is the most fundamental and the most contentious. It is difficult to see how it could be argued other than through the metapsychology. For Nagel, as for Freud, the objectivity of psychoanalytic subject matter and the causal nature of its explanations are the joint linchpins of its scientific status. They come together in Freud's conception of psychical processes as unitary processes with mental and physical 'sides'. This allows them to be seen as part of the causally-ordered material universe but prevents them from being reduced to ordinary physical processes. Each aspect is equally essential to their definition: their physical side links them into the world of matter, while their mental side sets them apart from ordinary physical processes. Thus the central concept and 'first principle' of psychoanalysis seems to hold the potential to meet Nagel's primary criteria of realism and antireductionism – criteria which Freud appears to share.

Both Nagel and Freud believe that empirical science can encompass psychoanalytic subject matter and the psychoanalytic form of explanation. We have already seen that Freud includes psychology in the 'natural sciences' (see p. 44 above). He also considers that 'every science is one-sided . . . physics does not diminish the value of chemistry; it cannot take its place but . . . cannot be replaced by it' (Freud 1926, S.E. 20, p. 231). Nagel stresses, correspondingly, that interpretative explanations are not a class on their own, but a type of causal explanation:

> The fundamental causal principle of commonsense psychology is that . . . you can discover causally relevant conditions (conditions that make a *difference* in precisely Grünbaum's sense) for a human action or thought or emotion by fitting it into a rationally coherent interpretation of the whole person as an intentional subject of this type – by seeing how from the person's point of view it is in some way *justified*.
>
> (Nagel 1994b, pp. 151–152 below, original emphases)

Nagel is taking causality as the overriding principle of empirical science. He is arguing that since interpretative explanations explain how one state of affairs leads from another, they too must be causal explanations; thus interpretative explanations can be part of a scientific approach. The problem then arises of the contradictory assumptions from which the mental and physical conceptions of reality start. To save the determinism of the physical sphere and the autonomy of the mental sphere from being mired in contradiction, Nagel considers it enough to say that their differences do not necessarily mean that one of the two is invalid.

> A psychological theory need not . . . be a rough sketch of the underlying physiological or physical structure. So long as there is no inconsistency at the

level of particular causal connections, it may be that both levels of description and explanation can be true, without anything like a reductive relation
between them.

(Nagel 1974, p. 13)

Nagel is proposing an alternative to the 'eliminative materialism' which proved
to underlie Grünbaum's physicalistic thinking (see p. 27 above). He is saying that
the mental realm does not have to be eliminated in favour of a wholly physical
picture of reality. Instead, the mental and physical conceptual schemes could be
seen as existing together, like patterns on a double-sided fabric. Only in the case
of outright contradiction would there be any need to choose between a mental and
physical explanation of the same event. Otherwise, the mental and physical
'templates' can be taken as equal but different forms of perception and understanding, both of which can be exploited by science.

This approach to their incompatibility is both crucial and debatable. It is the
basis of Nagel's and Freud's contention that meaning and matter, or as Freud
puts it, quality and quantity (Freud 1895, S.E. 1, pp. 307–310), can be explained
in principle, if not in practice, through the same causal structure. As such, it is the
axis of realism on which any reconciliation of the empirical and hermeneutic
approaches must turn. If each is a valid reflection of the same reality, there must
be a common causal principle that both go back to. Since this is the focus of the
final chapter, we will leave the causal question aside to concentrate on the related
issue of the objectivity of psychoanalytic subject matter. Our present purpose is
solely to ascertain whether Nagel's reconstructed claim is sufficiently coherent to
be advanced. Whether or not it succeeds must also be left for later.

Nagel sees phenomena as 'subjective' if they have to be defined from a
particular standpoint, and 'objective' if they can be defined.from no particular
perspective; this correlates with the usual way of understanding mental and
physical phenomena. At first sight, this seems to work against the scientific hopes
of psychoanalysis. Any claim to objectivity would appear to be ruled out by the
subjectivity that we have already identified as a defining characteristic of its
primary clinical subject matter. If psychoanalytic phenomena are experiential –
if they are concerned with unconscious conflicts involving wishing, fearing,
loving and hating – how can they be defined independently from the point of view,
whether conscious or unconscious, of the experiencing individual?[9] This is the
question that has to be resolved before psychoanalysis can even be considered as
an empirical science.

The argument for the objectivity of psychical processes

Freud rests the entire theoretical structure of psychoanalysis on the 'basic
assumption' of the link between the physical brain and the conscious mind (see
p. 13 above). He reasons that since consciousness is a real phenomenon, and since
the role of the brain in consciousness is sufficiently established to be accepted as

knowledge of something real, whatever connects the two must also exist in the objective sense that science demands. Nagel restates Freud's case for the objectivity of psychoanalytic knowledge, which we can now go through in some detail. The basis of the argument is that the primary language of psychoanalysis is the practical or 'mentalistic' language of the clinical theory. The metapsychological models and theories, with their physicalistic language, form a secondary layer developed to explain the clinical theory. The disparity between these two languages is crystallized in what I have been referring to as the 'metapsychology', the psychophysical unity on which the whole of Freud's psychoanalytic enterprise depends.

Nagel sets out Freud's position summarily in his review, and extensively in his earlier 'Freud's Anthropomorphism' (1974). Nagel explains in this paper that Freud uses the mentalistic language of practical psychology only by default. Freud's original aim was to explain psychological processes in terms of the physical processes he thought must underlie them (see Nagel 1974, pp. 13–14; Freud 1895, S.E. 1, p. 295; Grünbaum 1984, ch. 1). When this reductionist endeavour ran into the ground, Freud was left with only the language of experience to fall back on. But since he continued to accord a physical dimension to psychological processes, the primary language of psychoanalysis does not reflect the ontological status of its subject matter.

Nagel draws out the details and implications of Freud's position. He describes Freud as a 'sophisticated materialist' who 'believed that even conscious mental processes [are] also physical processes in the brain, though we know almost nothing about their physical character' (Nagel 1994a, p. 139 below). This belief led Freud to postulate another kind of process, related to the first kind, which does not appear to consciousness in any way:

> since the true nature of the mental processes that appear to consciousness is physical, with consciousness being just one added quality of them, there can be no objection to also describing as mental those intermediate processes, occurring in the same physical system, which do not appear to consciousness even though they may be in many respects physically and functionally similar to those that do.
>
> (Nagel 1974, p. 16)

Nagel is explaining that psychoanalysis is based on the assumption that there are unconscious mental processes. Freud argues that the composition and function of these processes are so similar to those of conscious mental processes that they can be expressed only by analogy with them. Even in the case of conscious mental processes, however, it is only their 'appearance', rather than the processes themselves, which one can be conscious of. As far as unconscious mental processes are concerned, not even their appearance is open to consciousness, but only some of their effects. The primary terminology of psychoanalysis is therefore at two removes from the processes it posits in its foundational hypothesis.

Thus the subject matter of psychoanalysis appears to be subjective, in that it can only be described in the experiential terms in which the subject matter most similar to it appears to consciousness. But it is conceived as objective, since these terms 'stand for' processes which meet the criteria for objectivity. They exist independently of the way in which they appear to consciousness. In themselves, they are as inaccessible to consciousness as any other reality behind appearance. They therefore do not depend for their definition on any particular perspective.

While Nagel largely accepts this ingenious explanatory strategy, he also detects a problem. A theory which is obliged to use mentalistic terms and concepts for what are also physical processes could not contribute directly to a fully objective account of reality. In particular, it would be unable to get outside the assumption of an individual perspective that its subjective terminology would carry.

> Since it appears to be part of our idea of the physical world that what goes on in it can be apprehended not just from one point of view but from infinitely many, because its objective nature is external to any point of view taken toward it, there is reason to believe that until these subjective features are left behind, the hypotheses of a mentalistic psychology will not be accepted as physical explanations.
>
> (Nagel 1974, p. 24)

This would mean that a theoretical system like psychoanalysis can never fully reflect the objective reality it is referring to, because objective realities stand outside particular standpoints and are independent of them.

Nagel nevertheless considers it possible, though by no means certain, that such a theory could contribute indirectly to an objective account of reality. Psychoanalysis might be able to clarify its field to the point where a less restrictive language could be developed, in which unconscious mental processes could be expressed directly rather than by analogy. This may not be attainable by enlarging the physicalistic frame of reference of mainstream empirical science, but only through the further evolution of the mentalistic framework of practical psychology. He points out that the features which unconscious mental processes share with conscious mental processes 'need not . . . be features describable in the terms of current neurophysiology. They may be describable only in the terms of a future psychology whose form will be in part determined by the development of psychoanalytic theory' (Nagel 1974, pp. 17–18). Thus psychoanalysis could be an interim theory, lying between the subjective framework of everyday psychology and the objective framework of the physical sciences and perhaps, of a future form of psychology.

Nagel stresses, however, that this outcome is by no means assured. 'Psychoanalytic theory would have to change a great deal before it comes to be regarded as part of the physical description of reality. And perhaps it . . . will never achieve the kind of objectivity necessary for this end' (ibid., p. 25). Nagel's hope is that psychoanalysis may help bring more precision to its mentalistic concepts, paving the way towards a more objective picture of its psychical domain. At the same time, he is voicing his doubts that things could go that smoothly.

Despite his reservations, it is on this basis that Nagel's case must rest. His essential argument is that psychoanalysis should be seen as an empirical science because although it is irreducible to physics, it is compatible with materialism. Its mentalistic framework prevents it from being reduced to a purely physical theory, but since its terms and concepts refer to processes which have a physical existence, it can count as a theory of objective reality. This explains, rather obliquely, how Nagel thinks psychoanalysis can meet his primary criteria of 'realism' and 'anti-reductionism' through the metapsychological equation of processes designated as mental on the one hand, and physical on the other.

Nagel's account is broadly consistent with the metaphysical views that seem to have endured throughout Freud's professional life. In 1895, Freud speaks of mental processes as neither reducible to physical processes nor separable from them, but as their 'subjective side' (Freud 1895, S.E. 1, p. 311).[10] In 1938, he restates this as: '[the] phenomena with which we were dealing . . . have an organic and biological side as well' (Freud 1938a, S.E. 23, p. 195). Nagel's petition for psychoanalysis to be accepted as an empirical science rests entirely on this hypothesis, but he has not examined this link to see if it stands up to scrutiny. Without further investigation, all Nagel has really shown is that psychoanalysis *may* be scientific. Whether or not it *is* scientific depends on whether the metapsychological foundation that Freud puts forward can be sufficiently endorsed by the 'intuitive plausibility' and 'rational coherence' of the interpretations it makes possible. Otherwise, it must be set aside as mere conjecture, generating hypotheses which can neither be confirmed nor refuted in any justifiably scientific sense.

Conclusion

Nagel's claim, like Grünbaum's, presupposes a metapsychological foundation; but it is here that the real problems start. The scientific status of psychoanalysis depends on finding a way of treating psychological processes 'objectively'. This means demonstrating the matchability in principle of psychological and physiological processes. If this could be established, the link between mentalistic and physicalistic explanations would follow. There is no avoiding this: without a material ground there is no way of getting from 'how things seem' to 'how things are'. Unless Nagel can make a convincing case for the regular and systematic correspondence between the mental and physical domains, he cannot defend psychoanalysis as an empirical science, innovative or not.

For Nagel, 'the main problem about the unconscious is not metaphysical'. His realist inclinations lead him to presume that experience and its unconscious substratum are ultimately understandable only through their inherence to matter. But as an antireductionist, he holds the position that psychological explanations are based on different principles from physical explanations; in which case, the objective physical reality of unconscious mental processes would not help to understand them.

Nagel's two primary conditions seem to be coming apart. If mentalistic concepts and explanations are neither reducible to the physicalistic level nor independent of it, what relation can he be envisaging between them? He can only be supposing that mentalistic explanations 'supersede' physicalistic explanations. This means that a psychological explanation would be the alternative form of a corresponding physical explanation, the exact psychological equivalent of physical terms that are definable, even if they have not yet been defined. Yet as he himself concedes, such constant and neat correspondence between these two contrasting realms is not in sight, although it is self-evident that some relationship must exist.

> Perhaps finally the physical explanations of the phenomena in question will not be reached by progressive refinement and exactness in our mentalistic understanding, but will come only in a form whose relation to mentalistic theories cannot be conceived by us.
>
> (Nagel 1974, p. 25)

Perhaps the full explanation of psychical processes may be found in physical terms which connect with mentalistic terms and concepts in as yet unthought-of ways.

However much Freud might want to make objective sense of what is subjective, Nagel is hinting that it may not be possible to do so in this way. Psychological and physical explanations may be set within conceptual systems which are irreducibly distinct: 'to assume that an objective psychology, whose concepts refer to physical phenomena, will roughly preserve the distinctions and categories embodied in commonsense mental concepts – is to assume a great deal' (ibid., p. 19). Certainly Freud, despite his best efforts, could never begin to formulate the regular relation between the 'qualitative' features of subjectively-perceived phenomena and the 'quantitative' features of materially-conceived phenomena on which his account depends. From the *Project* onwards, he strains towards this, eventually all but losing hope:

> Pleasure and unpleasure . . . cannot be referred to an increase or decrease of a quantity . . . It appears that they depend, not on this quantitative factor, but on some characteristic of it which we can only describe as a qualitative one . . . We do not know.
>
> (Freud 1924a, S.E. 19, p. 160)

His foundational conception of unitary processes which are mental yet physical, meaningful yet inaccessible to consciousness, may be nothing more than a conceptual *deus ex machina* to get him out of a tight spot. It may not be possible to forge a common language for mental and physical phenomena. Psychoanalysis may be unable to bring scientific status to 'commonsense psychology'.

Without examining the metapsychological foundations further, all that Nagel's expanded review can tell us for sure is that Grünbaum was right: whatever else may vindicate psychoanalysis, the principles of mainstream empirical science cannot do so. Nagel's more sensitive reading makes clear that interpretative explanations, validated by first-person 'evidence', are as necessary to psychoanalysis as its psychophysical foundation. But instead of justifying the scientific nature of psychoanalytic explanations, Nagel's two criteria end up working against each other. The glimmer of scientific hope that is kindled by the metapsychological possibility of objectivism is damped down by the antireductionism he so persuasively argues.

Nagel's arguments establish that in spite of Grünbaum's doubts, the (relative) permanence of the Freudian revolution suggests strongly that the basic concepts of psychoanalysis must be founded on something more than a series of lucky breaks. But it is through the 'cultural criterion' that Nagel persuades us of this, rather than through his account of psychoanalysis as an empirical science. The principle of psychophysical unity on which such status would depend cannot be embraced as it stands. But before we go on to examine it more closely, we should make sure that it is necessary to do so. If psychoanalysis is to find justification as an empirical science, the metapsychological question cannot be avoided. In a hermeneutic account, however, validation takes a different form. It goes back to the subject's way of knowing, rather than the independent existence of the object of knowledge. If psychoanalysis could be shown to belong to this theoretical category, Freud's psychophysical correspondence could legitimately be set aside.

The next step, therefore, is to consider Habermas' hermeneutic reading of psychoanalysis. Only if it proves inadequate or misconceived will there be any call to look further into the metapsychological foundation on which Freud's and Nagel's case depends.

Chapter 4

'Self-Reflection as Science'

Is psychoanalysis really a form of hermeneutics?

Introduction

Throughout the NYRB debate, no one considers whether psychoanalysis could be a science which is valid without being empirically based. Is it possible to have an evaluable theoretical system with subject matter which is not publicly observable, directly or indirectly, in practice or in principle?

The empirical approach is based on the idea of a reality which exists independently of the observer. Although, by definition, this reality cannot be directly apprehended, the sensory tracks it leaves allow its nature to be inferred. The hermeneutic approach, by contrast, rejects both the possibility and the rationality of excluding the knower from what can be known. The aim is not to attain fully impersonal knowledge, but to reach clarity about how knowledge develops and resides in human minds. For Crews, Grünbaum and Nagel, only the empirical approach holds epistemological authority. They are united in rejecting hermeneutic forms of validation, for psychoanalysis as for any subject worthy of being called a science (see Grünbaum 1984, ch. 1; Nagel 1994a, pp. 149–150 below). If a proposition, whether causal or interpretative, cannot be checked against some kind of tangible reality, they see it as remaining at the level of opinion. Unless it can be shown to be more than subjectively conceivable and testable, it cannot count as knowledge.

The problem of validation in the human sciences is a central concern of Jürgen Habermas. In *Knowledge and Human Interests* (1971) he develops an early and influential hermeneutic reading of Freud as part of an attempt to move beyond what he sees as a complacent objectivism in empirical science, allied with an uncritical subjectivism in the human or 'cultural' sciences. Habermas' thesis is that all disciplines should be grounded in the acknowledgment that what we call 'reality' has a dual nature. There is the reality which we take to exist outside ourselves and independently of ourselves, and there is also the reality which is lived and experienced subjectively. He suggests that these involve different ways of knowing which can be reconciled only through critical reflection: by getting clear about what an empirical-scientific approach already takes for granted, and what practical experiencing must itself presuppose. His larger aim is thus to build a critique of knowledge which can stand as a foundation for all subjects.

Psychoanalysis holds a key position in Habermas' project. Like Nagel, he sees it as a transformational subject, breaking new bounds in what can be known. For Nagel, its exclusivity lies in its promise of illuminating an as yet uncharted portion of the world. But for Habermas, it lies in having both its subject matter and its application centred in self-reflection. By this he means that psychoanalytic knowledge cannot be gained or applied automatically, but only through reflecting on its personal source and field. This sets it apart from normal empirical science, where the tradition of 'positivism'[1] can make critical thought appear unnecessary. From a positivist perspective, the established procedures of empirical science hold indisputable authority, and only knowledge gained in this way can be treated as real or 'positive' knowledge. This leads to the belief that knowledge can be sought and applied by following purely technical rules and procedures, with no consideration of their inbuilt biases and limitations. It is because psychoanalysis can never become a 'thought-free zone' that it appears to Habermas as an oasis of reason in the positivist desert, a 'science' which incorporates its own critique rather than excluding it.

Habermas' view of psychoanalysis stems from a different position on the metapsychology. He recognizes its foundational status, but rather than avoiding it, he confronts it head on. His essential claim is that Freud's move from the practical psychological level of the clinical theory to an unobservable physical level in the metapsychological models is a step too far. He points out that it is the potential for self-reflection within the analytic situation that sets the parameters for psychoanalytic theory, not its physiological particularities. Therefore, he argues, the foundations of psychoanalysis should also be psychological in nature. This means the metapsychological models and theories should be hermeneutically reconstituted, a task which he carries out by recasting them as the principles underlying the 'general interpretations', or clinical concepts and theories, which make up the clinical level of psychoanalytic theory.

On this reading, psychoanalysis loses all hope of acceptance as an empirical science. It becomes defensible only as a theory of how things appear, with nothing to say about what might exist independently. But Habermas does not see this as diminishing its value. On the contrary, he suggests that if Freud had not been seduced by the positivist dream – the dream that all knowledge could be subjugated to empirical methodology – he might have recognized psychoanalysis for what it is: a revolutionary new way of interpreting personal dysfunction, rather than a weak and aberrant psychophysiology.

I shall argue that Habermas successfully locates the subject matter of psychoanalysis in the symbolic realm, severely undermining Freud's grounds for theorizing it in the quasi-material terms of the metapsychological models and theories. His intricate account of its reflexive, self-critical structure leads to a bold vindication of the heart of its clinical theory. Broadly, then, Habermas' version of psychoanalysis wins out over those of Grünbaum, Freud and Nagel: psychoanalysis makes more sense as a hermeneutic theory than as an empirical science. But the price of greater coherence is smaller scope. The problem of connecting the mental and physical realms in a single theory, which was what led Freud to develop psychoanalysis in the first place, is shelved rather than solved. Denuded of its original function, the revised metapsychology has no way of articulating the connections Freud posits between the mental and the physical realms and their respective causal orders. Habermas' brilliant exposition leaves a crucial question hanging in the air. What must the psyche be like from the *outside* for psycho-analytic explanations to be meaningful?

Background

Habermas' conception of science

With Habermas, the term 'science' takes on a different slant. At times, he uses it in the usual way to refer exclusively to the empirical or 'empirical-analytic' sciences, both natural and 'cultural'; these are the physical sciences, and the social or 'human' sciences insofar as they depend on empirical (hypothetico-deductive) methodology. This approach to knowledge looks at the field of enquiry through a template of universal law and necessary causation, for the overall purpose of manipulating external causal factors to produce pre-chosen effects. But he also speaks of the 'hermeneutic' or 'historical-hermeneutic' sciences which seek to understand reality through a template of sharable meanings. They work by inter-preting symbolic structures rather than by analysing causal chains, and include the non-empirical aspects of the human sciences as well as the humanities. The most interesting, and also the most controversial as a category, are the 'critically-oriented' or 'critical-reflective' sciences, which turn the focus on habitual patterns of thought, including the templates themselves, with the aim of going beyond them. A science is 'critical' to the extent that it reflects on normally accepted premises. Apart from philosophy itself, Habermas includes psychoanalysis and Marxism in this group, as flawed prototypes which their authors misconceive as empirical sciences.

Habermas sees these different kinds of 'science' as springing from, and set within, particular 'human interests' or standpoints.

> The approach of the empirical-analytic sciences incorporates a *technical* cognitive interest; that of the historical-hermeneutic sciences incorporates a *practical* one; and the approach of the critically oriented sciences incorporates the *emancipatory* cognitive interest that . . . was at the root of traditional theories.
>
> (Habermas 1971, p. 308)

Each of these standpoints translates into a particular theoretical structure. The technical interest of empirical science leads to a subject–object relation between the enquirer and the field of enquiry. The hermeneutic approach, with its practical orientation, is built on an intersubjective or subject–subject configuration. The critical sciences, finally, are organized reflexively, turning back upon themselves in a continual renewal of their structures of thought. What makes a subject a science in Habermas' sense is the development of one or more of these orientations to the point where it can generate conclusions which are more than arbitrarily subjective. 'These cognitive interests . . . are, for all subjects of speech and action, the necessary conditions of the possibility of experience that can claim to be objective.' (Habermas 1973, pp. 8–9).[2]

Although Habermas is claiming 'objectivity' as the criterion of science, or valid knowledge, what he means by this is very different from what Nagel or mainstream empirical scientists mean. His different modes of enquiry all begin with human subjects actively engaged – with the world around them, with each other, or with their own thinking. There is thus no question of excluding the enquiring subject from any knowledge domain. The problem is rather how the empirical and hermeneutic approaches can maintain a sufficiently critical attitude to prevent stagnation in the face of their particular ambuscades.

'For the natural sciences, the fact of scientific progress poses the question how a universal relation can be known, given a finite number of established singular facts.' (Habermas 1971, p. 160). Habermas is making the same point as the philosopher David Hume, in his famous realization that the necessary causation expressed in universal laws is a theoretical conjecture based on a limited number of examples. Just because apples always seem to fall from trees does not in itself mean either that the theory of gravity is right, or that an apple may not behave differently tomorrow. 'For the cultural sciences', meanwhile, '[how] can the meaning of an individuated life structure be grasped and represented in inevitably general categories?' (ibid.). How can the broad and inclusive terms of a general theory do justice to the specificity of individual experience?

Habermas is suggesting that the pitfall of the empirical mode of enquiry is objectivism: the example of positivism shows how easy it is to forget the limits of what can be inferred from empirical data or sense experience.[3] In the hermeneutic mode, the corresponding danger is of a subjectivism which overlooks the complications of transferring concepts from specific individuals to people in general.

Discussion

Habermas' radical rethinking of Freud's legacy throws up two questions. How successfully does he defend his claim that psychoanalysis and its metapsychological foundation should be conceived in interpretative rather than empirical terms? And how convincingly does he argue that this enhances rather than diminishes its value? If a hermeneutic reconception of psychoanalysis is to have any chance of displacing Freud's own assessment of psychoanalysis as an empirical science, Habermas will have to establish both the necessity and the durability of such a reconception. He will need to demonstrate that Freud's presentation of psychoanalysis dictates rather than precludes a hermeneutic reading.

Additionally, he must show that although there can be any number of interpretations of a single material reality, it does not represent the dreaded slide into 'facile subjectivity'. This section assesses each of these conditions in turn.

Does Habermas show that psychoanalysis is primarily interpretative?

Both Nagel and Habermas see psychoanalysis combining causal and interpretative forms of explanation. Nagel, as we have seen, subsumes interpretation under causal explanation: 'Interpretation reveals causation because that's the kind of system a human being is' (Nagel 1994b, p. 290 below). He thus presents psychoanalysis as an empirical science which works through interpretation. For Habermas, the situation is reversed. He is fascinated by the way in which psychoanalysis incorporates causal explanations, but argues that these explanations fall outside the frontiers of empirical science. 'Freud's theory remains a scrap that the positivist logic of [empirical] science since has vainly tried to digest . . . But the hidden self-reflection that is the source of trouble cannot be conceptualized in this manner' (Habermas 1971, p. 189). Habermas is maintaining that the primary currency of psychoanalysis is semantic, or meaning-based, rather than causal. Its concepts and explanations arise within the practical realm of communication within and between people, rather than in the technical realm of instrumental or 'means-end' reasoning. Instead of an empirical science which operates through interpretation, he sees an interpretative science using causal explanation.

Habermas acknowledges that the causal form of psychoanalytic explanations makes them look like those of empirical science: 'psychoanalysis joins hermeneutics with operations that genuinely seemed to be reserved to the natural sciences' (1971, p. 214). Psychoanalysis aims not only to translate feelings, thoughts or actions into different terms, but also to explain how they arose in the first place. Habermas argues that the roles and contexts of psychoanalytic and empirical-scientific explanations are nonetheless different, in ways which underwrite the distinction between an empirical science and psychoanalysis as a critical-hermeneutic science. Freud's error, he says, was to take the resemblance between empirical-scientific and psychoanalytic explanations at face value. This led to his entrapment between the intersubjective nature of the discipline he founded and a prejudiced assumption that it could only be validly theorized as an empirical science. Psychoanalysis, as Habermas regards it, is an entirely practical body of interpretation lumbered with an unnecessary and inadequate empirical-scientific base.

Practically speaking, as Habermas observes, psychoanalysis is a system of interpretation. 'It provides theoretical perspectives and technical rules for the interpretation of symbolic structures' (ibid., p. 214). The first two[4] of his three psychoanalytic chapters argue that it resides exclusively in this dimension. He draws extensively on the analogy Freud makes between psychoanalytic interpretation and linguistic interpretation, and on his treatment of dreams and symptoms as arcane and shrouded texts. Neither Habermas nor Freud confines the linguistic to words: both include the whole range of communicable phenomena, from the primitive to the sophisticated. For Habermas, 'language' is the common pool of meaning and meaning structures running between words and other symbols, intentional behaviour and the physical expression of emotion. It is the ground on which verbal and non-verbal phenomena meet, drawing what would otherwise be disconnected pieces of experience and behaviour into a single personal episode. The 'grammar of ordinary language governs not only the connection of symbols, but also the interweaving of linguistic elements, action patterns, and expressions' (p. 217). Freud puts a similar thought rather more clearly. In psychoanalysis, 'language⁵ must be understood . . . to mean not merely the expression of thoughts in words, but also the language of gestures and every other mode of expression of psychic activity' (Freud 1913, S.E. 13, p. 176, quoted in Habermas 1971, pp. 218–219). At this point, Freud seems to be saying that psychical processes are necessarily symbolic.

If psychoanalysis were no more than the interpretation of symbolic structures, there would be no dispute about its hermeneutic classification. It is the pathological dimension of its subject matter that puts this into question. Where Grünbaum takes the causal power of repression as the central phenomenon of psychoanalysis, Habermas understands repression as the coming apart of the elements of 'language'. From his perspective, psychoanalysis is primarily concerned with breaks in the connections holding speech or symbol, action and emotional expression together.

> In the normal case, these three categories of expressions are complementary, so that linguistic expressions 'fit' interactions and both language and action 'fit' experiential expressions . . . In the limiting case [of interest to psychoanalysis], however, a language game⁶ can disintegrate to the point where the three categories of expressions no longer agree. Then actions and non-verbal expressions belie what is expressly stated.
>
> (Habermas 1971, pp. 217–218)

Habermas is saying that psychoanalytic 'symptoms' can be seen as purposive or intentional structures which have come adrift from the main flow of the subject's conscious life, concealing their meaning even from the subject. This makes them uniquely disturbing, yet their dislocation is neither arbitrary nor meaningless: 'the symbolic structures that psychoanalysis seeks to comprehend are corrupted by the impact of *internal conditions*. The mutilations have meaning *as such*.' (1971, p. 217, original emphases). This gives psychoanalysis a task which philological or linguistic hermeneutics is spared: it has to account for the gaps and distortions in its material, rather than simply filling them in. It is this, Habermas maintains, that leads to the combination of interpretation and causal analysis, setting psychoanalysis apart from both the 'empirical-analytic' and the 'exclusively hermeneutic' sciences (p. 189). Neither solely objectifying nor fully interpretative, it 'unites linguistic analysis with the psychological investigation of causal connections' (p. 217). Psychoanalytic explanations are at once causal and interpretative.

This is the point at which Habermas' conception of psychoanalysis diverges from that of Freud and Nagel. Although Freud repeatedly describes the work of psychoanalysis as 'translation', he locates the ultimate source of symptoms, or 'textual corruptions', beneath the level of 'language'. He sees the damage visited on symptomatic symbolic structures as a function of the warring drives or instincts, albeit at the behest of the ego. Psychoanalysis is built on the assumption that meaning extends deeper than we can ever know. But Freud takes all particular meanings, including those that lie behind the symptom, to be the outcome of psychophysical forces operating on the symbolic level from beneath.

The defining characteristic of a symbol is that it can be interpreted in different ways. Its meaning does not depend on its physical or structural characteristics, but on the conventions of the society or group for whom it is a symbol.[7] But the subterranean forces that Freud conceives of as drives (or instincts) cannot be said to function symbolically. Each instance carries no more than a single 'meaning', which Freud envisages as a particular point on the continuum of pleasure to unpleasure. Since the two major drive or instinct groups[8] are assumed to operate together, any particular instinctual impulse holds a meaning composed of a specific fusion of pleasure and unpleasure. The basis of each 'meaning' can thus be understood as an individual combination of pleasure and unpleasure.

Freud assumes that this unconscious yet experiential continuum must in some way correspond to an underlying physiological continuum related to the accumulation and discharge of energy. This is expressed in the third metapsychological principle, the capacity of the psyche to regulate itself through its modes of defence (see p. 12 above). It is also the source of Freud's continuing theoretical struggle to find a systematic relation between the 'quality' and 'quantity' of psychical processes (see p. 52 above). Although he was never able to pin down the exact form of association, Freud was in no doubt that a correlation must exist. On this assumption, each point on the pleasure–unpleasure scale can be taken to represent an exchange point between what can be experienced and what can be measured. Pleasure and unpleasure can then be treated as signs or markers of physiological states rather than as symbols grounded in cultural rules and conventions. By lining up an actual experiential scale with a hypothetical physiological scale, Freud formulates a possible mode of connection between the mental and physical conceptual worlds.

On the basis of this rather dubious link, Habermas observes, Freud defines psychoanalysis ultimately, though not unequivocally, as a 'causal' therapy. He implies that subjective phenomena must also have a physical point of access. Freud explains:

> Supposing, now, that it was possible, by some chemical means, perhaps, to interfere in this mechanism . . . this then would be a causal therapy in the true sense of the word . . . At present, as you know, there is no question of any such

method of influencing libidinal processes; with our psychical therapy we
attack at a different point in the combination . . .
(Freud 1916–1917, S.E. 16, p. 436, quoted Habermas 1971,
p. 171 below)

Freud seems to be saying, in a rather convoluted way, that if his psychological–
physiological correlation is right, it must be possible to influence instinctual
processes chemically as well as psychologically. A proper 'causal' therapy would
operate at the level of the measurable physical continuum which he sees as
underlying and linking into the psychical continuum of pleasure and unpleasure
(which in turn underlies conscious experience). Although psychoanalysis, he says,
does not intervene 'at what we know are the roots of the phenomena' (ibid., p. 171
below), the point at which it does so is further along the same 'combination', or
causal chain. Freud is suggesting, in effect, that psychoanalysis can be seen as an
indirect way of altering the physical determinants of experience. His explanation
indicates that he is situating the psychical and physical dimensions in the same
domain. Although he identifies psychical processes with symbolic or meaningful
processes, he tracks the causal connections which psychoanalysis investigates
back to the ordinary determinism of the physical world.

Habermas, by contrast, places them altogether within the symbolic realm.
He confirms the causal form of psychoanalytic explanations, but rejects Freud's
supposition that a physical intervention could be a direct alternative to a psychoanalytic intervention.

> Psychoanalysis does not grant us a power of technical control over the sick
> psyche comparable to that of biochemistry over a sick organism. And yet it
> achieves more than a mere treatment of symptoms, because it certainly does
> grasp causal connections.
>
> (Habermas 1971, p. 171 below)

But the causal connections that psychoanalysis grasps are not those of the physical
world. They belong to a different causal series, 'not at the level of physical events'
(ibid.). Symptoms, including bodily malfunction, can be understood as 'caused'
by a particular circumstance or event; but the power to cause symptoms does not
come from the material nature of the situation, but from the personal meaning
attached to it.[9] 'For the causal connection between the original scene, defense,
and symptom is not anchored in the invariance of nature according to natural
laws but only in the spontaneously generated invariance of life history' (ibid.,
p. 171 below). Habermas is arguing that it is personal history rather than the
laws of nature that explains the neurotic symptom – and in contrast to natural laws,
personal history cannot be predicted, because it only becomes 'fixed' as it takes
place.

In evidence, Habermas calls on the therapeutic power of psychological insight.
He reasons that if a neurotic symptom were physically caused, it could only be
physically cured. Recognizing the 'sense behind the symptom' could no more

change it than knowing how a wound was caused would make it heal. The mere possibility that mental and even physical states can be affected by entering into their meaning for the individual shows that a psychological causal power must be at work in the production and dissolution of symptoms. 'This is the causality of fate,[10] and not of nature, because it prevails through the symbolic means of the mind. Only for this reason can it be compelled by the power of reflection.' (Habermas 1971, p. 161 below).

Freud would hasten to object that this psychological power is not non-physical. On the contrary, the 'power of reflection' affects the body as well as the mind precisely because the psychical dimension is also the physical dimension, and psychological causation ultimately the same as physical causation. Habermas' response would be to challenge Freud to justify this shift from the experiential to the physical domain. In Habermas' analysis, the mind has the power to influence the body not because the mind is part of the body, but because the body is in a sense part of the mind. In the pathological situations that Freud seeks to explain, it is the body which is responding to mental pressures, not the mind to bodily pressures. Habermas points out that psychoanalytic theory was developed from Freud's experience in the therapeutic setting, which is characterized by its inter-subjective nature rather than by any physical property. He is implying that the only good reason for adding a theoretical foundation in a different dimension would be the increased understanding brought to the observed phenomena, on the basis of a clear link between them; but this, Habermas submits, is not what happens in psychoanalysis. Even the tripartite model of the mind as id, ego and super-ego, which assumes a physical base only tacitly and indirectly, adds nothing to our practical understanding of psychological phenomena: 'this theoretical exposition does not contain a single element that goes beyond the previous description of technique. The language of the theory is narrower than the language in which the technique was described.' (1971, p. 245).

Habermas' example could be questioned,[11] but his main point is that it is the practical context of psychoanalysis that authorizes its theoretical conclusions, not the other way round. All he considers Freud can legitimately infer from the analytic setting is the particular kinds of psychological states which appear within it, which can be made intelligible by an interpretative account of how minds in general tend to work.

> The basic categories of the new discipline [were] first derived from the ana-lytic situation and the interpretation of dreams . . . [These] metapsychological categories and connections were not only *discovered* under determinate conditions of specifically sheltered communication, they cannot even be *explicated* independently of this context.
>
> (Habermas, 1971, p. 158 below, original emphases)

Habermas is claiming that Freud's physicalistic models of mental processes are not legitimized by his observations. Without supporting evidence, he cannot deduce from what happens in the consulting room that the mind is 'really' a device for regulating a physical energy.[12] Nor is there any definite basis for the systematic matching of mental to physical events. 'The energy-distribution model only creates the semblance that psychoanalytic statements are about measurable transformations of energy. Not a single statement about quantitative relations derived from the conception of instinctual economics has ever been tested experimentally' (1971, p. 159 below). Habermas, like Grünbaum, is treating measurability as the essential criterion of empirical science; justifiably, since without a tangible link there is nothing to connect empirical observation and theoretical explanation. In psychoanalysis there is no possibility of such a link, Habermas argues, because the phenomena to be explained are structured by language, not by matter. They cannot be explained in the same way as events determined by phenomena which are measurable because they are material.

Habermas is accusing Freud of developing psychoanalysis as a way of understanding oneself, but theorizing it as though it were a way of understanding an object external to oneself. He notes, with Nagel, that the first involves immediate, first-person recognition, while the second depends on objective, third-person deduction. Nagel stretches his concept of empirical science to include interpretative explanation; but Habermas concludes that this debars psychoanalysis from classification as an empirical science.

> Freud erred in not realizing that psychology, insofar as it understands itself as a strict empirical science, cannot content itself with a model that keeps to a physicalistic use of language without seriously leading to operationalizable assumptions . . . [that is, to active testing] . . . The model of the psychic apparatus is so constructed that metapsychological statements imply the observability of the events they are about. But these events are never observed – nor *can* they be observed.
>
> (Habermas 1971, p. 159 below, original emphasis)

The id, ego and super-ego, the life and death drives, the self-regulatory function of repression – all these are concepts drawn from the psychoanalytic interpretation of experience. They can never be observed directly, nor deduced as the only possible explanation of anything that is observed directly. Habermas is saying that if the foundations of psychoanalysis can neither be observed nor measured, they can hardly be adopted as foundations for a science based on measurability.

Nagel, as well as Freud, would immediately rejoin that the ultimate ground of psychoanalytic concepts can only be physical, and must therefore be measurable, even if only potentially and at several removes. Just because this ground cannot as yet be identified does not mean that it does not exist. They would say that psychoanalysis is a way of understanding the psyche subjectively and objectively at the same time. Habermas would press his point by drawing out the contrast between the reflective stance of psychoanalysis and the technical stance of empirical science. Pursuing the therapeutic implications of the psychophysical definition of psychical processes, he considers Freud's musings on the possibility of short-circuiting psychoanalytic treatment by direct physical action:

> If analysis only *seems* to appear as an interpretation of texts and *actually* leads to making possible technical control of the psychical apparatus, then there is nothing unusual about the idea that psychological influence could at some point be replaced with greater effect by somatic techniques of treatment.
>
> (Habermas 1971, p. 155 below, original emphases)

He is observing that equating psychoanalytic intervention with physical intervention would reduce it to a technical operation. The subject would be treating his or her own mind as an 'apparatus' to stand outside, in order to control its workings by following pre-set rules. But this only serves to highlight Habermas' point that this is not the standpoint of psychoanalytic therapy. Now that the 'direct influence, by means of particular chemical substances' (Freud 1938a, S.E. 23, p.182, quoted Habermas 1971, p. 155 below) that Freud could only imagine has become routine, it is obvious that there is all the difference in the world between technical and psychoanalytic interventions into mental processes. Nagel himself argues to the effect that undergoing psychoanalysis is nothing like taking an antidepressant (Nagel 1994b, p. 153 below). Nor do physical or other technical methods of treatment[13] appear to enter at a 'deeper' level in the same causal series, but rather into a different causal series. There is no gaining of insight, because psychological factors are not part of the physical causal process. Where the aim of treatment is the simple amelioration of suffering, the technical approach makes sense: the cause of the symptom can readily be seen as a faulty 'apparatus' whose workings can be corrected by chemical or other means. But this is the antithesis of the psychoanalytic approach, where insight is valued for its own sake as much as for any relief it might bring. Yet Freud seems to be saying that psychological and physical interventions are different ways of doing the same thing.

Habermas argues that these passages, together with the physicalistic language of the metapsychological models, give the wrong impression of Freud's aims. He suggests that Freud was actually committed to facilitating psychological change through self-understanding, as opposed to imposing change by external means. He takes Freud's real estimation of psychoanalysis to be what is expressed in his overall aim of making what is unconscious conscious, so that what has been banished from consciousness is allowed into the realm of self-knowledge and personal responsibility: 'where id was, there ego shall be' (Freud 1932, S.E. 22, p. 80).[14]

This aim, Habermas argues, excludes psychoanalysis from empirical science: their theoretical structures are irredeemably different. Psychoanalysis is structured on a subject–subject relation, and its orienting framework is practical. It is set in the sphere of communication between people and within people, for the purpose of inter- and intra-personal understanding through meanings held in common. Empirical science, by contrast, operates on a subject–object configuration. It is set in the framework or 'interest' of technical or instrumental action, with the aim of performing operations on external objects in order to achieve anticipated effects. In tacking an empirical-scientific foundation on to an interpretative body of theory, Habermas is accusing Freud of conceptual scavenging.

Habermas presses home the incompatibility of the two categories by showing us what it means to put psychoanalytic concepts into a strictly empirical framework.

> Some [psychoanalytic assumptions] have been newly formulated in the framework of behavioristically oriented learning psychology . . . More sophisticated is the attempt to take the personality model developed by ego psychology . . . and reformulate it . . . in terms of modern functionalism. In both cases the new theoretical framework makes possible the operationalization of concepts; in both cases it requires verification of the derived hypotheses under experimental conditions.
>
> (Habermas 1971, p. 159 below)

Putting psychoanalytic concepts into an empirical framework means removing them from psychoanalysis itself and transporting them into a physicalistic theoretical framework such as that of Grünbaum, with all the limitations that this brings. The reflective approach is abandoned to the extent that empirically testable hypotheses are involved. Of course this supports his point. Empirical-scientific knowledge cannot be gained without the trial-and-error of the experimental method, because the objects of potential knowledge are by definition set against the subject who encounters them. For this reason, reflection alone cannot lead to understanding. In psychoanalysis, however, the object of investigation is part of the reflecting subject, and psychoanalytic knowledge can arise only by practical rather than technical means; otherwise, as Habermas says, it would not be psychoanalysis.

> As long as the theory derives its meaning in relation to . . . self-reflection, its application is necessarily practical. It effects the reorganization of the action-orienting self-understanding of socialized individuals, which is structured in ordinary language.
>
> (Habermas 1971, p. 155 below)

Psychoanalytic knowledge, he is saying, is intrinsically practical knowledge, set in the realm of meaning and communication.

Approaching the relation between psychoanalysis and empirical science from the other direction confirms their incompatibility. The practical orientation towards reality is diametrically opposed to the perspective of empirical science. Technical and psychoanalytic interventions can never 'amount to the same thing':

In this role [i.e. insofar as it remains in the sphere of self-reflection] . . . psychoanalysis can never be replaced by technologies derived from other theories of the empirical sciences . . . For psychopharmacology only brings about alterations of consciousness to the extent that it controls functions of the human organism as objectified natural processes. In contrast, the experience of reflection induced by enlightenment [or personal illumination] is precisely the act through which the subject frees itself from a state in which it had become an object for itself.

(Habermas 1971, p. 155 below)

What Habermas is getting at is that the subject–object organization of empirical science leads potentially to knowledge of everything except what is indistinguishable from the enquiring subject. This cannot include psychoanalysis, because psychoanalysis is directed towards dissolving the illusion that makes part of the self appear as other than ('an object for') the self. Habermas suspects that some recognition of this kind was behind Freud's resistance to empirical tests:[15]

Freud surely surmised that the consistent realization of the program of a 'natural-scientific' or even rigorously behavioristic psychology would have had to sacrifice the one intention to which psychoanalysis owes its existence: the intention of enlightenment, according to which ego should develop out of id.

(Habermas 1971, pp. 159–160 below)

Habermas' arguments hold up only if there is no alternative to conceiving psychoanalysis on a subject–subject configuration. He himself harbours no doubts:

The thesis that psychoanalytic knowledge belongs to the category of self-reflection can be easily demonstrated . . . For analytic treatment cannot be defined without recourse to the experience of reflection. Hermeneutics derives its function in the process of the genesis of self-consciousness . . . Repressions can be eliminated only by virtue of reflection.

(Habermas 1971, p. 228)

Interpretation, he is saying, depends on reflexive consciousness – on turning one's attention back upon oneself not as an external object but as an experiencing subject. It is this that constitutes the self-reflection on which both psychoanalysis as a whole and the lifting of repression in particular depend. If this is so, then psychoanalytic insight cannot be gained of anything lying outside the possibility of self-reflection, even if it lies within the possibility of empirical discovery. And if *this* is so, it is because repression cannot be conceived as a technical operation enacted on an external object. It can only be seen as the dynamic expression on the part of the subject of a wish to eject one of its constituent symbolic structures – a wish, a memory, an intention – outside its own parameters. Habermas is conveying all this when he defines insight as the lifting of repression, repression as the opposite of 'self-formation', and psychoanalysis as releasing self-formation.

This line of argument is plausible and persuasive, both with reference to Freud's expressed views and independently of them. If what is 'ejected' were a detachable component, repression could succeed. It is quite possible to eliminate specific mental elements by destroying the brain-cells on which they depend. But the nature of the repressed is that it tends to return to consciousness. The process of repression may depend on physicality, but whatever it consists of cannot be on a par with physical processes. If psychoanalytic knowledge were knowledge of any-thing that could be defined as external to the reflecting self, it would be derivable in more than one way. As it is, it depends entirely on the first-hand recognition of alienated structures of the self, manifested in consciousness or in the resumption of the 'self-formative processes'. The potential for insight in psychoanalytic treatment is indeed undermined to the exact extent that what is rejected is treated as other than the ejector. Habermas seems to prove his point that psychoanalysis depends on its subject and its object being the same, and that this prevents it from being classed as an empirical science.

Does Habermas show that psychoanalysis is more than arbitrarily subjective?

What then can psychoanalysis be based on, if not the empirical principle that it investigates something that exists independently of its investigation? What autho-rizes its theories of psychical structures and process, and how, in this context, can the 'causality of fate' by which they are supposedly determined be anything more than a piquant phrase? Habermas answers these questions by changing the meaning of key psychoanalytic terms. He retains the term 'metapsychology' for the principles presupposed by psychoanalytic observations, while altering its content. Since he sees these foundational principles as interpretative rather empirical in nature, working out what they must be is a solely conceptual task. He pursues this to the point of affording psychoanalysis a new kind of validation.

'General Interpretations'

Habermas has successfully argued that the foundations of psychoanalysis cannot consist in any physiological condition. He therefore proceeds to translate its 'first principles' from the physicalistic language of empirical theory to the 'meta-hermeneutics' of a critical-hermeneutic theory. Like Freud, he includes the deeper levels of the clinical theory, and whatever must be taken to govern it. But where Freud tries to explain psychoanalytic concepts physicalistically, Habermas looks to the patterns underlying the meaning structures with which psychoanalysis is concerned. He conceives these symptomatic structures as 'privatized' symbolic structures. They are no longer sharable, even within the subject's own conscious-ness, because they have become dislocated from the network of common meanings through which ordinary communication and normal psychology work. Instead, they have a logic of their own, which Habermas characterizes as the logic behind psychoanalytic interpretation: 'Metapsychology unfolds *the logic of interpretation in the analytic situation of dialogue*' (1971, p. 160 below, original emphasis). Under his new definition, the metapsychology consists of '*a general interpretation of self-formative processes*' (ibid., original emphasis). By this, he means not a clinical interpretation, but the interpretative patterns which underlie all specific psychoanalytic interpretations and are embodied in all psychoanalytic concepts.

Although Habermas does not go into detail, the most fundamental 'general interpretation' must be the principle of an unconscious level of experience which follows different rules and patterns from the conscious level. This forms the basis of a network of 'general interpretational' theories, ranging from revised versions of the metapsychological models to Freud's programme of libidinal organization and the clinical-level theories of resistance, repression and transference. Together, these provide an interpretative frame through which the linkage between the manifest symptom and its unconscious meaning can become apparent.[16]

Thus Habermas' 'general interpretations' are a recasting of Freud's metapsychological principles in frankly hermeneutic terms: 'Metapsychology deals with . . . the connection between *language deformation and behavioral pathology*' (1971, p. 160 below, original emphasis) Instead of postulating a hypothetical link between experience and physiology, Habermas presents a simpler explanatory strategy which links symptom and meaning directly at the level of language. He rejects outright the physicalistic thinking on which Freud's metapsychological models and theories are based.

Empirical principles and hermeneutic principles

Thus Habermas' and Freud's versions of psychoanalysis are set on different foundations. Habermas explains the differences as a function of the structural disparity between empirical and hermeneutic theories and their respective concepts of causality. He argues that the critical-hermeneutic nature of psychoanalytic theory arises in the convergence of theoretical elements which empirical science keeps apart. This passage (pp. 164–173 below) holds the key to his whole critique. A powerful vindication of psychoanalysis emerges in his dazzling exposition of the fusion of the enquiring subject, the object of investigation and the explanation itself.

Habermas strikes a startling demarcation between the governing principles of empirical-scientific and psychoanalytic theories. In empirical science, the phenomena under investigation and the theoretical system itself occupy different spheres; but in psychoanalysis, they are the same. The law-based explanations of empirical science are made in language, not in physical events: they exist in a different dimension from the phenomena which they investigate. This is true even of the human or cultural empirical sciences, where the objects of enquiry have a non-physical dimension. Their delineating boundaries are still marked by publicly observable signs, and the phenomena to be explained still stand apart from the explaining of them.

Habermas explains that this rule does not apply to psychoanalysis. In psychoanalytic practice, the explanatory link becomes the event to be explained. At the moment of insight, the 'general interpretation' (the psychoanalytic concept) and the principles configured in it come alive. The concept or interpretative pattern exists as a felt experience rather than as a deductive theoretical proposition. It is this that sets psychoanalytic concepts and explanations apart from their empirical-scientific counterparts. The hypotheses of empirical science are confirmed by applying them to something external to the hypotheses themselves; but the interpretational hypotheses of psychoanalysis are verified only by becoming real. 'The process of inquiry can lead to valid information only via a transformation in the patient's self-inquiry' (p. 165 below). This personal transformation underwrites the general psychoanalytic concepts and principles which any particular interpretation might contain.

Nagel assumes that the retrodictive nature of interpretative explanations reflects the predictive nature of hypothetico-deductive explanations. He argues that their common causal nature justifies the empirical-scientific standing of psychoanalysis. But Habermas shows that the causality of psychoanalytic interpretation is not the causality of physics, but the causality of personal intention. The symbolic structures that make up interpretative causal structures are not the same as those which make up physical causal structures. They cannot be countered by the manipulation of physical cause and effect; or rather, what physical manipulation can change is no more than the material condition on which symbolic structures depend. The structures themselves can be reached only through the recognition that puts an end to their dissociation from the main body of the consciously accessible self and its capacity for influencing and regulating itself.

This can happen, Habermas contends, only because the empirical phenomenon to be explained – the symptom or 'irrational' state of mind which exists independently of any explanatory hypothesis – is at the same time an intentional structure. As such, the causal links between the 'initial causal conditions' and the 'event to be explained' proceed in the symbolic, not the physical realm. The action or state of mind is significant only in view of its meaning, which is itself determined by the meaning attributed to the circumstances from which it arose. The physical movements performed and the material state of affairs are causally irrelevant.

On these considerations, Habermas concludes that the 'general interpretations' of psychoanalysis are not equivalent to the 'general theories' of an empirical science. By themselves, and unlike empirical theories, 'general interpretations' explain nothing; they are merely ways of articulating particular psychological states. They become explanatory only when they form part of an intentional structure which the subject recognizes as her own. Then, 'understanding itself obtains explanatory power' (1971, p. 170 below).

Again, Habermas' reasoning seems to work out. It is only the subject's realization that she holds an intention which has Oedipal, or oral, or projective dynamics that actualizes the explanatory potential of these concepts. And this actualization takes place on the basis of the principles underlying meaning structures, not principles underlying physical structures. *What* the individual realizes is an actual dynamic in her mental process, brought to life in a form which is both the same as and different from the fragments of experience which it gathers together. *That* she is realizing it gives an explanatory dimension to the dynamic itself, and the abstraction or 'general interpretation' embodied in it. Interpretations are transformative when they become real; and since all particular interpretations exemplify a 'general interpretation', transformative interpretations or realizations serve to endorse not only themselves, but also the theoretical concepts intrinsic to them.

Thus it is only in an actual lived dynamic that a 'general interpretation' exists as something real; and if it is real, it is also explanatory. The intentional structure within it provides the 'causal story' linking the initial causal conditions (the event perceived as impossible to assimilate) and the symptomatic state or event (the action or experience insofar as it represents an intelligible response to the disturbing nature of the situation). Physical structures lie outside this particular causal chain. 'General interpretations' are causally explanatory, but the dimension in which they operate cannot be reduced to the physical dimension; and since they only become causally explanatory in particular instances, they cannot be classed as empirical-scientific theories.

These are also the grounds on which Habermas presents psychoanalysis as a critical-hermeneutic science with significance beyond itself. It acts as a beacon for all hermeneutic theorizing by showing how interpretations can be both particular and universal. They can be subjective without being arbitrarily subjective, and general without being purely abstract: 'General interpretations can abstractly assert their claim to universal validity because their derivatives are additionally determined by context' (1971, pp. 172–173 below). Because it is an abstraction, the same 'general interpretation' can appear in many different guises; thus it is not solely particular. Neither is it just an abstraction, because in becoming explanatory it also becomes real: the phenomenon to be explained is incarnated in its explanation. 'Narrative explanations differ from strictly deductive ones in that the events or states of which they assert a causal relation is [*sic*] further defined by their application' (p. 173 below). The theories of empirical science offer causal explanations independently of the context in which they are applied; but 'general interpretations' become causally explanatory only in the particular conditions in which they are applied. This means they do not function as empirical-scientific theories.

This makes the general principles of psychoanalytic explanations valid to the extent that they are causally explanatory, and causally explanatory only on the basis of their interpretative potency. Any single psychoanalytic explanation rests on what is held in common by innumerable particular interpretations, tested in every new instance in which it appears. In relation to the psychoanalytic programme of instinctual development, for example:

> Only the *metapsychologically founded and systematically generalized history*
> of infantile development . . . puts the physician in the position of so com-
> bining the fragmentary information obtained in the analytic dialogue that
> he can reconstruct the gaps of memory and hypothetically anticipate the
> experience of reflection of which the patient is at first incapable.
>
> (Habermas 1971, p. 164 below, original emphasis)

Habermas is saying that particular interpretations depend on 'general interpretations' (on psychoanalytic concepts),[17] and that these presuppose hermeneutic
rather than empirical principles. 'General interpretations', and the principles on
which they are founded, can be relied on to the extent that they lead to an enhanced
coherence in the reflecting subject's sense of who she is: 'The interpretation of the
case is corroborated only by the successful continuation of an interrupted self-
formative process' (p. 164 below).

Thus psychoanalysis gains a new solidarity with itself when it is conceived as
an intersubjective path to deepening the understanding of one's own subjectivity,
and thereby that of others. This makes it incompatible with the technical approach
of an empirical science, but without depriving it of epistemological authority: there
is simply no other path to psychoanalytic knowledge. In psychoanalysis, '[there]
can be no substitute for [the experience of reflection], including a technology,
unless technology is to serve to unburden the subject of its own achievements'
(1971, p. 155 below). Any purely technical solution can only be at the expense of
the insight which psychoanalytic reflection can bring.

Conclusion

Habermas' case rests on the division between empirical-theoretical and practical
ways of knowing, and also on their epistemological parity. If both are equally
legitimate foundations of knowledge, then psychoanalysis is not disadvantaged
by falling under the practical rather than the empirical-theoretical heading; but
neither, of course, is it advantaged by this. Habermas' presentation of psychoanalysis is fairly irresistible, especially the first time one finally understands it;
but the absence of something like the Freudian metapsychology forces upon it a
number of questions and detractions, two of which are relevant here. The first
concerns the kind of objectivity that psychoanalytic concepts hold; the second,
their capacity for linking different theoretical domains. Although these have failed
to be endorsed by empirical-scientific conceptions of psychoanalysis, under a
critical-hermeneutic reading they are dealt a stunning blow.

Reconstituting 'metapsychology' as 'metahermeneutics' means deriving both
the content and the validation of psychoanalytic concepts entirely from their
realization in experience. And since the ground of hermeneutic understanding
is cultural rather than material, this means the experience of a finite number
of individuals. Bernstein points out in his critical study that the 'meta' in 'metahermeneutics' does nothing to change this: 'depth hermeneutics remains

hermeneutics – historical, contextual, productive' (Bernstein 1995, p. 58). Because the hermeneutic domain is practical communication itself, the cultural relativity which affects all theorizing has a double impact. Any kind of theory must be limited by the terms in which it is expressed and the background assumptions of those terms.[18] But hermeneutic theories are also limited to the linguistic community whose symbolic structures they are attempting to interpret. There is no reason to believe that these structures must be the same in other communities, although they may be; but the more universal they appear to be, the more likely they are to be seen as physically- rather than culturally-determined. This makes the potential field of application much narrower for hermeneutic theories than for empirical theories.

For psychoanalysis, this magnifies the already weighty question of how far its concepts can be applied outside the social groupings from whose self-reflection they emerged. This is already a significant issue in transcultural work, but the objectivity question goes further. When the terms of reference of Westernized societies develop beyond their present paradigm, the psychoanalytic perspective will lose its intuitive resonance for a critical mass of humanity. Not only will psychoanalysis no longer be 'true', but also what it refers to will no longer be 'real', not even in retrospect.[19] Habermas has demonstrated that without a basis in experience, psychoanalytic concepts have no ontological milieu; no conceptual sea, as it were, in which to swim. Freud inaugurated a theory which he intended to be universal on the basis of the ground it shared with physiology. He expected it to undergo improvement and development, but he did not foresee its demise until human beings evolve beyond their present form. On Habermas' cultural foundations, the universality to which psychoanalysis can hope to lay claim is drastically curtailed.

Habermas convincingly locates much of what is most essential to psychoanalysis within the symbolic arena. On its relation to other arenas, however, he stays silent. The 'unconscious', for example, is truncated to what is already configured as potential communication: he has no time for sub-symbolic determinants of mental life. '[Freud's] distinction between word-presentations and asymbolic ideas is problematic, and the assumption of a non-linguistic substratum ... is unsatisfactory' (1971, p. 241).[20] What then would make these explanatory forays more satisfactory? All Habermas seems to offer is the tacit proposal that the problems they address be ruled out of court. In the same way, he upholds Freud's theory of the drives or instincts as 'necessary', but goes on to derive them from the practical situations they are supposed to explain. Even animal instincts are referred back to a 'linguistically interpreted, albeit reduced human world' (1971, p. 161 below).[21] But if instinct theory is secondary to language theory, he cannot then explain instinctual factors through meaning alone. Habermas' account begs the question of how to explain or conceive those factors which are assumed to shape linguistic structures and experience.

Habermas would sharply demur that neither speculation nor knowledge about the biological conditions of psychical processes should be confused with psychoanalysis proper. It would belong to something more like the academic psychology that Freud contrasts with psychoanalysis as the 'physiology of the sense organs' (see p. 44 above). Habermas certainly demonstrates that psychoanalysis hangs together far better when it is conceived in wholly practical terms. But however originally he does this, and although it is not his predominant aim, there is nothing particularly remarkable about bringing a recalcitrant theoretical system to order by lopping off its most fractious parts. Habermas' critique explains why a rigorously hermeneutic account is not only adequate but also mandated for a practical psychoanalysis centred in self-reflection. Theoretically, however, he presents a shrunken subject.

This is not to deny the interpretative and communicational bedrock of all theorizing, which Habermas, like Kuhn, insists on. Nor does it justify the actual substratum, physiological or structural, that Freud gives psychoanalysis in his metapsychological models and theories. It merely underlines that neither a hermeneutic nor an empirical-scientific framework can encompass the whole of Freud's idea of the psychoanalytic. Habermas shows how much neater this idea is if the empirical part is excised. But Freud's theoretical project seems precisely to be to commence the slow march towards internal consistency without sacrificing either the interpretive or the objectifying aspects of his concepts and theories. He intends psychoanalysis to '[act] as an intermediary between biology and psychology' (see p. 13 above).

If the sphere of biology is what is somatic and without meaning, and the sphere of psychology is what is mental regardless of its physicality, then the psychical, as the site of their interchange, must contain elements of both. It must be conceived as physical without being devoid of meaning, and psychological without being non-bodily. Since these are properties which are normally defined against each other, Freud's 'science of psychoanalysis' stands for their potential compatibility. Its true foundational principles must be both empirical and hermeneutic. In the face of Freud's idiosyncratic metapsychological vision, for Habermas as for Grünbaum and for Nagel, the question of the relation between the causality of intention and the causality of matter arises anew.

This brings us to the end of the critical part of the enquiry. Conventional theoretical frameworks have failed to solve the riddle of the nature and legitimation of psychoanalysis. The next chapter develops a response to the impasse we have reached, in a move from argument and counter-argument to reconstruction and construction. The main finding of the enquiry is that psychoanalysis goes beyond the standard theoretical frameworks; its foundations cannot be those of either an empirical or a hermeneutic science. The proposal coming out of this is that psychoanalysis holds within it a different kind of foundational approach, which starts from the metapsychological ambiguity that Freud places at its heart. Our final task is to engage directly with the philosophical conundrum of psychoanalysis, to draw out one form that this new foundational approach could take.

Chapter 5

The apparatus of the soul

How can mental and physical explanations coincide?

Introduction

'The apparatus of the soul'.[1] Freud uses this arresting phrase as a direct alternative to the more usual 'psychic apparatus'. It encapsulates the ambiguity of psychoanalysis in a particularly striking way. How can the 'soul' or psyche, so redolent with personal unity, be channelled through something as mechanistic as an 'apparatus'? Yet how can subjective processes *not* be mediated physically, with all the limitation this entails? The gap between the interpretative and the objectifying currents of psychoanalysis shows little sign of narrowing. A way has not yet emerged of extracting objective information about the psyche from the first-person data on which it must depend. Psychoanalysis shows us far more of what it is like from the inside to be a psychical being; but inferring what the psyche and its mode of being must then be like from the outside remains tantalizingly elusive.

Neither a scientific nor a hermeneutic conception of the psychical can match the originality of Freud's metapsychological thinking. In Grünbaum's external perspective, its experiential qualities are lost. His inductivist criterion of science conceals a physical model of reality which is unable to encompass the subjectivity of psychoanalytic subject matter. Without the mental–physical link embodied in Freud's metapsychology, he cannot advance psychoanalysis as even a failing empirical science; and without the first-person evidence he rejects, psychoanalytic propositions can neither be refuted nor confirmed with confidence.

Where Grünbaum's reading is physically reductive, Habermas' is mentally reductive. He sets out the practical vindication of psychoanalysis with panache, but the theoretical depletion that goes with it amounts to a mutilation of the psychoanalytic landscape. The enhanced cohesion that a hermeneutic reconception of the metapsychology brings to psychoanalysis is offset by the loss of its essential bridging function. We can appreciate Habermas' practical validation of psychoanalysis as self-reflection while resisting his theoretical conclusion that any substantive implications are of necessity out of reach.

Nagel's position is the closest to Freud's: he too seems to be trying to have it both ways. He justifies psychoanalysis as an extension of 'commonsense psychology' with its interpretative mode of explanation and validation. But he also defends it as an empirical science, on the grounds that it aims to infer hard information on the psyche from its subjective data. The psychophysical unity that Freud's metapsychology stands for must be central to fulfilling this aim. Psychoanalytic knowledge cannot be accepted as fully objective, nor can psychoanalysis be endorsed as empirical science, except on the basis of a principle showing how mental and physical explanations can coincide. Yet no such principle has been pinned down.

This leaves us with the central question unanswered. How are we to understand and evaluate the imperfect vision of psychophysical unity the metapsychology holds? Should its mental and physical aspects be understood in tandem, or in unison? Is the underlying principle of psychophysical unity coherent, or is it a conceptual illusion which breaks apart under scrutiny? If mental and physical phenomena can only be conceived as arising from different viewpoints, there can be no prospect of a psychophysical foundation. The most that could be achieved is coordination between mental and physical explanations, with psychoanalysis as the practical strand of a group of disciplines with theories at both the physiological and the psychological levels. Coherent foundations would become thinkable only if a way can be found to express what lies between these levels in unitary form.

This chapter explores the viability of a unitary conception of psychoanalysis, and develops the rudiments of one possible form that its foundations could take. If the concept of the psychical is the condition on which psychoanalysis rests, what are the conditions on which the concept of the psychical rests? The aim is to develop the practical and theoretical basis which psychoanalysis assumes and on which it can be legitimated. The practical condition would be the active principle underpinning a unified concept of the psychical. The theoretical condition would state the substantive features which must be presupposed about the kind of being which has 'psychical' potential, and the primary category of the reality that such beings must inhabit. These key foundational elements would constitute the psychophysical equivalent of the hermeneutic principle with its basis in the mind, and the empirical principle with its starting-point in matter.

This foundational picture is developed in three stages. The first section of the chapter looks beneath the surface of Freud's theories for the roots of their strange categorial ambiguity. Rather than conceptual incoherence, we find a philosophical context and *modus operandi* which point towards a foundational approach which begins *before* the divisions into physical and mental, body and mind, empirical and hermeneutic. The second section develops a conceptual framework which reflects these foundational fragments, based on the intimate association between psychoanalysis and the 'pre-theoretical' psychology of everyday living. This allows the practical foundational principle to be drawn out. The third section fills out the theoretical or substantive implications of the practical foundation and links it into a broader theoretical ground. In the evolving metaphysical picture, the ground of the psychical is neither the mind of hermeneutic approaches

nor the body of empirical approaches. It can only be the person, as the irreducibly psychophysical holder of the psychical reality from which all knowledge
derives.

These elements make up the skeleton of a unitary foundational approach in
which the mental and physical conceptual schemes can find a potential meeting-
place. Although it is a hypothetical development, it indicates that a psychophysical
foundational approach is not intrinsically hybrid. Psychoanalysis is not condemned
to be practically coherent but theoretically anomalous. It can also appear as a
unique form of enquiry which illuminates the ground of unity beneath the empirical
sphere of matter and the interpretational sphere of the mind.

Tracing Freud's foundations

Freud's writings contain explicit and implicit foundational elements. He offers a
practical vindication of psychoanalysis and gives indications of the philosophical
perspective from which his work should be viewed. These two strands form the
practical and philosophical layers of an approach towards reality with elements
of both the empirical-scientific and hermeneutic modes. Between these levels,
however, a hiatus opens up: at the level of specific foundational content, no definite
statements can be found. The metapsychology represents the mediation of 'matter'
and 'mind', but the principle[2] and the primary category on which their mediation
stands are left unstated.

This section of the chapter approaches the ambiguities in Freud's thought from
the 'top down' and from the 'bottom up'. It discusses the practical strength and
theoretical weakness of his explicit justification for psychoanalysis in general and
his concept of the psychical in particular. His underlying philosophical position is
reconstructed from allusions that Freud makes from time to time. We arrive at
Freud's practical vindication of psychoanalysis and his underlying philosophy,
leaving the gap between the two to be filled in.

Freud's explicit justification of psychoanalysis

The psychophysical unity of the psychical is the bedrock of Freud's theories.
Without unconscious mental processes there can be no psychoanalysis; and without a bodily milieu, 'unconscious mental processes' is a contradiction in terms
(see p. 45 above). It is to this concept, rather than to any particular theoretical
expression of it, that psychoanalysis must look for its legitimation.

Freud presents his work as a scientific enterprise whose primary concepts need
only a limited defence. He argues that psychoanalysis must begin with a ready-
made conception of the psychical; it is up to 'philosophy' to account for it:
'Psychoanalysis makes a basic assumption [that there are unconscious mental
processes], the discussion of which is reserved to philosophical thought but the
justification for which lies in its results' (1938a, S.E. 23, pp. 144–145). He believes

that a unitary conception of psychical processes is needed to fill a gap in our understanding of the world, and that the explanations it engenders constitute sufficient justification. But this is not a straightforward addition to an existing scientific model, and cannot simply be grafted on to conventional foundations and existing bodies of scientific theory. Freud's concept of the psychical represents a fresh theoretical departure which requires a new foundational principle to underwrite the mental–physical unity it represents. For this to be fulfilled, more than practical justification is required.

In a three-pronged defence of the concept of unconscious mental processes, the shortfall in Freud's strategy becomes clear. He deems that 'our assumption of the unconscious is *necessary* and *legitimate*, and that we possess numerous proofs of its existence' (1915a, S.E. 14, p. 166, original emphases). It is legitimate, Freud argues, in that it involves no new way of thinking. We already make exactly the same 'inference' in attributing consciousness to others as we do in imputing unconscious states and processes to ourselves (ibid., pp. 169–170). As 'proof', he calls on 'post-hypnotic suggestion' to demonstrate not just the existence of unconscious states of mind, but also their motivational power.[3] Freud's arguments are sound as far as they go, but that is not far enough to justify such far-reaching theoretical innovation. The 'legitimacy' he claims for his assumption is only equivalent to the legitimacy of everyday psychological thinking. This may make it practically viable, but hardly scientifically so. Equally, actions carried out under the influence of earlier hypnosis 'prove' no more than the dynamic function of unconscious states; which again, does nothing to establish their objective psychophysical existence.

Freud's most compelling argument is for their conceptual 'necessity', on the grounds that conscious states and processes cannot be explained without them: 'to require that whatever goes on in the mind must also be known to consciousness is to make an untenable claim' (ibid., p. 167). The ordinary experience of memory and the evanescence of the contents of consciousness make 'latent states of mental life' a necessary inference. Apart from hypnosis, psychoanalytic phenomena from dreams and symptoms to slips and self-deception suggest active processes rather than fixed states. So far, so uncontentious; in practice, we do indeed assume that mental life rests on an unconscious substratum. The issue, as Freud points out, is how this should be conceived: as physical 'dispositions' to produce conscious phenomena, or as unconscious mental states and processes which also have a physical realization.

Again, Freud adopts a pragmatic approach. Traditionally, philosophy had taken the 'physical disposition' line; but Freud points out that these unconscious states and processes are only psychologically understandable. There is no doubt about their physical *existence*; but

> As far as their physical characteristics are concerned, they are totally inaccessible to us: no physiological concept or chemical process can give us any notion of their nature . . . On the other hand, we know for certain that they

have abundant points of contact with conscious mental processes . . . and all
the categories which we employ to describe conscious mental acts . . . can be
applied to them.

(Freud 1915a, S.E. 14, p. 168)

Freud is saying that physical concepts do not illuminate the nature of psychical
processes, while psychological concepts do. He concludes that rejecting the idea
that what is mental can also be unconscious either 'begs the question . . . or else
it is a matter of convention, of nomenclature' (ibid., p. 167). For that, he has little
time.[4]

Freud's arguments bear out the explanatory 'expedience' (ibid.) of unconscious
mental processes in everyday life and psychoanalysis alike; and if no more than
practical vindication were required, he might have done enough. But without
a conceptual bridge between the mental and physical domains, psychoanalytic
knowledge cannot be recognized as objective knowledge of an independent reality.
The question is not the ontological nature of psychical processes – as Freud
observes, we assume them to be both mental and physical – but their conceptual
category and organization. Neither mentalistic nor physicalistic foundations
will do. Freud's hope is to introduce not only a new descriptive label, but also a
new explanatory framework:[5] '*psychical* reality is a particular form of existence
not to be confused with *material* reality' (1900, S.E. 5, p. 620, original emphases),
any more than it is with consciousness. This means he cannot simply 'shrug his
shoulders' at the conceptual anomaly his notion of psychical reality evinces.[6]
The riddle of their conceptual domain and causal order must at some point be
unravelled.

Despite his embargo on philosophizing, Freud's defence carries some theoretical weight; and the way in which it does so illustrates his idiosyncratic approach.
He is claiming, essentially, that if a unitary conception of psychical processes is
such that it cannot be rebutted, then they have to be allotted a space in our overall
world view. On practical grounds alone, they enter into the realm of objectifiable
knowledge. Like ordinary physiological processes, they have to be considered as
existing independently of any particular perspective.

Freud's claim remains persuasive. Although psychical processes can neither be
measured through the body nor experienced in consciousness, they are nevertheless a necessary presupposition of ordinary practical life. Everyday experience
proceeds on a joint commitment to the material nature of reality and the relative
coherence of mental life. These are convictions which we are simply not at liberty
to reject. We cannot make our way in the world as animate beings without taking
the world to be physically real; and we cannot live as persons without treating
ourselves and others as holders of values, emotions, thoughts and intentions which
hang together to make personal rather than mechanical sense. In the same way, no
one 'decides' to extend this mental coherence to unconscious levels. In realizing
the meanings and motivations in our experiencing and acting, we find that we have
done so.

Given the infiltration of biological knowledge into everyday thinking, specific 'theoretical' conclusions follow. The vast majority of us have no choice but to assume the mind–brain connection which forms Freud's starting-point.[7] Although, like him, we can give no account of this connection,[8] we 'know' that it holds. We therefore also 'know' that there must be some way of conceiving *how* it holds. It must be possible to conceptualize not just their grounds of difference, but also the ground on which they are the same. Freud's concept of the psychical assumes and inhabits this ground.

It is this that induces Nagel to treat psychoanalysis as a scientific subject, and this that is lacking in Habermas' much tidier account. But Freud's method of persuasion is quite different from that of a normal empirical science. He invites us to discover the independent existence ascribed to psychical processes not through any physical signs they give off, but through the practical grasp of reality we are unable to relinquish. It is practical reasoning, not scientific deduction, that leads us to conclude that unconscious mental processes are real; and common sense, rather than observation and experiment, that tells us that they must be physical as well as mental in nature.

This way of approaching 'reality' holds elements from each theoretical category. It shares a destination with empirical science, but takes a hermeneutic route. If this eccentric validational tactic were confined to Freud's central concept alone, it would constitute no more than an *ad hoc* solution to a gritty theoretical puzzle. Psychoanalysis would still have to look to empirical science or hermeneutics for its substantive, as opposed to merely practical, foundation. We find, however, that the same two-sided thread runs throughout Freud's thought. At every level, he seems to see 'reality' as objective, but not as independent of the mind. By following the undertow of his thinking, we arrive at a perspective on reality in which both appear as true.

Freud's philosophical outlook

Freud does not set out the background to his thinking explicitly, but it can be gathered from remarks, asides, and the general tenor of his ideas. Just as his concept of the psychical owes its vindication more to ordinary reflection than to mainstream empirical science, so too does the materialism he seems to espouse so strongly.[9] Freud does not reduce the mental to the physical, as a normal scientific realist would do. His position is that in the last resort, we have nothing to go on but our ideas of things and what can be inferred from this: 'The processes with which [psychoanalysis] is concerned are in themselves just as unknowable as those dealt with by other sciences, by chemistry or physics, for example' (1938a, S.E. 23, p. 158). From this perspective, 'reality' does not go back to either the physical or the mental realm, as these are normally understood. It is rather that the physical and mental realms themselves go back to the way reality is registered within the human psyche. What we call reality exists primarily as something within the psyche, and only secondarily as something outside it.

Freud remains a realist, since he believes that there is a level of reality beyond consciousness which shapes our conscious perceptions; this reality can be inferred from our perceptions, but cannot be experienced directly. But he is not a physical realist. The primary reality is not, for him, a material reality existing independently of the human mind, but a psychical reality existing in the depths of the human psyche. This means that in the strictest sense, 'reality' cannot be analysed down to actual energy and hard matter, however these might be conceived, although something like them probably exists. All we can be sure of, through the indirect medium of reflection on experience, is whatever 'experience' itself can be analysed down to.

For Freud, this absolute bedrock consists of psychic units,[10] linked together into networks, as the form in which the unconscious basis of experience is registered. According to Freud's three metapsychological principles or 'forms of organization', these networks carry features that are registered as spatial, dynamic and quantitative in nature. It is these features, or properties, that define and ground the most basic element of reality. In normal empirical science, this is 'matter', or 'energy'; but in Freud's metapsychological picture, the most primitive element is not physical but psychophysical in nature. The mental and physical forms of perception branch off from it, rather than being separated from the start. Thus both physical reality and psychological reality have their source in psychical reality, with its metapsychological forms of organization.[11] Freud's 'basic assumption' of the original unity of the psychical and the physical is founded in their common ground of registration in the mind.

This orientation is as evident in Freud's earliest works as in his latest. His pre-psychoanalytic *Project for a Scientific Psychology* is usually taken to be the most physically reductive of his works. He announces his intention 'to *represent* psychical processes as quantitatively determinate states of specifiable material particles' (Freud 1895, S.E. 1, p. 295, added emphasis) – not to show that they *are* such particles. Equally, he identifies the fundamental category of science as 'quantitativity', or measurability, far more often than as 'matter'. There are regular though not wholly consistent[12] indications that Freud takes the ground of what can be known scientifically to reside not in the world itself, but in what is recorded in the mind in quantitative terms.

If the ground of scientific knowledge is what can be recorded in the mind in quantitative terms, then the ground of knowledge *per se* must be simply what is recorded in the mind. The 'qualitative' features of consciousness must also be foreshadowed in the psyche. Though Freud could never arrive at the principle or formula which could explain the relationship between the quantitative and qualitative aspects of reality, some form of connection must plainly exist. Perceptions of both mental and physical reality must go back to the same psychical ground. This makes the metapsychological principles significant not just as the basis of psychical life, but as the basis of everything that is considered 'reality'.[13] The 'fundamental hypothesis' of the spatial conception of psychical processes is also Freud's first precept of knowledge.[14] In Freud's philosophical outlook, the principles of the psychical come before the principles of matter. Through psychoanalysis, '[we] venture . . . to transform metaphysics into metapsychology' (1901, S.E. 6, p. 259).

We can now see how Freud's philosophical foundations diverge not only from those of Grünbaum and Habermas, but also from those of Nagel. Both Freud and Nagel believe that the ultimate validation of knowledge lies in the reality that it reflects, but each situates this 'reality' in a different place. In Nagel's straightforward physical realism, knowledge is justified through a material reality that is assumed in advance to be impacting on the mind. He endorses subjective knowledge not because the mind is the locus of reality, but because he believes that it reflects the real, mind-independent state of affairs well enough. In Freud's more subtle 'psychical' realism, this additional presumption is not made. Reality goes back only to what appears to the psyche, directly or through the processes of thought. The practical nature of his thinking goes 'all the way down'.

Nothing in this prevents Freud, or us, from supposing that there must be a real world impacting on the mind to give these psychical registrations in the first place. Nor can we or should we avoid treating these as external reality itself for all practical purposes, including science and psychoanalysis. But because the psychical runs through every level of existence, the order of reality is not the same as that of a conventional empirical science. Freud's starting-point is that a reality which is wholly independent of the mind can only be taken as a matter of faith: it cannot be established theoretically. Theoretical accounts of reality begin with the inference or principle that psychical activity itself is spatially organized. This intrinsic spatial functioning is dimly and indirectly apprehended as 'endo-psychic perception' (1901, S.E. 6, p. 258), which Freud rather confusingly explains is a form of 'knowing' which 'naturally has nothing of the character of perception'. He is striving to express that the psyche's own form of organization must condition, or systematically affect, its subsequent perceptions. In that sense, it can be said to perceive itself 'endo-psychically', or from within.

This psychical registration is the most primitive layer that Freud believes reality can be traced back to. Above this layer he places the domain of matter and mind as we take it to be 'objectively', on the basis of observation together with the logical reasoning through which we can partially excise our grossest individual projections. The most superficial level of reality is everyday conscious perception, including the apprehension of consciousness itself. Normal scientific realism assumes the series: *external world – matter – mind as appearance to consciousness*, with each domain being understood as an offshoot of the one before. In Freud's psychical realism, we have the different series, *psychical reality – matter and mind – consciousness*. The mind-independent world is treated as a supposition of the conscious mind, rather than as the primary reality.

This means that Freud's psychoanalysis is set within an approach towards reality which carries elements of both hermeneutic and empirical thinking. Like hermeneutics, it begins with the perceiver, but like empirical science, it acknowledges the primacy of 'matter' over 'consciousness'. Instead of the brute alternatives of physical or mental theorization, it moots the possibility of a 'psychical' theorization. The psychical is set *before* the theoretical dichotomy into the external viewpoint of empirical science and the internal viewpoint of hermeneutics. It therefore holds both physical and mental aspects.

Towards a psychical foundational approach

The 'psychical realism' at the root of Freud's thought appears to hold the empirical-hermeneutic meeting-ground that his theories call for and which they seem to herald. To be true to this unitary approach, the full foundations of psychoanalysis should show how psychoanalytic concepts can be theoretical without being abstractions, and 'real' but not merely material. The practical hallmark of Freud's thinking should be reflected in both their active and substantive aspects. But as things stand, these psychophysical foundations exist only in part and in promise. Freud's writings give no more than the strategy and the ground of a possible new approach. Its application can be made out in Freud's practical method of establishing the objectivity of psychical processes; the philosophical ground emerges in his siting of objective reality in the psyche rather than in the world outside the mind. But the theoretical stratum between these two layers is missing: the hierarchy of foundational principles and concepts on which the theoretical explanations of all the different classes of phenomenon must rest. For psychoanalysis itself, this means whatever the concept of the psychical must presuppose, about itself and about the kind of being to which the term can apply. Beyond psychoanalysis, it means whatever must be presupposed about the reality inhabited by such a being.

The task is now to begin to evolve this missing layer by identifying the foundational principle and fundamental category on which the concept of the psychical, as the core of psychoanalysis, rests. Given the range of nuances within Freud's writings, there must be many ways in which these could be developed. All that can be done here is to develop one shape for the foundations which are beginning to emerge from within psychoanalysis itself. The purpose of the next two sections is expository rather than critical: the aim is to sketch in the overall shape of the alternative foundations for psychoanalysis rather than to examine them in detail. There is therefore little or no scrutiny of the ideas put forward, not because their close discussion is unimportant, but solely because it lies outside the scope of this particular enquiry.

The practical foundation of psychoanalysis

This section develops the practical framework and foundational principle on which psychoanalysis can be legitimized. To reflect the practical pre-eminence in Freud's thinking, they should be located before the mental–physical division, and should form the basis for the theoretical foundation, rather than the other way round. Their reconstruction makes substantial use of the work of Sebastian Gardner, a British philosopher whose interests in the philosophy of mind include the philosophy of psychoanalysis (Gardner 1993). His precise philosophical articulation of psychoanalytic concepts and assumptions conveys an intuitive 'feel' for his subject. Nevertheless, the focus of the section is not Gardner's thought itself, but what it can contribute to practical foundations which are consistent with Freud's 'psychical' approach.

The first part of this section sets out the grounds for a conceptual framework which is 'neutral' with regard to the empirical and hermeneutic theoretical modes. The second tests its viability by investigating what this perspective reveals about the central concept of the psychical. The third discusses the 'psychical' causal mode as one which carries features of both physical and mental causality. Together, they provide the grounds for a psychophysical framework and principle on which the practical legitimation of psychoanalysis can rest.

Psychoanalysis and commonsense psychology: the 'neutral' theoretical mode

Psychoanalysis begins and ends in the practical domain. The interpersonal setting is the generator of its concepts and the source of their validation. Without the ordinary ways of interpreting subjective states and processes, there would be nothing for psychoanalysis to grip on to: psychoanalytic explanation starts where our normal explanatory resources give out. Everyday practical psychology must be our starting-point; but everyday practical psychology is by definition pre-theoretical. It allows for reflection and self-reflection as well as the immediacy of initial impressions, but it precedes the separation into the hermeneutic and empirical modes on which theoretical systems divide. This augurs well for what might be sharable, but badly for what must be foundational. How can 'common sense' or its components be a source of legitimation?

Nagel, as we have seen, attributes some of the validational authority of psychoanalysis to its continuity with 'commonsense psychology'. In doing so, he joins the unwilling Grünbaum in confirming that 'common sense' must possess a degree of validity in its own right. This, again, is something that we cannot really question. All theories and explanations begin with ordinary perception and reflection, and all are justified in terms which are ultimately translatable into everyday language. The pre-theoretical knowledge of common sense may be unreliable, but as the starting-point and end-point of knowledge, it cannot be completely set aside. Nagel's primary allegiance, however, is to fully objective knowledge ('some questions have right and wrong answers'). He endorses subjective knowledge as potentially objective because he sees it as a window on to the real, mind-independent state of affairs which science can go on to ratify or refute.[15] Objective existence means, for him, not a particular kind of existence in the mind, but existence independently of being perceived. From this perspective, 'commonsense psychology' can offer psychoanalysis a temporary toehold, but only physical science could afford it a solid base.

Sebastian Gardner, by contrast, suggests boldly that everyday practical psychology is not just a major but the *only* relevant conceptual ground for psychoanalysis. 'Psychoanalytic explanation is shown to be a coherent extension of everyday forms of psychological explanation, and scepticism about psychoanalysis is met by exhibiting this continuity' (1993, frontispiece). There are no breaks, Gardner says, between the practical ways of knowing used by commonsense psychology and by psychoanalysis; so doubting the one means doubting the other. '[There] can be no pretending that psychoanalytic theory is defensible except on the assumption that ordinary psychology is cogent' (Gardner 1993, p. 202). He is proposing that psychoanalysis derives its entire practical authority from its continuity with ordinary psychological thinking. It is this that holds the key to the 'neutral' conceptual framework from which a psychophysical conception of psychoanalysis must stem.

For Gardner, the essence of psychoanalysis is practical psychological explanation which makes use of the idea of unconscious motivation. Like Grünbaum and Habermas, he is setting psychoanalysis at the clinical level rather than any deeper. This practical focus restricts his scope, but his 'ordinary' approach leaves more room for theoretical manoeuvre than Habermas' outright hermeneutic stance. Where Habermas takes the hermeneutic fork at the crossroads of theoretical categories, Gardner tracks back to before the crossroads itself. By attaching the central concept of psychoanalysis to ordinary practical psychology, he gives psychoanalysis a non-contentious (or pre-contentious) starting-point. The corresponding drawback is its apparent demotion as a theoretical discipline. If psychoanalysis is continuous with ordinary psychological thinking, surely it too must be a 'pre-theoretical' subject, delivering only flimsy knowledge.

Gardner explains that their continuity is a matter of conceptual domain rather epistemological respectability, with affinity running both ways. While the practical concepts of psychoanalysis are in a sense 'pre-theoretical', psychoanalysis itself is not. Methodical evaluation protects psychoanalytic explanations from arbitrariness, although they are arbitrated in the same way as their ordinary psychological counterparts. Psychoanalysis, in return, 'repays ordinary psychology for its extension, by assisting in its vindication' (1993, p. 231). Thus practical psychology justifies psychoanalytic ways of knowing, while psychoanalytic theorization can validate some of the intuitive insights of ordinary psychology. It is only when this dual relation is misunderstood, Gardner suggests, that psychoanalysis begins to look like 'bad science', or 'paradoxical misapplication of ordinary psychology' (p. 226).

This suggests that we may not be obliged to class psychoanalysis as either an empirical or a hermeneutic science. Cast as a distinctive adjunct to ordinary practical psychology, its conceptual ambiguity begins to seem less strange. Rather than being a deficient conventional theory, it can be seen as a theoretical system dealing directly with material from the 'pre-theoretical' domain, and therefore using the conceptual framework of this domain. Psychoanalytic concepts are not like other theoretical concepts, which can be divided along empirical or hermeneutic lines. Like their 'ordinary' prototypes of character, emotion and motive, we have to treat the processes, structures and states they refer to as 'real'. This is justifiable, because although they are unconscious, they have 'real psychological grounds': each psychical structure or process corresponds to a 'real piece of the . . . mind' (p. 149). Gardner is restating what Habermas has already demonstrated, that clinical concepts such as projection, transference and repression have to be understood as psychological *phenomena* as well as psychological *concepts*.

This puts psychoanalytic concepts into a different order from the '*intrinsically theoretical* properties and entities' of other theoretical systems, whether empirically derived concepts like the laws of gravity, or hermeneutically-derived concepts such as grammatical structures. These concepts are 'intrinsically theoretical' in that they are 'not open to being fixed epistemically in a direct, non-theoretical way, and in some sense owe their existence to the theory which constructs them' (p. 220). They cannot be experienced directly because they are not themselves phenomena, but ways of explaining phenomena. But the concepts of psychoanalytic and ordinary psychology are phenomena which may become explanatory. It is in this sense that they are 'pre-theoretical'.

This means that they can only be known ('fixed epistemically') and validated directly. 'Nothing purely logical can compel recognition of psychoanalytic explananda',[16] Gardner remarks, which is why those of Grünbaum's persuasion are unlikely ever to be convinced (p. 228). More rigorously even than Habermas, Gardner is defending psychoanalysis as reflection on a self, by a self; directly, or by attunement with another. This sets psychoanalytic thinking apart not only from the technical application of empirical-scientific theories, but also from the esoteric application of hermeneutic theories. The first requires knowledge of the hidden workings of the physical world; the second, knowledge of special symbolic forms. Although psychoanalysis is, like them, an evaluable system of ideas, both system and ideas are practical. Establishing their 'truth' is a matter of recognition rather than either deduction or indoctrination.[17]

This strategy begins to look promising. Locating the psychoanalytic domain *before* the differentiation of the mental and physical conceptual categories gives a more solid starting-point than an outright hermeneutic or empirical stance. Although psychoanalysis can be seen as extending everyday psychology in quite novel ways, there need be no theoretical schism between the two: no break between appearance and underlying reality other than what is already assumed in ordinary psychology. '[The] upshot of psychoanalytic interpretation of persons should . . . be likened to the adding of detail and deeper perspective in a growing, palimpsestic, but single picture – rather than a process of stripping-away to reveal a "true" image' (p. 201). Gardner is saying that psychoanalysis does not set itself up as a rival to the commonsense picture of the mind, but rather as a way of taking it further. In the realm of ordinary and psychoanalytic psychology, the theoretical level is continuous with the practical level.

The picture of psychoanalysis conveyed by Gardner reflects the substance and the spirit of Freud's 'psychical realism' with uncanny accuracy. Both are conceptually safe, because they claim less, rather than more, than any alternative. In Freud's 'psychical' approach, locating objective reality in the psyche means *not* taking the extra step of transferring it to a world outside the psyche. This cannot be refuted, since the burden is on the scientific realist to prove, impossibly, that the material reality we think we know really does exist outside the mind or psyche. Equally, allying psychoanalytic thinking to ordinary ways of knowing means *not* transferring it beyond the point at which theoretical knowledge starts. Again, in any disagreement, the onus is on 'the critic of psychoanalytic explanation to demonstrate that its epistemology [its ground of knowledge] differs in kind from that of ordinary psychology' (p. 233).[18]

Gardner's exposition provides the basis for taking the implicit pre-theoretical framework of ordinary psychology as a legitimate practical framework for a psychophysical conception of psychoanalysis. Whether it can also be accepted as a potential theoretical framework depends, however, on whether it delivers a better understanding of the concept of the psychical, particularly its causal mode, than either the empirical or the hermeneutic alternative.

The 'neutral' account of the psychical

While the practical legitimacy of the 'neutral' conceptual framework rests on the continuity of ordinary and psychoanalytic ways of thinking, its theoretical viability depends on their discontinuity. Theoretical status can be accorded only if psychoanalysis can be shown to reach a level of reality beyond that which is open to ordinary psychology. Gardner is confident on this score: 'On the one hand . . . psychoanalytic concepts are natural extensions of the ways of thinking of ordinary psychology . . . On the other, psychoanalytic theory is not just a terminological reformulation of ordinary psychology' (ibid., p. 87). Although psychoanalysis builds on ordinary psychology, it is not simply another way of saying what ordinary psychology already says: 'it explains things that ordinary psychology cannot explain, and does so by employing a distinctive form of explanation which is foreign to ordinary psychology' (ibid.).

The crucial question is whether this 'distinctive form of explanation' throws up any hint of reconcilability between the physical and mental conceptual schemes. If so, the conceptual framework of ordinary psychology would gain validation as a potential theoretical framework, and we would be on the way to discovering the principle underlying Freud's concept of the psychical as the junction of the mental and the physical dimensions.

Propositional psychology

But first, we need to set the context of the discussion. Gardner sees psychoanalysis as philosophically significant in its own right. Its main contribution, he suggests, is to extend one of the standard philosophical definitions of mental phenomena beyond the level of rationality. This overall approach is known as 'propositional psychology': the field of processes and states that contain a proposition, or proposal. These are, by definition, mental states and processes, but they do not necessarily include all aspects of what can be experienced. Emotions, beliefs and intentions are propositional, because they 'say' something: I want this, think that, intend to do the other. But reflex actions and any 'raw sensation' component of mental phenomena are not,[19] because they do not hold a statable meaning, or proposition. Since they can be fitted into a purely physical chain of linear cause and effect, phenomena of this kind can count as physical phenomena instead.

Thus propositional psychology defines a phenomenon as 'mental' if can be fitted into a rationally coherent system of meaningful elements. Just as physical phenomena become comprehensible when set within the physical causal network, so mental phenomena (defined as 'propositional attitudes') can be understood by setting them within the personal nexus of values, aims and tendencies which make up each individual's mental 'set'. What holds this network together is not the hypothetico-deductive logic of physical systems, but the 'human' logic underwriting the rationality of mental states and processes. Unlike the logic of the physical world, the logic of rationality is not invariable, but neither is it purely individual. It reflects each human group's shared 'common sense' interpretations of the physical and human worlds. For an action to count as rational, it has to be possible for others as well as oneself to see it as a realistic means to an end which fits in well enough with the individual's values, beliefs and plans. Equally, beliefs, emotions and other states of mind can be judged as rational only if they are seen as understandable responses to a particular interpretation of the circumstances which is reasonably consistent with the rest of that person's mental set, or outlook.

The main point is that propositional psychology treats what is mental as synonymous with what is rational. From this perspective, explaining an emotion, a thought, a belief or a piece of behaviour means finding or hypothesizing a 'reason' for it. 'Because it attributes reasons for action', explains Gardner, 'propositional psychology is also *rational psychology*' (p. 250, original emphasis). The 'reason' is the mental equivalent of the physical cause: reasons are the currency of rationality in the same way that causes are the currency of determinism. Where physical causes are made up of prior events, reasons are typically a composite of conscious wants or desires,[20] and consciously accessible beliefs and intentions; it is rational to turn on the tap if one is thirsty and believes that water will come out. Without a viable reason, actions or states of mind do not 'make sense'. They cannot be brought into the realm of rational psychology on which propositional accounts of the mind rely.

Psychoanalysis as pre-propositional psychology

Psychoanalysis, of course, deals routinely with exactly this kind of mental phenomenon – with actions, thoughts and states of mind that on the face of it have no reason, no 'good' reason, or which even appear to be 'against all reason'. Propositional psychology pushes 'irrational' phenomena like neurotic symptoms to the very edge of the mental sphere. It cannot see them as special mental processes which reveal the deeper levels of the mind, but only as deviant processes which indicate a breakdown or complication of normal mental functioning.

Gardner sets out the wider view that psychoanalysis takes. He describes the 'distinctive form of explanation' which psychoanalysis provides as 'a new form of intentional[21] explanation at the personal level . . . achieved by an extension of ordinary psychology, grounded on the supposition that there exist kinds of mental state that do not interact rationally' (p. 115). He is saying that rationality is not all there is to the mind. Psychoanalysis enables us to understand actions and states of mind which we experience, but cannot ordinarily explain. It does so, remarkably, by positing a causal link between mental phenomena which reflects neither the determinism of the physical world nor acting, feeling, or thinking 'for a reason'.

Strange as it may sound, this kind of causal link is already familiar to ordinary pre-theoretical psychology as the 'power of desire to malform belief' (p. 36).[22] Gardner is alluding to the 'wishful thinking' of everyday life. We know we are prone to believe what we want to believe, against the available evidence and particularly when we find our desires disturbing; our self-deception can be both unconscious and complete. A kind of desire seems capable of acting as the irrational cause of a false belief, an 'effect' which is neither generally predictable, like physical causality, nor a credible means to any rational end, like propositional causality. Psychoanalysis 'exploits, with much greater intensity, the same resources' (ibid.) to develop a theoretical account of what is already accepted as a prevailing human tendency.

This peculiar causal action is the key to the mediation of the physical and mental conceptual schemes. Propositional psychology can explain irrational actions and states of mind only as aberrations of propositional processes – as normal mental functioning gone wrong. Psychoanalysis offers a new explanation of irrationality as the manifestation of an underlying layer of 'primitive' mental states and processes. It sees 'propositional attitudes as embedded in a structure, a constitution, which is psychological but not propositional, and capable of influencing propositional attitudes in organised ways' (ibid.).[23] Gardner is paraphrasing psychoanalytic insights in more precise philosophical terms. He is suggesting that psychoanalysis explains 'irrational' mental processes not as faulty mental processes,[24] but as outbreaks of a pre-rational realm pushing through the veneer of rationality. This is, of course, the psychical domain, lying between the non-propositional level of ordinary physiological processes and the propositional level of ordinary rationality.

Gardner defines this most primitive level of mental functioning as the 'motivational state'. This is not a conscious state of wanting or desire, but the unconscious ground from which these and other rational motivational elements arise. 'Propositional desires are generated out of motivational states with the aid of beliefs about the world . . . motivational states are states that *cause* people to have desires' (p. 117, original emphasis).[25] Very often, these states are thought of in biological terms. The cause of thirst, for example, would normally be said to be the organism's need for fluid. While this is not untrue, Gardner is indicating that there must be an intervening stage. At some point, the subjective inclination to seek fluid develops out of the objective state of bodily dehydration. He is effectively endorsing Freud's practical justification for the 'basic assumption' of processes which connect physical requirement and conscious experience. By presenting psychoanalysis as 'pre-propositional psychology', he is underwriting Freud's pragmatic judgement that a psychological approach to processes which are typically cast in biological terms facilitates fuller, more convincing explanations.

The simplest motivational states are what psychoanalysis terms 'wishes'.[26] These are 'conative [purposive] states whose causes . . . are simple universal biological requirements, the most basic instinctual demand' (p. 120). The 'wish' is distinguished from its physical cause by its mental content: a wish is by definition a wish *for* something. It is unconscious, but it carries a picture, or engram, of what would fulfil it; which, with the merest shift of perspective, engenders a picture of the fulfilment itself, as though it had occurred. Although Gardner does not say so, this implies that a physical cause is not enough. There must also be a cultural causal strand, however minimal. The same biological state can give rise to different wishes, depending on cultural convention and individual preference and experience. One person's 'motivational state' of hunger could involve a picture of devouring food which would be found repellent by another person, or in another society. The tendency to 'wish' may be biologically determined, but every instance of 'wishing' carries conditions of fulfilment which cannot be explained by biology alone.

In representing the conditions and realization of fulfilment, the leap into symbolism is made. What would otherwise be a simple physical state gains a psychological dimension. It is this that opens the door to the elaboration of basic wishes for physical satisfaction into more sophisticated wishes for less concrete forms of satisfaction. Gardner explains that simple motivational states can develop into 'motivational states with a more psychologically complex, less biological character [which] can play the same role' (p. 120). Motivational states can hold pictures of fame and fortune as well as purely physical gratification. Thus 'wishes are a sort of hybrid: they have the *force* of pre-propositional states of instinctual demand, whilst being able to draw on the *complexity of content* of propositional states' (p. 124, original emphases). They mark the point at which a physical urge gains meaning. The mental and the physical, the social and the biological, come together at the very ground of psychical life.

The wish, then, is the 'stuff' of the pre-propositional psychical domain. Gardner's philosophical analysis supports the partial autonomy of this domain: it cannot be simply assimilated to either a normal physical framework or to an ordinary rational psychological framework. The next task is to investigate the causal mode by which one psychical process leads to another, with a view to discovering the causal principle involved. This is the acid test which will show whether this way of understanding psychoanalysis reflects an approach which is genuinely unitary, rather than falling at the last minute into either empirical-scientific or hermeneutic principles. If successful, it would constitute the practical foundation for a psychophysical conception of psychoanalysis.

The 'psychical' causal mode

Like physical 'causes' and rational 'reasons', motivational states are embedded in a causal structure. In Gardner's analysis, the motivational state is the 'cause' of a conscious or pre-conscious propositional desire which can be fulfilled through rational thought and action. But this is not the first thing it gives rise to. The most immediate 'effect' of a wish (or 'conative state') is the picture or 'hallucination'[27] of fulfilment implicit in it. The link between wish and wish fulfilment is direct, non-linear, non-rational and non-arbitrary: 'content is straightforwardly trans-posed from a wish into a representation of the wish as fulfilled' (p. 120). In this sideways transferring of content, we see a conjoint causal mode at work. It lacks the predictability of outcome of physical determinism, yet it is the inevitable consequence of putting a normal human organism in a normal social environment. Like physical cause and effect, the movement from wish to wish fulfilment is instantaneous, unmediated and outside conscious awareness. Like acting for a reason, the contents of the wish and wish fulfilment depend not only on the physical characteristics of the motivational state, but on how it is 'felt'; it is a matter of individual-social interpretation. As an embodied process, the 'psychical' causal mode emerges from the causal structure of the physical world. As a symbolic process, it manifests the human intentionality which bends the physical order to individual perception and volition.

From a propositional vantage point, the wish can be thought of as the precursor of a rational desire, and the picture of its fulfilment as the irrational prototype of a rational belief. Prior to this level, the mental and the physical are only for-mally distinct, and the wish is only separable from the picture of its fulfilment in a theoretical sense: in 'psychical' reality, desiring cannot be distinguished from believing, or causes (including reasons) from their effects. The point at which rationality enters into mental life is the point at which the 'event causality' of the physical world can be thought of as diverging from the 'intentional causality' of the mental world. In one sense this point is virtual, dissolving under the spotlight of attention into either mental or physical causality. In another sense it must also be real, because there is a definite point at which the mental dimension differentiates out from the physical dimension, and mental explanations diverge from physical explanations. The psychical causal order is set before this divergence. Again, it means *not* proceeding forward into either theoretical modality.

Because psychical activity is neither conscious nor rational, it is not 'thought' as such, but rather 'mentation'. It has to be defined as a presupposition of propositional thinking, but it also feeds directly into the rational level through the workings of what psychoanalysis terms 'phantasy'. A minimal openness to feedback induces motivational states to connect with each other to form a characteristic stream. This is the flow of phantasy, the personal, wish-fulfilling story-lines which run beneath the surface of consciousness, pressing on propositional rationality in the same purposive but unrealistic way as the wishes that make it up.[28]

Phantasy is the 'primary content of unconscious mental processes . . . the "mental expression" of instinct' (Isaacs 1943, p. 81, quoted in Gardner 1993, p. 142). It is also the medium of communication between pre-propositional and propositional states. Insofar as we are desiring and believing beings, phantasy provides us with a reality that we are able to latch on to because it speaks to our own particular interests; without the wish-fulfilling element it provides, reality would hold no significance for us. Insofar as we aspire to rationality, however, phantasy is a 'kind of mental grit' clogging up the rational processes and distorting our perceptions. It gives us a personal stake in events at the price of a less than realistic estimation of the circumstances.

The configurations of phantasy are largely unconscious, but unlike the wholly unconscious psychoanalytic wish, they can be open to observation. Their most transparent manifestations are the touchingly obvious dreams of early childhood; they are obvious because unlike the dreams of later life, wish and wish fulfilment are largely undisguised. Freud's own examples include his daughter of 19 months, calling out a list of her favourite foods in her sleep;[29] and his small nephew, who dreamed of eating the very same cherries he had been forced to hand over for his uncle's birthday (Freud 1900, S.E. 4, pp. 130–131).[30] But they can also be made out in the 'quasi-manifestations' of phantasy in waking life. 'This form of intro-spectability is mid-way between ordinary consciousness of one's mental states, and madness, the direct invasion of consciousness by unconscious content, as in psychosis' (Gardner 1993, p. 219). Gardner is trying to get across its 'as-if', almost impersonal quality. 'Quasi-manifestation necessarily lacks the sense of agency which usually accompanies mental life, but may nevertheless have a negative connection with the will: quasi-manifestation may facilitate a minimal ability to hinder the influence of phantasy' (ibid.).[31]

We can discern the phantasy conditioning our consciousness in experiences like the dim sense we may get of being impelled to act, react or perceive in a particular, perhaps characteristic, perhaps apparently self-defeating way; as though it were something that happens to us, rather than something that we 'do'. Like remembering one's dreams, sensitivity to this dimension can grow, especially within an interpretative milieu such as the psychotherapeutic setting. It may then become possible to gain a small but genuine degree of control over psychical causal action; though often only with considerable psychological effort, the force of phantasy can be to some extent contained, resisted or reflected on. This, together with its 'internal recognisability' (ibid.), constitutes the connecting thread between phantasy and consciousness, and the pre-propositional and propositional worlds. 'Irrational' actions and states of mind can be understood as protrusions of pre-propositional functioning into ordinary rationality, often to the bewilderment of all concerned. Through the power of self-reflection, these primitive mental elements may be drawn towards or even into the propositional network of rationality and conscious choice: 'where "It" was, there "I" shall be'.

Thus the movement from wish to wish-fulfilment reveals a causal mode which arises before the division into external and internal reality makes any sense. Something like desire causes something like belief, in a purposive but non-rational way. As an extension of the 'pre-theoretical' domain of everyday psychological thinking, this proposition can be justified by both conceptual and perceptual means; as a necessary presupposition and as an observable reality. The concept of the psychical, with its 'pre-theoretical' causal mode, is implicit in ordinary psychological knowledge. The wish, or motivational state, is the ground of all conscious desires and beliefs, emotions and intentions: the condition of rationality is irrationality. The 'quasi-manifestability' of phantasy means that the psychical is not a purely theoretical conjecture, but must be attributed as tangible an existence as any other object of first-person perception. Phantasies are no less real than emotions, ideas or intentions.

The practical principle of pre-rational psychical processes now falls into our hands. In Freudian terminology, it is the 'pleasure principle', contrasting with the 'reality principle' of ordinary rationality. Freud's terms encapsulate the focus and intention of the psychical domain but leave its underlying principle unspecified. Continuing Gardner's philosophical re-articulation of psychoanalytic terms and concepts, we might call this principle the principle of fulfillability, of wishes and therefore also of desires. This is the kernel of practical knowledge embodied in the dual structure of biologically-derived wish and culturally-derived wish-fulfilment. Its pre-hermeneutic, pre-empirical derivation represents the point of meeting between the physical and the mental, the cultural and the biological. This principle is the ground of human subjectivity, and the practical foundation of the concept of the psychical. It is conceptually necessary, because without it, there would only be an abstract symbolic order and a blind biological urge.

This way of looking at psychoanalysis brings clarity to Freud's vision of the psychical as an authentic third domain, lying between what is physically given and what is mentally constructed. The inevitability and lack of volitional control characteristic of physical causality have not yet separated out from the creation of individual meaning characteristic of intentional causality. As Freud proposed, the psychical process is an original unity which can only secondarily be dissected into mental and physical 'sides'.

The practical foundation of psychoanalysis

With this, the practical legitimation of psychoanalysis is complete. Its practical foundation is implicit in the intimate connection and significant disjuncture between psychoanalytic and everyday psychology. Psychoanalysis draws practical validity from the ordinary forms of psychological knowing which it shares and on which everyday living depends. Its 'distinctive mode of explanation' in terms of unconscious motivation is not derived from anything alien to ordinary psychology, but is presupposed in ordinary explanations of motivation through the everyday concepts of desire, belief and intention. The new dimension that psychoanalysis brings to ordinary psychology is thus a legitimate addition.

Analysing this dimension reveals a causal process which is recognizable to ordinary psychology but which goes beyond its terms. Although the material that psychoanalysis deals with is 'pre-theoretical' by nature, it can claim to be a theoretical system (with a practical foundation) on the grounds that it reaches beneath the level of 'appearances' to expand the 'pre-theoretical' understanding of its field. The principle of the fulfillability of wishes defines the practical bedrock of human subjectivity. Even more than we are rational or physical beings, we are wishing beings.

This reading of psychoanalysis reflects a conceptual framework which is 'neutral' with regard to the empirical and hermeneutic theoretical modes. Set within the domain of 'pre-theoretical' practical psychology, psychoanalysis requires 'neither hermeneutic reconstruction, nor the scientifically oriented criticism which analytic philosophers have tended to accord it' (Gardner 1993, frontispiece). On the contrary, the advocates of empirical and hermeneutic readings of psychoanalysis could find a meeting-point by moving back to this position which is presupposed by each of theirs.

The theoretical foundation of psychoanalysis

If practical foundations were all that psychoanalysis needed, our job would be done. Any deeper theorization would go beyond its parameters, and since it could only go in either an empirical-scientific or a hermeneutic direction, we would be little better off. A misleading theorization may be worse than none; but without a theoretical setting of its own, psychoanalysis remains stranded in a hermeneutic classification. A purely practical foundation leaves psychoanalysis shifting on the sands of cultural relativity, grounded in the practical ways of thinking of particular cultural groups rather than in anything more essentially 'human'. But the psychophysical unity of the metapsychology stands for the link between the subjective and objective worlds. Its dual aspect goes back to the psychical realism beneath the surface of Freud's thinking. This implies a more substantive ground than practical legitimation can supply.

Like any practical account, however, the 'neutral' conception of psychoanalysis carries theoretical implications. As well as taking forwards some of its practical assumptions, the concept of the psychical is a refinement of an existing pre-theoretical picture in ordinary psychology. This picture is peripheral to Gardner's enquiry, but it is not absent from it. He gives his brief attention to the question of the foundational category and substantive presupposition of ordinary and psychoanalytic psychology. This can only be the 'person',[32] which Gardner readily defines as a 'psychophysical being' with 'substantial unity' (ibid.); a subject of experience with a palpable existence, which can only secondarily be divided into 'parts'.[33] Since neither psychoanalytic nor ordinary psychology can be based on either a mechanical or a disembodied primary category, this preliminary definition seems cogent and apt.

The validation of the normal theoretical approaches rests on their respective foundational principles and categories; but since the psychophysical approach is set prior to these, the validation of psychophysical foundational elements must rest on something more basic. If psychoanalysis is to count as a theoretically-grounded system, the concept of personhood must be shown to be a justifiable primary category with the potential to link into a wider theoretical ground than psychoanalysis alone. Establishing this means going outside psychoanalysis into more open philosophical terrain. As the last section draws from Gardner's work, this section draws significantly from a text by one of the most eminent British philosophers of recent times. Peter Strawson's philosophical interests do not include psychoanalysis and its problems; they centre, rather, on the foundations of ordinary thought, approached from the practical perspective of logic and the substantive perspective of metaphysics.

The first part of this section makes use of his best known metaphysical study to set out the theoretical and foundational credentials of the concept of the person as the psychophysical ground of the concepts of the human body and mind. This fulfils the minimal requirements for a reconstruction of the foundational elements of a psychophysical conception of psychoanalysis. But this psychophysical ground is confined to personhood. It underwrites the meeting-point of human physiology and the human mind or psyche, but falls short of Freud's vision of the prior unity of the very concepts of matter and mind.

The second part takes forward this foundational reconstruction, contrasting Freud's philosophical ground with Nagel's underlying approach (Nagel 1986, 1998). This development suggests that a general psychophysical mode of theorization is conceivable. The primary principle and category on which the psychophysical conception of psychoanalysis is founded could in principle be extended into an approach with a wider applicability than psychoanalysis alone. Freud's psychical realism could form the basis for a theorization of all aspects of reality, developing directly out of the psychophysical concept of personhood as the ground not just of the mind–body division, but also of the matter–mind dichotomy.

The concept of the person

Strawson's *Individuals* (1959) is an analytical *tour de force* which has served as a vital reference point for any number of philosophical enquiries over the years. There is no opportunity, in this context, to do justice to its subtlety and detail. The only aspect which is relevant to this study is his analysis of the concept of the person. Our purpose is to make a first investigation into the viability of this concept as a foundational category which carries theoretical as well as practical weight, and is more fundamental than the concepts of either the human body or the human mind.

Individuals is subtitled 'An Essay in Descriptive Metaphysics'. This refers to the branch of metaphysics which describes and analyses our picture of reality, as opposed to explaining how it came about or suggesting modifications. 'Descriptive metaphysics is content to describe the actual structure of our thought about the world, revisionary metaphysics is concerned to produce a better structure' (Strawson 1959, p. 9). From the perspective of this enquiry, descriptive metaphysics is more basic than revisionary metaphysics, or indeed than any other theoretical enquiry. Before one can improve on or develop a picture of reality, one must be clear exactly what it is. If we believe, with Strawson, that the 'human' picture of reality is not infinitely variable, it becomes all the more important to identify what the essential elements are, and how they connect with each other:

> there is a massive central core of human thinking which has no history – or none recorded in histories of thought; there are categories and concepts which, in their most fundamental character, change not at all. Obviously these are not the specialities of the most refined thinking. They are the commonplaces of the least refined thinking; and are yet the indispensable core of the conceptual equipment of the most sophisticated human beings.
>
> (Strawson 1959, p. 10)

Strawson is pointing towards what is universal to human beings, as opposed to what is culturally variable. The fundamental nature of his work can make his propositions appear trivial or obvious: 'metaphysics is the finding of reasons . . . for what we believe on instinct' (p. 247).[34] This is particularly so when limitations of space prevent us from including the close logical reasoning by which he justifies his conclusions. Yet his findings are essential to our project: the task of metaphysics is to clarify, examine and account for the terms that other subjects take for granted. Since the psychophysical basis of psychoanalysis cannot rest on any existing theoretical foundation, conceptual analysis offers the only way of setting psychoanalysis on firm conceptual ground.

Particulars

Strawson's opening proposition is that our overall conceptual scheme – the framework in which our perceptions have their place – depends on the idea of 'particulars'.[35] Unless particular phenomena can be distinguished in the general perceptual flow, nothing specific could be identified or re-identified. The possibility of 'particulars' is thus a condition of all mental activity, from pre-rational 'mentation' and unconscious phantasies to propositional emotion and rational thought. The 'basic particulars', Strawson continues, are 'objects . . . which are, or possess, material bodies – in a broad sense of the expression' (p. 39).[36] These are physical objects on the one hand, and 'persons' on the other. Without these fundamental categories, there would be no way of noticing or referring to anything at all. Nothing specific could be talked about, and there would be neither subjects of experience nor objects of perception.

Having analysed the necessary criteria for 'material bodies', Strawson concludes that their fundamental place is a logical consequence of the way in which perceptual reality is organized:

> This conclusion should be in no way surprising or unexpected, if we recall that our general framework of particular-reference is a unified spatio-temporal system of one temporal and three spatial dimensions, and reflect once more that, of the available major categories, that of material bodies is the only one competent to constitute such a framework. For this category alone supplies enduring occupiers of space possessing sufficiently stable relations to meet, and hence to create, the needs with which the use of such a framework confronts us.
>
> (Strawson 1959, p. 56)

Strawson is saying that only material objects can act as overall orientation points in the general framework of space and time, since only 'particulars' which are physically identifiable and reidentifiable take up space and endure through time. This justification is inevitably circular. It can equally be argued that the concept of material bodies depends on our spatio-temporal system, or that our spatio-temporal system depends on the concept of material bodies. Their mutual necessity is as far as the analysis of our normal conceptual scheme can go.

Despite its primary position, the category of 'material body' is not the only 'basic particular'. It does not constitute the basis for all that we experience, perceive or know. The category of 'material bodies' underpins the conceptualization of publicly observable phenomena, but it cannot ground the essential subjectivity of phenomena which are only privately observable. Thus 'mental' phenomena, such as sensations, thoughts and emotions, assume a second primary category; Strawson argues that 'the category of persons . . . [is] in a different though related way basic' (p. 246). It cannot be the result of bringing the categories of body and mind together, but has to be the ground from which these categories emerge. The idea of a mind (and hence a disembodied mind) and the idea of a body (and hence a de-animated body) can be extracted from the idea of a person, but the full concept of the person cannot be derived from either of these. The concept of the person refers to an original unity with both mental and physical properties. By logic and by definition, it cannot go back to a 'basic particular' of either 'material body' or 'mind':[37]

> the concept of the pure individual consciousness . . . cannot exist as a primary concept in terms of which the concept of a person can be explained or analysed. It can only exist, if at all, as a secondary, non-primitive concept, which itself is to be explained, analysed, in terms of the concept of a person

... What I mean by a concept of the person is the concept of a type of entity such that *both* predicates ascribing states of consciousness *and* predicates ascribing corporeal characteristics, a physical situation etc. are equally applicable to a single individual [i.e. example] of that single type.[38]

(Strawson 1959, pp. 102–103, original emphases)

The '*both . . . and*' must represent a primary unity rather than a secondary amalgamation, since 'states of consciousness could not be ascribed at all unless they were ascribed to persons' (ibid.). Unless we have a concept of the person, we would not be able to conceptualize experience or consciousness either: there would be nowhere for them to go.

Thus Strawson's analysis reveals the conceptual structure beneath the ordinary idea of personhood. The possibility of 'particulars' defines the condition of all mental activity, which itself can proceed only on the basis of the two fundamental categories of 'material bodies' and 'persons'. This means that the primary category of psychoanalysis does not have to be the 'mind' of hermeneutic approaches or the 'body' of empirical approaches. It could in principle be founded directly on the concept of the person as their unitary psychophysical ground.

The theoretical properties of the person

The conceptual primacy of the concept of the person may be clear, but its empirical content is not. The next step is to begin to identify the substantive properties on which the category of the person depends: 'what it is in the natural facts that makes it intelligible that we should have this concept' (p. 111). Strawson proposes two fundamental 'person-predicates'. These are things that can be said of persons, but not of 'material bodies' as such. An interesting consequence of this is that non-human creatures are left to be attached as subcategories to one of the two primary categories.[39] This point is too complex to pursue here, but we should note that although the properties of personhood do not necessarily exclude all other animals, they begin with human beings and apply primarily to human personhood; thus non-human creatures and other animate beings may variously be conceived as 'persons-minus' (or 'material bodies-plus'), rather than conforming to every aspect of the criteria for either category.

Strawson's two 'person-predicates' substantiate the logical concept of personhood as a basic psychophysical unity from which secondary concepts such as mind and body are derived. First, there is the seemingly 'natural fact' that 'persons' can sometimes recognize each other's subjective intentions through bodily movement alone. Strawson is thinking of simple meaningful actions such as 'going for a walk', 'coiling a rope', 'writing a letter' (ibid.). These descriptions mark out the category of persons from the category of material bodies in a fundamental way.[40] They are crucially significant conceptually because they traverse the physical–mental, public–private dichotomy:

> They release us from the idea that the only things we can know about without observation or inference, or both, are private [i.e. mental] experiences; we can know, without telling by either of these means, about the present and future movements of a body. Yet bodily movements are certainly also things we can know about by observation and inference.
>
> (Strawson 1959, p. 111)

Strawson is referring to the standard division between empirical-scientific and hermeneutic ways of knowing. Empirical science depends on deduction and inference, because the phenomena it investigates are observable from the outside but not from the inside. In general, these are physical phenomena, going back to the 'basic particular' of 'material bodies'. Hermeneutic theories depend on interpretation through empathic resonance, because they are concerned with phenomena which are perceptible from the inside but not, in themselves, from the outside. These are meaningful or mental phenomena which go back to the secondary (i.e. not basic) concept of 'mind' or 'consciousness'.

The intentional states and actions that Strawson puts forward hold elements of each. They carry meaning, but no leap of imagination is required to say that you can see someone 'writing a letter', or 'coiling a rope'. Yet it is not the recognizability of the actions themselves that constitutes the 'natural fact'. In cultures without writing or ropes, Strawson's examples would not be self-evident. It is rather the necessity of such mutual recognition within cultural groups that is the fundamental property or 'natural fact' of personhood. Thus intentionality can be put forward as a universal attribute of persons which is psychophysical in nature, because it is set within the ground from which the concepts of body and mind branch off.

The second fundamental 'person-predicate' is implied by the first. It derives directly from the conclusion, familiar to psychoanalysis and anthropology, that 'persons' have an intrinsic need to relate to other persons. This 'natural fact' is reflected in the 'conceptual fact' that the concept of a person in the singular, and the concept of 'persons' in the plural, depend upon each other. Without the idea of a class of beings of which oneself is one, personhood would never become conceptualized at all:

> There would be no question of ascribing one's states of consciousness, or experiences, to anything, unless one also ascribed, or were ready and able to ascribe, states of consciousness, or experiences, to other individual entities of the same logical type [the same category].
>
> (Strawson 1959, p. 104)

There would literally be no call to do so: without assuming the parallel subjectivity of other people, one's own subjective experience would be simply what it is, without qualification and without limit.

At the same time, the degree of overlap must be finite, or the concept of the individual would disappear into the mass. 'It sometimes happens, with groups of human beings, that, as *we* say, their members think, feel and act "as one" . . . [It] is a condition for the existence of the concept of the individual person, that this should happen only sometimes' (p. 114 emphasis original). The second 'natural fact' which makes the concept of personhood intelligible is that the 'person' can be understood only as a 'person-amongst-persons'. Logically and experientially, there is an enduring tension between the individual and the group, belonging and individuation. Neither can be forgone, yet they pull in opposite directions.

The substantive foundation of psychoanalysis

The objective picture is now a little clearer. The concept of the 'person-amongst-persons' is an original unity of body and mind. It constitutes the immediate theoretical underpinning of psychoanalysis, and stands as a foundational category and keystone of any 'human' conceptual scheme. The 'biocultural' constituents of personhood include intentionality and our individual-social human nature. The observable intentionality described by Strawson is a sign of rational states and actions; as such, it belongs to the 'propositional network' of conscious rationality. But it also forms the template for the unobservable intentionality of psychical states and processes. It is these processes, rather than their rational counterparts, which mark the boundary of personhood: it is possible to be a person without being rational, but unless there is the capacity to wish, there is only a person-in-waiting. The fulfillability of wishes opens up the connection with the external-internal world, without which there would be nothing to value or recognize within it. Thus intentionality belongs to personhood at the most primitive level of psychical functioning, within a conceptual frame which is set prior to the major theoretical divisions.

Each psychophysical property depends upon the other. The recognizability of intentionality implies a communicational setting, just as communication implies the recognizability of intentionality. Without a cultural milieu, we would be unable to develop the capacity to wish from which our first connections with reality are forged. Only through the wish and its picture of fulfilment can we tune into the psychophysical ground of communication, negotiate its subsequent separation into mental states and physical signs, and foster its further development into propositional thought and desire. But symbolic functioning is not a matter of information alone. Induction into personhood requires more than a lexicon of meanings. A human organism can only enter into the social arena as a 'person-amongst-persons'; and a necessary condition of this is being treated as such, even before we know that this is what we are, or could become.[41] There is no short-circuiting the equal necessity for personhood of biological and social factors.

These biocultural properties, or 'natural facts', bring experiential substance to the 'logically primitive' (conceptually basic) concept of the person. This gives it credence as a foundational category in its own right which is capable of theoretical development from a position preceding the major severances into mental and physical, subjective and objective, autonomous and determined. The final step is to extend this theoretical line by uncovering the connection between the concept of the person and Freud's underlying philosophical ground.

A psychophysical context for psychoanalysis

There is a crucial discrepancy between the framework of Strawson's analysis and that of Freud's psychical realism. The first goes back to two 'basic particulars'; the second, just to one. The framework of everyday practicality assumes a pre-theoretical distinction between persons and things, and intentional causality and physical causality, but the 'psychical' picture of reality has no such distinction. The psychophysical foundation is unitary, with a primary category and causal principle which are conceptually prior to the matter–mind divide. This seems to be the natural philosophical context for psychoanalysis; but the question then arises of whether a single-category framework is capable of supporting theoretical development.

In one sense, we have seen that it is not. The psychical domain is the pre-rational domain, and theorization is necessarily rational. At least within the dominant Western system, theorization formalizes the fundamental distinction between persons, who act upon the physical world, and the physical world, which persons act upon. But the issue is not whether the whole of Western thought should be demolished and set upon a different course. It is more a matter of bringing the epistemological muscle of empirical and hermeneutic thinking to bear upon the pre-differentiated ground that they themselves presuppose. Just as psychical structures and processes can only be identified from the viewpoint of conscious-ness, so the unitary ground of psychoanalysis can only be discerned from a dualistic vantage point. As the divergent categories of matter and mind draw into view, so also does their unitary common source. This is the conceptual ground on which psychoanalysis builds.

There is a precedent for a single-category framework which is neither pre-theoretical nor pre-rational. Empirical science goes back to the single 'basic particular' of 'material bodies', from which a fundamental substance is inferred. The strict empiricist approach of eliminative materialism assumes that a basic concept of matter (or energy) is sufficient to explain not just physical phenomena, but mental phenomena too (see pp. 26–28 above). Although this approach is rejected in this enquiry, a reasonable philosophical case can still be made for according conceptual priority to material bodies over persons: if persons were not also material bodies, they could not be identified as persons, or at all. The example of empirical science shows that it is possible to develop a single-category theo-retical framework out of a critique of the normal conceptual divisions.

This raises the possibility of a parallel single-category framework, not to displace the established modes of thought but as a critical adjunct to them. As well as 'material bodies' being prior to 'persons', there is a sense in which persons can be seen as logically prior to material bodies. Conceptually, the idea of a material body (or matter) can be derived from the psychophysical idea of a person, but the full idea of a person cannot be derived from that of matter, or a material body. Empirically, we have to learn that some 'bodies' are not animate, where we do not have to learn that others are; bodily animacy is, after all, the first thing we can possibly 'know'.[42] From this standpoint, logically and in experience, 'persons' hold priority over 'material bodies', rather than the other way round.

A wholly psychophysical framework could in principle be developed, with the concept of the 'person-amongst-persons' as an alternative ground of thought.[43] We cannot second-guess what its form of knowledge might look like, or make comparisons or contrasts with any existing formulation. But psychophysical theorization would not have to be confined to what is now thought of as 'human' studies (the humanities and human sciences). The concept of the person would mediate between theoretical development into the non-human material world on the one hand, and the non-material human world on the other. The inanimate and mental fields could still be theorized, through principles and subcategories in which concepts from causality to matter would appear in a different light. The transformations between inanimate, animate, psychical and rational states might look more self-evident and less mysterious, and the categories we now call 'matter' and 'mind' less antithetical. The 'person-amongst-persons' holds them together; the mental/physical distinction wrenches them apart.

Nagel's entrancement with Freud's thinking may be partly due to their shared vision of the obvious yet theoretically inexplicable ground of unity between the physical and mental dimensions. Nagel's term for this is 'dual-aspect theory' (1986), a development that he forecasts but places far into the future. He suggests that the mental and physical schemes could be reconciled by exchanging explanation of one in terms of the other for explanation of both in terms of a single primary category with a 'dual aspect'. This would entail a revolution in how we think of matter as well as mind, which he can only imagine arising from new theoretical developments: 'any fundamental discoveries we make about how it is that we have minds, and what they really are, will reveal something fundamental about the constituents of the universe as a whole' (1986, p. 53). Instead of reductionism, there would be an expansion in our view of the reality of which we are a part.

Nagel is only too conscious of the plethora of questions this throws up: 'how can a mental unit have physical parts?' '[How] could *any* properties of the chemical constituents of a brain combine to form a mental life?' (1986, pp. 50–51) These are paradoxes, due to the limitations of our current ways of thinking as well as to the boundaries of scientific knowledge. The terms and concepts of a paradigm which has not yet arrived cannot, by definition, be thought up beforehand. Yet, Nagel (1998) argues, a space awaiting its development already exists in our ordinary, pre-theoretical thinking. We assume that the reality from which mental and physical phenomena emerge is single and intact, but we can give no account of this. For our own peace of mind, we need either to understand why we cannot explain mental and physical phenomena together, or find a way of doing so.

In everyday intuition, the link between the mental and the physical is assumed, yet strangely tenuous. It is neither a contradiction nor a tautology to say that every mental state or event is the same phenomenon as the corresponding bodily state or event.[44] The ideas of a human body without a human mind (a zombie), and a human mind without a human body (a conscious robot) are perfectly thinkable; but the ideas of liquid that is not wet, or water which is not a combination of hydrogen and oxygen, are not. 'We conceive the body from outside and the mind from inside, and see no internal connection, only an external one of correlation or perhaps causation' (1998, p. 346). We should be satisfied only when the continuity between physical and mental reality is as transparent to us as that between a substance and its chemical composition, or a mind and its propositional network. Only then will our everyday thinking make sense.

Nagel's hope is that his own philosophical work might help engender 'the ancestor of a credible solution' (ibid., p. 338). But it is just possible that this already exists in Freud's concept of the psychical as pertaining not to mind, nor to body, but to persons. When the concept of the 'person-amongst-persons' is taken as foundational, the intuitive connectedness that Nagel seeks seems closer. An initial check seems at least not to rule this out. It is easier to attribute 'mind' (or at least 'mentation') to a conscious robot than it is to see one as a 'person'. Equally, a sense of the psychical as the confluence of physiology and (minimal) culture makes it harder to envisage a normal human organism, in a normal social environment, being devoid of the capacity to 'wish'. The category of the 'person-amongst-persons' is irreducibly psychophysical; it cannot be divided into mental and physical parts.

But these considerations are not at hand for Nagel. Because he accords ultimate priority to reality conceived as independent of the mind, he privileges physical theory over practical conceptualization. This means that he can only look ahead, to scientific and conceptual developments which have not yet come about; it does not occur to him to look beneath, behind or to one side of our familiar conceptual assumptions.[45] Freud does the reverse; and in subordinating empirical conclusions to practical reasoning, he makes their shared objective seem a fraction more accessible. Whether it would turn out that way is a question beyond the scope of the present, rudimentary enquiry. All we can say at this point is that a psychophysical theoretical approach which extends beyond the person is not unthinkable. The seed from which it could develop is contained within the unarticulated sense of a unitary reality which is assumed in practical living and registered in the depths of the psyche. To that extent, psychoanalysis can be endorsed as a theoretical development of a previously untheorized reality, in which the ground of unity between the mental and physical worlds can almost be envisaged.

Chapter 6

Conclusions

Though much remains to be done, this takes us to the limit of our enquiry. The route we have been following is only one way of tracing the foundations which seem to be implicit in psychoanalysis. There must be other forms that they could take, since Freud does not in the end defend psychoanalysis as a normal empirical science in which interpretation must take second place. He offers, rather, an implied critique of empirical science as the theorization of a reality which is not mind-independent but necessarily interpreted.

Freud's practical method of theoretical development is the epistemological principle on which psychoanalysis is built. This is not a sign of conceptual incoherence, but imposed by its practical subject matter. There is no other way of realizing his aim of developing as objective a theory as possible of the implicit 'inner' person. The insights of psychoanalysis go beyond everyday psychology, but their legitimation depends on what they share. This begins with an immediate form of knowing which cannot be contradicted, although it can be revised after reflection. It continues with the objects of this practical knowing, which have to be treated as 'real': even unconscious states and processes are recognizable only through their resonance in consciousness. And because they are part of the undivided reality that practical living assumes, these 'real' phenomena are set within a conceptual framework in which the division into empirical and hermeneutic theoretical modes has not yet been formalized.

Thus the psychoanalytic concept of the psychical cannot be arrived at from the physical starting-point of matter, or from the hermeneutic basis of mind. It arises out of the ordinary idea of the person, the ground and origin of the concepts of both body and mind. This concept is utterly foundational, irreducibly psychophysical, yet capable of theoretical development without diverging into either the hermeneutic or the empirical path. Its active principle of the fulfillability of wishes is the point at which biology becomes subjective and therefore culturally sensitive; its substantive ground includes the primary psychophysical properties of the external recognizability of intentionality and the individual-social nature of human beings. They reflect each other and their common 'biocultural' ground.

These practical-theoretical foundations do not have to end in psychoanalysis. The theoretical properties of personhood could extend into further theoretical development within the primary psychophysical framework to form the basis for a psychophysical picture of reality. This would be the theoretical articulation of Freud's psychical realism, the conclusions of practical reasoning about the only reality available to us. Experience and reflection take us all the way from ordinary psychological thinking, to distinctively psychoanalytic thinking, to the psychical ground of any 'human' reality. The fragile thread between what is purely causal, general and physical, and what is solely interpretative, individual and mental, can expand into a theoretical vista. Its watchword is *reculer pour mieux sauter*.[1] At every step, it goes beyond its predecessors by stepping back before them.

Where does this leave psychoanalysis? What kind of a subject is it, and what is its legitimate source of authority? From conventional perspectives, it has no easy classification. Marooned between the two theoretical hemispheres, it combines the practical immediacy of hermeneutics with the accent on substantive conclusions of empirical science. On Freud's explicit foundations, psychoanalysis appears a maverick subject; but when these foundations are developed, its very ambidextrousness brings its critical edge to the fore. Psychoanalysis then gravitates most naturally towards other branches of enquiry in which critique takes precedence over dogma.[2] Perpetually hovering between the practical and the theoretical, the hermeneutic and the empirical, it challenges our ingrained theoretical habits as much as our customary views of ourselves.

More rigorously even than Habermas, psychoanalysis defines itself as reflection on a self, by a self;[3] directly, or by attunement with another. Psychoanalysis is most secure on the basis that there is no specialized arena, no technical or linguistic model of knowing or knowledge to which it must accede.[4] It is not a hermeneutic theory, since its material is treated as 'real' rather than 'merely' symbolic. Neither is it an empirical science, because its concepts and explanations must be reachable, and reached, through reflection alone. Perhaps it could be described as a systematic enquiry into the unspoken explanation of oneself, at a generalized level, and taking both mental and physical convictions into account.

The subject matter of psychoanalysis, its method and its underlying nature are all centred in reflection, making psychoanalytic thinking even less fixed and more 'critical' than psychoanalytic theory itself. In psychoanalysis more than in any other subject, theoretical consolidation and theoretical renewal pull against each other. Experience and reflection lead to both the establishment and the challenge of theoretical concepts and structures. The only theory that can be made use of psychoanalytically is theory that has been assimilated and modified to become personal knowledge.[5] The extent to which psychoanalytic concepts are taught or learned, rather than recognized or reached through reflection, is the extent of the loss of their critical-reflective potential. This does not mean that psychoanalytic thought is confined to the 'lowest common denominator'; just that interpretations have to be individually rather than generally inspired, and should arise from the subjective or intersubjective situation rather than straight from the theoretical preconceptions of the individual.[6]

The psychophysical account of psychoanalysis is not put forward as the only possible reading. Nor does it adjudicate between different psychoanalytic modalities. The proliferation of psychoanalytic approaches is in part a function of its unique categorial status, but it also reflects the variable resonances of individuals, groups and cultures. Given the equal necessity for personal and intellectual conviction in this most subjective of theoretical fields, a range of readings will probably always coexist within it. While adherents of each approach will champion their own modality, all hold something of value for psychoanalysis as a whole.

Empirical approaches keep before us the dangers of treating psychoanalytic theory as proven fact. It is never justifiable to gloss over uncomfortable empirical findings or ignore discrepancies between personal assumptions and new scientific developments. Hermeneutic approaches, by contrast, hold the priority of the practical in focus. Centred in reflection and self-reflection, they remind all psychoanalytic approaches that whatever new discoveries take place, personal insight and resonance are not optional extras but the heart of the psychoanalytic process. Psychoanalysis is an enquiry into the unconscious ground of personhood; this prevents both positive and negative external findings from translating straightforwardly into firm conclusions about its theory or practice.[7]

The special contribution of the psychophysical approach is to mark the common ground beneath the theoretical divergences. Our habitual conceptual dualism makes this a tantalizingly elusive vision. The psychophysical conceptualization begins with the disjunctures of subjective conviction and external knowledge which the normal theoretical division tends to mask; the resolution that it offers is conceptual rather than actual, and potential rather than achieved. But in the fleeting realization of the unity of the psychical domain, psychoanalysis gains a coherence beyond either of the traditional approaches. The central concept of the psychical leads transparently to and from its practical method of validation and underlying conceptual framework. Its psychophysical foundations sustain the conjunction rather than the opposition of subjective and objective modes of thought. They do not cancel out their mutual exclusiveness, but they call up a forum in which their usually contradictory insights can be contemplated together.

Almost imperceptibly, the hermeneutic and empirical-scientific territories extend towards each other. Nagel's ground of objectivity transfers from the world outside the mind to its registration in the mind. Habermas' sphere of reflection reaches beyond self-reflection into what we take to be an independent reality. Partially and indistinctly, they come together in that actual and potential world that can only be held within. Unlike a world conceived as independent of its perception, the 'psychical' world changes as our registration of it changes; no aspect of it more so than the psychophysical beings that we take ourselves to be. Unlike phenomena that exist only in the experiencing of them, this aspect of reality is barely open to us. We assume that our psychical nature is given and constructed, caused and co-created. But apart from the minute and tendentious shading of phantasy into consciousness, we can neither detect it as an external object nor shape it as an internal object. Yet we have to hold a space for it in our view of what exists.

The psyche and its processes are just an aspect of the whole. The rest of what we call reality must also have its 'psychical' underlay. It too must configure at a point before theoretical categorization begins; it too must be subjectively objective. The psychical sense of objectivity lies midway between the hermeneutic sense of what subjectivities hold in common, and the empirical-scientific sense of independence from the mind. When we analyse its nature, we can only shift between the two. Before we try to do so, we can almost glimpse its wholeness. It is this elusive oneness that the conception of the psychical invokes.

The opening dialogue of our enquiry asks, 'whatever is man?' But this perpetual question now looks a little different. The three critiques suppose that psychoanalysis must be approaching it in the deceptively simple terms that Socrates puts forward. They presume that human subjectivity must be understood as either physical or mental in its nature. Alcibiades' discomfort reverberates a conflict which many must share. Whatever the conceptual necessity of a mental or a physical theorization, we feel we should not have to choose between them in our minds, because in our lives we cannot: we can only choose the person.

We can now see why empirical-scientific or hermeneutic readings of psychoanalysis fail to satisfy. They enter into the theorizing process too late to encompass the whole of what psychoanalysis has to offer. The concept of the psychical implies foundations in which mental and physical explanations can in principle converge. The place at which the psychical arises is the place in which the 'soul' meets with its concrete 'apparatus'. The question of *how* mental and physical explanations coincide cannot be answered, by psychoanalysis or anything else. It becomes, instead, the question of *where* they coincide. The answer seems to be: before they begin to diverge.

Part II

The three critiques

Critique of Psychoanalysis

Adolf Grünbaum

This paper is an entry in The Freud Encyclopaedia: Theory, Therapy and Culture, *edited by Edward Erwin (2002).*

Introduction

The most basic ideas of psychoanalytic theory were initially enunciated in Josef Breuer and Sigmund Freud's 'Preliminary Communication' of 1893, which introduced their *Studies on Hysteria*. But the first published use of the word 'psychoanalysis' occurred in Freud's 1896 French paper on 'Heredity and the Aetiology of the Neuroses' (1896, p. 151). Therein Freud designated Breuer's method of clinical investigation as 'a new method of psycho-analysis'. Breuer used hypnosis to revive and articulate a patient's unhappy memory of a supposedly *repressed* traumatic experience. The *repression* of that painful experience had occasioned the first appearance of a particular hysterical symptom, such as a phobic aversion to drinking water. Thus, Freud's mentor also induced the release of the suppressed emotional distress originally felt from the trauma. Thereby Breuer's method provided a catharsis for the patient.

The cathartic *lifting* of the repression yielded relief from the particular hysterical symptom. Breuer and Freud believed that they could therefore hypothesize that the *repression*, coupled with affective suppression, was the crucial cause for the development of the patient's psychoneurosis (1893, pp. 6–7; 1893–1895, pp. 29–30).

Having reasoned in this way, they concluded in Freud's words: 'Thus one and the same procedure served simultaneously the purposes of [causally] investigating and of getting rid of the ailment; and this unusual conjunction was later retained in psychoanalysis' (1924b, p. 194).

In a 1924 historical retrospect (1924b, p. 194), Freud acknowledged the pioneering role of Breuer's cathartic method: 'The cathartic method was the immediate precursor of psychoanalysis; and, in spite of every extension of experience and of every modification of theory, is still contained within it as its nucleus.'

Yet Freud was careful to highlight the contribution he made himself after the termination of his collaboration with Breuer. Referring to himself in the third person, he tells us: 'Freud devoted himself to the further perfection of the instrument left over to him by his elder collaborator. The technical novelties which he introduced and the discoveries he made changed the cathartic method into psycho-analysis' (1924b, p. 195).

These extensive elaborations have earned Freud the mantle of being the *father* of psychoanalysis.

By now, the psychoanalytic enterprise has completed its first century. Thus, the time has come to take thorough *critical* stock of its past performance qua theory of human nature and therapy, as well as to have a look at its prospects. Here I can do so only in broad strokes.

It is important to distinguish between the validity of Freud's work qua *psycho-analytic* theoretician, and the merits of his earlier work, which would have done someone else proud as the achievement of a lifetime. Currently, Mark Solms, working at the Unit of Neuro-surgery of the Royal London Hospital (Whitechapel) in England, is preparing a five-volume edition of *Freud's Collected Neuro-scientific Writings* for publication in all the major European languages. One focus of these writings is the neurological representation of mental functioning; another is Freud's discovery of the essential morphological and physiological unity of the nerve cell and fiber. They also contain contributions to basic neuroscience such as the histology of the nerve cell, neuronal function, and neurophysiology. As a clinical neurologist, Freud wrote a major monograph on aphasia (Solms and Saling 1990). As Solms points out in his preview *An Introduction to the Neuro-Scientific Works of Sigmund Freud* (unpublished), Freud wrote major papers on cerebral palsy that earned him the status of a world authority. More generally, he was a distinguished pediatric neurologist in the field of the movement disorders of childhood. Furthermore, Freud was one of the founders of neuropsychophar-macology. For instance, he did scientific work on the properties of cocaine that benefited perhaps from his own use of that drug. Alas, that intake may well also account for some of the abandon featured by the more bizarre and grandiose of his psychoanalytic forays.

As Solms has remarked (private conversation), it is an irony of history that Freud, the psychoanalyst who postulated the ubiquity of bisexuality in humans, started out by deeming himself a *failure* for having had to conclude that eels are indeed bisexual. In a quest to learn how they reproduce, one of Freud's teachers of histology and anatomy assigned him the task of finding the hitherto elusive testicles of the eel as early as 1877, when he was twenty-one years old. After having dissected a lobular organ in about four hundred specimens in Trieste, Freud found that this organ apparently had the properties of an ovary no less than those of a testicle. Being unable to decide whether he had found the ever elusive testicles, Freud inferred that he had failed, as he reported in a rueful 1877 paper.

In 1880, he published a (free) translation of some of J.S. Mill's philosophical writings (Stephan 1989, pp. 85–86). Yet he was often disdainful of philosophy (Assoun 1995), despite clearly being indebted to the Viennese philosopher Franz Brentano, from whom he had taken several courses: The marks of Brentano's (1995) quondam representationalist and intentionalist account of the mental are clearly discernible in Freud's conception of ideation. . . . And the arguments for the existence of God championed by the quondam Roman Catholic priest Brentano further solidified the thoroughgoing atheism of Freud, the 'godless Jew' (Gay 1987, pp. 3–4).

History and logical relations of the 'dynamic' and 'cognitive'

Species of the unconscious

Freud was the creator of the full-blown theory of psychoanalysis, but even well-educated people often don't know that he was certainly *not at all* the first to postulate the existence of *some kinds or other of unconscious mental processes*. A number of thinkers did so earlier to explain conscious thought and overt behavior for which they could find no other explanation (1915a, p. 166). As we recall from Plato's dialogue *The Meno*, that philosopher was concerned to understand how an ignorant slave boy could have arrived at geometric truths under mere questioning by an interlocutor with reference to a diagram. And Plato argued that the slave boy had not acquired such geometric knowledge during his life. Instead, he explained, the boy was tapping prenatal but *unconsciously stored* knowledge, and restoring it to his conscious memory.

At the turn of the eighteenth century, Leibniz gave psychological arguments for the occurrence of *subthreshold* sensory perceptions, and for the existence of unconscious mental contents or motives that manifest themselves in our behavior (Ellenberger, 1970, p. 312). Moreover, Leibniz (1981, p. 107) pointed out that when the contents of some forgotten experiences subsequently emerge in our consciousness, we may *misidentify* them as *new* experiences, rather than recognize them as having been unconsciously stored in our memory. As Leibniz put it (1981, p. 107):

> It once happened that a man thought that he had written original verses, and was then found to have read them word for word, long before, in some ancient poet . . . I think that dreams often revive former thoughts for us in this way.

As Rosemarie Sand has pointed out (private communication), Leibniz's notion anticipates, to some extent, Freud's dictum that '*The interpretation of dreams is the royal road to a knowledge of the unconscious activities of the mind*' (1900, p. 608).

Before Freud was born, Hermann von Helmholtz discovered the phenomenon of 'unconscious inference' as being present in sensory perception (Ellenberger 1970, p. 313). For example, we often unconsciously infer the *constancy* of the *physical* size of nearby objects that move away from us, when we have *other* distance cues, although their *visual* images decrease in size. Similarly, there can be unconsciously inferred constancy of brightness and color under changing conditions of illumination, when the light source remains visible. Such unconscious *inferential compensation* for visual discrepancies also occurs when we transform our *non*-Euclidean (hyperbolic) binocular *visual* space into the 'seen' Euclidean physical space (Grünbaum 1973, pp. 154–157).

Historically, it is more significant that Freud also had other precursors who anticipated some of his key ideas with impressive *specificity*. As he himself acknowledged (1914b, pp. 15–16), Arthur Schopenhauer and Friedrich Nietzsche had speculatively propounded major psychoanalytic doctrines that he himself reportedly developed independently from his clinical observations only thereafter. Indeed, a new German book by the Swiss psychologist Marcel Zentner (1995) traces the foundations of psychoanalysis to the philosophy of Schopenhauer.

Preparatory to my critical assessment of the psychoanalytic enterprise, let me emphasize the existence of major differences between the unconscious processes hypothesized by current cognitive psychology, on the one hand, and the unconscious contents of the mind claimed by psychoanalytic psychology, on the other (Eagle 1987). These differences will show that the existence of the *cognitive* unconscious clearly fails to support, or even may cast doubt on, the existence of Freud's psychoanalytic unconscious. His so-called *dynamic* unconscious is the supposed repository of repressed forbidden wishes of a sexual or aggressive nature, whose re-entry or initial entry into consciousness is prevented by the defensive operations of the ego. Though socially unacceptable, these instinctual desires are so imperious and peremptory that they recklessly seek immediate gratification, independently of the constraints of external reality.

Indeed, according to Freud (1900, pp. 566–567), we would not even have developed the skills needed to engage in cognitive activities if it had been possible to gratify our instinctual needs without reliance on these cognitive skills. Thus, as Eagle has pointed out (1987, p. 162):

> Freud did not seem to take seriously the possibility that cognition and thought could be inherently programmed to reflect reality and could have their own structure and development – an assumption basic to cognitive psychology. After World War II, the psychoanalyst Heinz Hartmann was driven, by facts of biological maturation discovered *non*-psychoanalytically, to acknowledge in his so-called 'ego psychology' that such functions as cognition, memory and thinking can develop autonomously by innate genetic programming, and independently of instinctual drive gratification.
>
> (Eagle 1993, pp. 374–376)

In the cognitive unconscious, there is great rationality in the ubiquitous computational and associative problem-solving processes required by memory, perception, judgment, and attention. By contrast, as Freud emphasized, the wish content of the dynamic unconscious makes it operate in a highly illogical way.

There is a further major difference between the two species of unconscious (Eagle 1987, pp. 161–165): the dynamic unconscious acquires its content largely from the unwitting repression of ideas in the form they originally had in consciousness. By contrast, in the generation of the processes in the cognitive unconscious, neither the expulsion of ideas and memories from consciousness nor the censorious denial of entry to them plays any role at all. Having populated the dynamic unconscious by means of repressions, Freud reasoned that the use of his new technique of free association could *lift* these repressions of instinctual wishes, and could thereby bring the repressed ideas back to consciousness *unchanged*. But in the case of the cognitive unconscious, we typically cannot bring to phenomenal consciousness the intellectual processes presumed to occur in it, although we can describe them theoretically.

For example, even if my life depended on it, I simply could not bring into my phenomenal conscious experience the elaborate scanning or search process by which I rapidly come up with the name of the Russian czarina's confidante Rasputin when I am asked for it. Helmholtz's various processes of 'unconscious inference' illustrate the same point. By glossing over the stated major differences between the two species of unconscious, some psychoanalysts have claimed their compatibility within the same genus without ado (Shevrin et al. 1992, pp. 340–341). But Eagle (1987, pp. 166–186) has articulated the extensive modifications required in the Freudian notion of the dynamic unconscious, if it is to be made compatible with the cognitive one.

More important, some Freudian apologists have overlooked that even after the two different species of the genus 'unconscious' are thus made logically *compatible*, the dynamic unconscious as such cannot derive any *credibility* from the presumed existence of the cognitive unconscious. Nonetheless, faced with mounting attacks on their theory and therapy, some psychoanalysts have made just that fallacious claim. Thus, the Chicago analyst Michael Franz Basch (1994, p. 1) reasoned in vain that since neurophysiological evidence supports the hypothesis of a *generic* unconscious, 'psychoanalytic theory has passed the [epistemological] test with flying colors'. On the contrary, we must bear in mind that evidence for the cognitive unconscious does not, as such, also furnish support for the dynamic unconscious as such.

Has psychoanalytic theory become a staple of Western culture?

In appraising psychoanalysis, we must also beware of yet another logical blunder that has recently become fashionable: The bizarre argument recently given by a number of American philosophers (e.g., Nagel 1994a, 1994b) that the supposed pervasive influence of Freudian ideas in Western culture vouches for the validity of the psychoanalytic enterprise. But this argument is demonstrably untenable (Grünbaum 1994).

Even its premise that Freudian theory has become part of the intellectual ethos and folklore of Western culture cannot be taken at face value. As the great Swiss scholar Henri Ellenberger (1970, pp. 547–549) has stressed in his monumental historical work, *The Discovery of the Unconscious*, the prevalence of vulgarized *pseudo*-Freudian concepts makes it very difficult to determine reliably the extent to which *genuine* psychoanalytic hypotheses have actually become influential in our culture at large. For example, *any* slip of the tongue or other bungled action (parapraxis) is typically yet incorrectly called a 'Freudian slip'.

But Freud himself has called attention to the existence of a very large class of lapses or slips whose psychological motivation is simply *transparent* to the person who commits them or to others (1916–1917, p. 40). And he added commendably that neither he nor his followers deserve any credit for the motivational explanations of such perspicuous slips (1916–1917, p. 47). In this vein, a psychoanalyst friend of mine provided me with the following example of a pseudo-Freudian slip that would, however, be wrongly yet widely called 'Freudian': A man who is at a crowded party in a stiflingly hot room starts to go outdoors to cool off but is confronted by the exciting view of a woman's *décolleté* bosom and says to her: 'Excuse me, I have to get a *breast* of *flesh* air'. Many otherwise educated people would erroneously classify this slip as Freudian for two *wrong* reasons: First, *merely* because it is motivated, rather than a purely mechanical *lapsus linguae*, and, furthermore, because its theme is sexual.

Yet what is required for a slip or so-called parapraxis to qualify as *freudian* is that it be motivationally *opaque* rather than transparent, precisely because its psychological motive is repressed (1916–1917, p. 41). As the father of psychoanalysis declared unambiguously (1901, p. 239): If psychoanalysis is to provide an explanation of a parapraxis, 'we must not be aware in ourselves of any motive for it. We must rather be tempted to explain it by "inattentiveness", or to put it down to "chance".' And Freud characterized the pertinent explanatory unconscious causes of slips as 'motives of unpleasure'. Thus, when a young man forgot the Latin word '*aliquis*' in a quotation from Virgil, Freud diagnosed its interfering cause as the man's distressing unconscious fear that his girlfriend had become pregnant by him (1901, p. 9). *If* that latent fear was actually the motive of the slip, it was surely *not apparent* to anyone.

Once it is clear what is *meant* by a *bona fide* Freudian slip, we need to ask whether there *actually exist* any such slips at all, that is, slips that *appear* to be psychologically *unmotivated* but are actually caused by repressed, unpleasant ideas. It is very important to appreciate how difficult it is to provide cogent evidence for such causation. K. Schüttauf et al. (1997) claim to have produced just such evidence. They note that, according to psychoanalytic etiologic theory, obsessive-compulsive neurosis is attributable to an unconscious conflict whose repressed component features anal-erotic and sadistic wishes, which are presumably activated by regression. Then they reason that when such conflict-laden material is to be verbalized by obsessive-compulsive neurotics, Freudian theory expects a higher incidence of misspeakings (slips of the tongue) among them than among normal subjects. And these researchers report that all their findings bore out that expectation.

This investigation by Schüttauf et al. (1997) differs from Bröder's (1995) strategy, which was designed to inquire into 'the possible influence of unconscious information-processing on the frequency of specific speech-errors in an experimental setting'. Thus, Bröder and Bredenkamp (1996, Abstract) claim to have produced experimental support for the 'weaker Freudian thesis' of verbal slip-generation by unconscious, rather than repressed, thoughts: 'Priming words that remain unconscious induce misspeaking errors with higher probability than consciously registered ones.'

As for the soundness of the design of Schüttauf et al. (1997), Hans Eysenck (private communication to Rosemarie Sand, March 1, 1996; cited by permission to her) has raised several objections:

(1) 'as the author [Schüttauf] himself acknowledges, this is not an experiment, as ordinarily understood; it is a simple correlational study . . . correlation cannot be interpreted as causation, which he unfortunately attempts to do'. (2) The members of the experimental group were severely neurotic, while the control group were normals. But 'the proper control group would have been severely [disturbed] neurotics suffering from a different form of neurosis than that of obsessive compulsive behaviour'. (3) 'Freudian theory posits a causal relationship between the anal stage of development and obsessive compulsive neurosis; the author does not even try to document this hypothetical relationship.' (4) '[O]bsessive-compulsive neurotics suffer from fear of dirt and contamination, so that on those grounds alone they would be likely to react differentially to stimuli suggesting such contamination . . . It is truly commonsensical to say that people whose neurosis consists of feelings of dirt will react differentially to verbal presentations of words related to dirt.'

Naturally, I sympathize with Schüttauf and his coworkers in their avowed effort (Section 4) to escape my criticism (Grünbaum 1984, pp. 202–205) of an earlier purported experimental confirmation of Freud's theory of slips by M.T. Motley (1980). I had complained that the independent variable Motley manipulated in his speech-error experiments did *not* involve *unconscious* antecedents – only conscious ones. As Schüttauf et al. (1997) tell us, precisely to escape my criticism of Motley, they relied on Freud's etiology of obsessive-compulsive neurosis to infer that subjects who exhibit the symptoms of that neurosis fulfill the requirement of harboring repressions of anal-sadistic wishes. Thus, *only* on that etiologic assumption does their use of compulsive subjects *and* their manipulation of words pertaining to anal-sadistic themata warrant their expectation of a higher incidence of verbal slips in this group than among normals.

Surely one could not reasonably expect the authors themselves to have carried out empirical tests of the etiology on which their entire investigation is *crucially predicated*. But nonetheless Eysenck's demand for such evidence is entirely appropriate: without independent *supporting* evidence for that etiology, their test is definitely not a test of Freud's theory of slips of the tongue, let alone – as they conclude – a confirmation of it.

Thus, as long as good empirical support for the Freudian scenario is unavailable, we actually don't know whether any *bona fide* Freudian slips exist at all. Just this lack of evidence serves to undermine Nagel's thesis that cultural influence is a criterion of validity. After all, if we have no cogent evidence for the existence of genuinely Freudian slips, then Freud's theory of bungled actions ('parapraxes') might well be false. And if so, it would not contribute one iota to its validity, even if our entire culture unanimously believed in it and made extensive explanatory use of it: When an ill-supported theory is used to provide explanations, they run the grave risk of being bogus, and its purported insights may well be *pseudo-insights*.

A second example supporting my rejection of Nagel's cultural criterion is furnished by the work of the celebrated art historian Meyer Schapiro of Columbia University. Schapiro saw himself as greatly influenced by Freud in his accounts of the work of such painters as Paul Cézanne, who died in 1906 (Solomon 1994). Of course, Schapiro never actually put Cézanne on the psychoanalytic couch. But he subjected artists indirectly 'to his own [brand of speculative] couch treatment' (Solomon 1994). In his best known essay, Schapiro 'turns the Frenchman into a case history'. Indeed, a recent tribute to Schapiro's transformation of scholarship in art history (Solomon 1994) says that his 'accomplishment was to shake off the dust and open the field to a style of speculation and intellectual bravura that drew . . . most notably [on] psychoanalysis' (Solomon 1994, p. 24). Reportedly, 'his insights into . . . the apples of Cézanne' (Solomon 1994, p. 24) make the point that Cézanne's 'depictions of apples contain [in Schapiro's words] "a latent erotic sense".'

But if apples are held to symbolize sex unconsciously for Cézanne or anyone else, why doesn't *anything else* that resembles apples in some respect (e.g., being quasi-spherical) do likewise? Yet we learn that Schapiro's (1968) publication 'The Apples of Cézanne' is 'His best known essay' (p. 25). Alas, if Schapiro's claim that Cézanne was 'unwillingly chaste' is to be a psychoanalytic insight gleaned from his art, rather than a documented biographical fact, Schapiro's psychodiagnosis is an instance of what Freud himself deplored as '"Wild" Psycho-Analysis' (1910, pp. 221–227). In any case, *pace* Nagel, such art-historical invocation of Freud, however influential, does nothing, I claim, to enhance the *credibility* of psychoanalysis.

For centuries, even as far back as in New Testament narratives, both physical disease and insanity have been attributed to demonic possession in Christendom, no less than among primitive peoples. That demon theory has been used, for example, to explain deafness, blindness, and fever as well as such psychopathological conditions as epilepsy, somnambulism, and hysteria. Our contemporary medical term 'epilepsy' comes from the Greek word '*epilepsis*' (*seizure*) and reflects etymologically the notion of being seized by a demon. Since exorcism is designed to drive out the devil, it is the supposed *therapy* for demonic possession. In the Roman Catholic exorcist ritual, which has been endorsed by the present pope and by the late John Cardinal O'Connor of New York, the existence of death is blamed on Satan. And that ritual also survives in baptism as well as in blessing persons or consecrating houses.

How does the strength of the cultural influence of such religious beliefs and practices compare to that of Freud's teachings? Though Freud characterized his type of psychotherapy as '*primus inter pares*' (1933, p. 157), he conceded sorrowfully: 'I do not think our [psychoanalytic] cures can compete with those of Lourdes. There are so many more people who believe in the miracles of the Blessed Virgin than in the existence of the unconscious' (1933, p. 152). Clearly, the psychoanalytic and theological notions of etiology and of therapy clash, and their comparative cultural influence cannot cogently decide between them. But if it *could*, psychoanalysis would be the loser! This alone, I claim, is a reductio ad absurdum of the thesis that the validity of the psychoanalytic enterprise is assured by its wide cultural influence.

Nor can Nagel buttress that thesis by the dubious, vague declaration that psychoanalysis is an 'extension' of common sense. As I have shown elsewhere (Grünbaum 2005), the term 'extension' is hopelessly unable to bear the weight required by his thesis, if actual psychoanalytic theory is to square with it. What, for example, is *commonsensical* about the standard psychoanalytic etiologic explanation of male diffidence and social anxiety by repressed adult '*castration anxiety*' (Fenichel 1945, p. 520), or of a like explanation of a male driver's stopping at a *green* traffic light as if it were red (Brenner 1982, pp. 182–183)? Common sense rightly treats such explanations incredulously as bizarre, and rightly so: As I have shown (Grünbaum 1997), these etiologic explanations rest on quicksand, even if we were to grant Freud's Oedipal scenario that all adult males unconsciously dread castration by their fathers for having lusted after their mothers.

Critique of Freudian and post-Freudian psychoanalysis

Let me now turn to my critique of the core of Freud's original psychoanalytic theory and to a verdict on its fundamental modifications by two major post-Freudian sets of hypotheses called 'self-psychology' and 'object relations theory'.

The pillars of the avowed 'cornerstone' of Freud's theoretical edifice comprise several major theses: (1) Distressing mental states induce the operation of a psychic mechanism of repression, which consists in the banishment from consciousness of *unpleasurable* psychic states (1915b, p. 147). (2) Once repression is operative (more or less fully), it not only banishes such negatively charged ideas from consciousness, but plays a *further* crucial multiple causal role: It is *causally necessary* for the pathogens of neuroses, the production of our dreams, and the generation of our various sorts of slips (bungled actions). (3) The 'method of free association' can identify and lift (undo) the patient's repressions; by doing so, it can identify the pathogens of the neuroses and the generators of our dreams, as well as the causes of our motivationally opaque slips; moreover, by lifting the pathogenic repressions, free association functions therapeutically, rather than only investigatively.

Freud provided two sorts of arguments for his cardinal etiologic doctrine that repressions are the pathogens of the neuroses: His earlier one, which goes back to his original collaboration with Josef Breuer, relies on purported *therapeutic successes* from lifting repressions; the later one, designed to show that the pathogenic repressions are sexual, is drawn from presumed re-enactments ('transferences') of infantile episodes in the adult patient's interactions with the analyst during psychoanalytic treatment.

It will be expositorily expeditious to deal with Freud's earlier etiologic argument below, and to appraise the subsequent one, which goes back to his 'Dora' case history of 1905, after that. But also for expository reasons, it behooves us to devote an introduction section to his account of the actuation of the hypothesized mechanism of repression by 'motives of unpleasure'.

Negative affect and forgetting

As Freud told us, 'The theory of repression is the cornerstone on which the whole structure of psycho-analysis rests. It is the most essential part of it' (1914b, p. 16). The *process* of repression, which consists in the banishment of ideas from consciousness or in denying them entry into it, is itself presumed to be unconscious (1915b, p. 147). In Freud's view, our neurotic symptoms, the manifest contents of our dreams, and the slips we commit are each constructed as 'compromises between the demands of a repressed impulse and the resistances of a censoring force in the ego' (1925, p. 45). By being only such compromises, rather than fulfillments of the instinctual impulses, these products of the unconscious afford only *substitutive* gratifications or outlets. For brevity, one can say, therefore, that Freud has offered a unifying 'compromise model' of neuroses, dreams, and parapraxes.

But what, in the first place, is the *motive* or cause that initiates and sustains the operation of the unconscious mechanism of repression *before* it produces its own later effects? Apparently, Freud assumes *axiomatically* that distressing mental states, such as forbidden wishes, trauma, disgust, anxiety, anger, shame, hate, guilt, and sadness – all of which are *unpleasurable* – almost always actuate, and then fuel, *forgetting* to the point of repression. Thus, repression regulates pleasure and unpleasure by defending our consciousness against various sorts of *negative affect*. Indeed, Freud claimed perennially that repression is the paragon among our *defense* mechanisms (Thomä and Kächele 1987: vol. 1, pp. 107–111). As Freud put it dogmatically: 'The tendency to forget what is disagreeable seems to me to be a quite universal one' (1901, p. 144), and 'the recollection of distressing impressions and the occurrence of distressing thoughts are opposed by a resistance' (1901, p. 146).

Freud tries to disarm an important objection to his thesis that 'distressing memories succumb especially easily to motivated forgetting' (1901, p. 147). He says:

> The assumption that a defensive trend of this kind exists cannot be objected to on the ground that one often enough finds it impossible, on the contrary, to get rid of distressing memories that pursue one, and to banish distressing affective impulses like remorse and the pangs of conscience. For we are not asserting that this defensive trend is able to put itself into effect *in every case*.
>
> (Freud 1901, p. 147, italics added)

He acknowledges as 'also a true fact' that 'distressing things are particularly hard to forget' (1916–1917, pp. 76–77).

For instance, we know from Charles Darwin's autobiography that his father had developed a remarkably retentive memory for painful experiences (cited in Grünbaum 1994), and that a half century after Giuseppe Verdi was humiliatingly denied admission to the Milan Music Conservatory, he recalled it indignantly (Walker 1962, pp. 8–9). Freud himself told us as an adult (1900, p. 216) that he 'can remember very clearly', from age seven or eight, how his father rebuked him for having relieved himself in the presence of his parents in their bedroom. In a frightful blow to Freud's ego, his father said: 'The boy will come to nothing.'

But Freud's attempt here to uphold his thesis of motivated forgetting is evasive and unavailing: Since some painful mental states are vividly remembered while others are forgotten or even repressed, I claim that *factors different from their painfulness determine whether they are remembered or forgotten*. For example, personality dispositions or situational variables may in fact be causally relevant. To the great detriment of his theory, Freud never came to grips with the *unfavorable* bearing of this key fact about the mnemic effects of painfulness on the tenability of the following pillar of his theory of repression: When painful or forbidden experiences are forgotten, the forgetting is tantamount to their repression *owing to their negative affect*, and thereby produces neurotic symptoms or other compromise formations. Thomas Gilovich, a professor of psychology at Cornell University, has done valuable work on the conditions under which painful experiences are *remembered*, and on those *other* conditions under which they are forgotten.

The numerous and familiar occurrences of vivid and even obsessive recall of negative experiences pose a fundamental *statistical* and explanatory challenge to

Freud that neither he nor his followers have ever met. We must ask (Grünbaum 1994): Just what is the *ratio* of the forgetting of distressing experiences to their recall, and what *other* factors determine that ratio? Freud gave no statistical evidence for assuming that forgetting them is the *rule*, while remembering them is the exception. Yet as we can see, his theory of repression is devastatingly undermined from the outset if forgettings of negative experiences do not greatly outnumber rememberings statistically. After all, if forgetting is not the rule, then what *other* reason does Freud offer for supposing that when distressing experiences are actually forgotten, these forgettings are instances of genuine repression due to affective displeasure? And if he has no such other reason, then, a fortiori, he has no basis at all for his pivotal etiologic scenario that forbidden or aversive states of mind are usually repressed and thereby cause compromise formations.

Astonishingly, Freud thinks he can parry this basic statistical and explanatory challenge by an evasive dictum as follows: 'mental life is the arena and battle-ground for mutually opposing purposes [of forgetting and remembering] (1916–1917, p. 76) . . . ; there is room for both. It is only a question . . . of what effects are produced by the one and the other' (p. 77). Just that question cries out for an answer from Freud, if he is to make his case. Instead, he cavalierly left it to dangle epistemologically in limbo.

The epistemological liabilities of the psychoanalytic method of free association

Another basic difficulty, which besets all three major branches of the theory of repression alike, lies in the epistemological defects of Freud's so-called fundamental rule of free association, the supposed microscope and X-ray tomograph of the human mind. This rule enjoins the patient to tell the analyst without reservation whatever comes to mind. Thus it serves as the fundamental method of clinical investigation. We are told that by using this technique to unlock the floodgates of the unconscious, Freud was able to show that neuroses, dreams, and slips are caused by repressed motives. Just as in Breuer's cathartic use of hypnosis, it is a cardinal thesis of Freud's entire psychoanalytic enterprise that his method of free association has a twofold major capability, which is both investigative and therapeutic: (1) It can *identify* the unconscious causes of human thoughts and behavior, both abnormal and normal, and (2) by overcoming resistances and lifting repressions, it can remove the unconscious pathogens of neuroses, and thus provide therapy for an important class of mental disorders.

But on what grounds did Freud assert that free association has the stunning investigative capability to be *causally probative* for etiologic research in psychopathology? Is it not too good to be true that one can put a psychologically disturbed person on the couch and fathom the etiology of her or his affliction by free association? As compared to fathoming the causation of major somatic diseases, that seems almost miraculous, *if at all true*. Freud tells us very clearly

(1900, p. 528) that his argument for his investigative tribute to free association as a means of uncovering the causation of neuroses is, at bottom, a *therapeutic* one going back to the cathartic method of treating hysteria. Let me state and articulate his argument.

One of Freud's justifications for the use of free association as a *causally probative* method of dream investigation leading to the identification of the repressed dream thoughts, he tells us (1900, p. 528), is that it 'is identical with the procedure [of free association] by which we resolve hysterical symptoms; and there the correctness of our method [of free association] is warranted by the coincident emergence and disappearance of the symptoms'. But as I have pointed out elsewhere (Grünbaum 1993, pp. 25–26), his original German text here contains a confusing slip of the pen. As we know, the patient's symptoms hardly first emerge simultaneously with their therapeutic dissipation. Yet Strachey translated Freud correctly as having spoken of 'the coincident emergence and disappearance of the symptoms'. It would seem that Freud means to speak of the resolution (German: *Auflösung*), rather than of the emergence (*Auftauchen*), of the symptoms as coinciding with their therapeutic dissipation. Now, for Freud, the 'resolution of a symptom', in turn, consists of using free association to uncover the repressed pathogen that enters into the compromise formation that is held to constitute the symptom. This much, then, is the statement of Freud's appeal to therapeutic success to vouch for the 'correctness of our method' of free association as causally probative for etiologic research in psychopathology.

To articulate the argument adequately, however, we must still clarify Freud's original basis for claiming that (unsuccessful) repression is indeed the pathogen of neurosis. Only then will he have made his case for claiming that free association is etiologically probative, because it is uniquely capable of uncovering repressions. The pertinent argument is offered in Breuer and Freud's 'Preliminary Communication' (1893, pp. 6–7). There they wrote (p. 6, italics in original):

> For we found, to our great surprise at first, that *each individual hysterical symptom immediately and permanently disappeared when we had succeeded in bringing clearly to light the memory of the event by which it was provoked and in arousing its accompanying affect, and when the patient had described that event in the greatest possible detail and had put the affect into words.* Recollection without affect almost invariably produces no result. The psychical process which originally took place must be repeated as vividly as possible; it must be brought back to its *status nascendi* and then given verbal utterance.

Breuer and Freud make an important comment on their construal of this therapeutic finding:

> It is plausible to suppose that it is a question here of unconscious suggestion: the patient expects to be relieved of his sufferings by this procedure, and it is

this expectation, and not the verbal utterance, which is the operative factor. This, however, is not so.

(p. 7)

And their avowed reason is that, in 1881, i.e., in the 'pre-suggestion' era, the cathartic method was used to remove *separately* distinct symptoms, 'which sprang from separate causes' such that any one symptom disappeared only after the cathartic ('abreactive') lifting of a *particular* repression. But Breuer and Freud do not tell us why the likelihood of placebo effect should be deemed to be lower when several symptoms are wiped out *seriatim* than in the case of getting rid of only one symptom. Thus, as I have pointed out elsewhere (Grünbaum 1993, p. 238), to discredit the hypothesis of placebo effect, it would have been essential to have comparisons with treatment outcome from a suitable control group whose repressions are *not* lifted. If that control group were to fare equally well, treatment gains from psychoanalysis would then be placebo effects after all.

In sum, Breuer and Freud inferred that the therapeutic removal of neurotic symptoms was produced by the cathartic lifting of the patient's previously ongoing repression of the pertinent traumatic memory, not by the therapist's suggestion or some other placebo factor (see Grünbaum 1993: ch. 3 for a very detailed analysis of the placebo concept). We can codify this claim as follows:

> T. Therapeutic Hypothesis: Lifting repressions of traumatic memories cathartically is *causally relevant* to the disappearance of neuroses.

As we saw, Breuer and Freud (1893, p. 6) reported the immediate and permanent disappearance of each hysterical symptom after they cathartically lifted the repression of the memory of the trauma that occasioned the given symptom. They adduce this 'evidence' to draw an epoch-making inductive *etiologic* inference (p. 6), which postulates 'a causal relation between the determining [repression of the memory of the] psychical trauma and the hysterical phenomenon'. Citing the old scholastic dictum '*Cessante causa cessat effectus*' (When the cause ceases, its effect ceases), they invoke its contrapositive (p. 7), which states that as long as the effect (symptom) persists, so does its cause (the repressed memory of the psychical trauma). And they declare just that to be the pattern of the pathogenic action of the repressed psychical trauma. This trauma, we learn, is *not* a mere *precipitating* cause. Such a mere '*agent provocateur*' just releases the symptom, 'which thereafter leads an independent existence'. Instead, 'the [repressed] memory of the trauma . . . acts like a foreign body which long after its entry must continue to be regarded as an agent that is still at work' (p. 6).

The upshot of their account is that their observations of positive therapeutic outcome upon the abreactive lifting of repressions, which they interpret in the sense of their therapeutic hypothesis, spelled a paramount etiologic moral as follows:

E. Etiologic Hypothesis: An ongoing repression accompanied by affective suppression is causally necessary for the initial pathogenesis *and* persistence of a neurosis.

(This formulation of the foundational etiology of psychoanalysis supersedes the one I gave at the hands of a suggestion by Carl Hempel and Morris Eagle [in Grünbaum 1984, p. 181, last paragraph]. The revised formulation here is faithful to Breuer and Freud's reference to 'accompanying affect' [p. 6] apropos of the traumatic events whose repression occasioned the symptoms.)

Clearly, this etiologic hypothesis *E* permits the *valid deduction* of the therapeutic finding reported by Breuer and Freud as codified in their therapeutic hypothesis *T*: the cathartic lifting of the repressions of traumatic memories of events that occasion symptoms engendered the disappearance of the symptoms. And as they told us explicitly (p. 6), this therapeutic finding is their 'evidence' for their cardinal etiologic hypothesis *E*.

But I maintain that this inductive argument is vitiated by what I like to call the *'fallacy of crude hypothetico-deductive ("H-D") pseudo-confirmation'*. Thus note that the remedial action of aspirin consumption for tension headaches does not lend H-D support to the outlandish etiologic hypothesis that a hematolytic aspirin *deficiency* is a causal *sine qua non* for having tension headaches, although such remedial action is validly deducible from that bizarre hypothesis . . . Wesley Salmon (1971) called attention to the fallacy of inductive causal inference from mere valid H-D deducibility by giving an example in which a deductively valid pseudoexplanation of a man's avoiding pregnancy can readily give rise to an H-D pseudoconfirmation of the addle-brained attribution of his nonpregnancy to his consumption of birth-control pills. Salmon (1971, p. 34) states the fatuous pseudoexplanation: 'John Jones avoided becoming pregnant during the past year, for he had taken his wife's birth control pills regularly, and every man who regularly takes birth control pills avoids pregnancy.'

Plainly, this deducibility of John Jones's recent failure to become pregnant from the stated premises does not lend any credence at all to the zany hypothesis that this absence of pregnancy is *causally attributable* to his consumption of birth-control pills. Yet it is even true that any men who consume such pills *in fact* never do become pregnant. Patently, as Salmon notes, the fly in the ointment is that men just do not become pregnant, whether they take birth-control pills or not.

His example shows that neither the empirical truth of the deductively inferred conclusion and of the pertinent initial condition concerning Jones nor the deductive validity of the inference can provide bona fide confirmation of the causal hypothesis that male consumption of birth-control pills prevents male pregnancy: That hypothesis would first have to meet other epistemic requirements, which it manifestly cannot do.

Crude H-D confirmationism is a paradise of spurious causal inferences, as illustrated by Breuer and Freud's unsound etiologic inference. Thus, psychoanalytic narratives are replete with the belief that a hypothesized etiologic scenario embedded in a psychoanalytic narrative of an analysand's affliction is *made credible* merely because the postulated etiology then permits the logical deduction or probabilistic inference of the neurotic symptoms to be explained.

Yet some apologists offer a facile excuse for the fallacious H-D confirmation of a causal hypothesis. We are told that the hypothesis is warranted by an 'inference to the best explanation' (Harman 1965). But in a careful new study, Salmon (2001) has argued that 'the characterization of nondemonstrative inference as inference to the best explanation serves to muddy the waters . . . by fostering confusion' between two sorts of why-questions that Hempel had distinguished: *Explanation*-seeking questions as to why something is the case, and *confirmation*-seeking why-questions as to why a hypothesis is *credible*. Thus, a hypothesis that is pseudoconfirmed by some data cannot be warranted qua being 'the only [explanatory] game in town'. Alas, 'best explanation'-sanction was claimed for psychoanalytic etiologies to explain and treat the destructive behavior of sociopaths *to no avail* for years (cf. Cleckley 1988, Section Four, esp. pp. 238–239 and 438–439).

I can now demonstrate the multiple failure of Freud's therapeutic argument for the etiologic probativeness of free association in psychopathology, no matter how revealing the associative contents may otherwise be in regard to the patient's psychological preoccupations and personality dispositions. Let us take our bearings and first encapsulate the structure of his therapeutic argument.

First, Freud inferred that the therapeutic disappearance of the neurotic symptoms is *causally attributable* to the cathartic lifting of repressions *by means of the method free associations*. Relying on this key therapeutic hypothesis, he then drew two further major theoretical inferences: (1) The seeming removal of the neurosis by means of cathartically *lifting* repressions is good inductive evidence for postulating that repressions accompanied by affective suppression are themselves *causally necessary* for the very existence of a neurosis (1893, pp. 6–7), and (2) granted that such repressions are thus the essential causes of neurosis, *and* that the method of free association is uniquely capable of uncovering these repressions, this method is uniquely competent *to identify the causes* or pathogens of the neuroses. (Having convinced himself of the causal probativeness of the method of free associations on therapeutic grounds in the case of those neuroses he believed to be successfully treatable, Freud also felt justified in deeming the method reliable as a means of unearthing the etiologies of those other neuroses – the so-called narcissistic ones, such as paranoia – that he considered psychoanalytically *untreatable*.)

But the argument fails for the following several reasons: In the first place, the durable therapeutic success on which it was predicated did not materialize (Borch-Jacobsen 1996), as Freud was driven to admit both early and very late in his career (1924c/1925, p. 27; 1937a, pp. 216–253). But even insofar as there was transitory therapeutic gain, we saw that Freud *failed* to rule out a rival hypothesis that undermines his attribution of such gain to the lifting of repressions by free association: The ominous hypothesis of placebo effect, which asserts that treatment ingredients *other than* insight into the patient's repressions – such as the mobilization of the patient's hope by the therapist – are responsible for any resulting improvement (Grünbaum 1993, ch. 3). Nor have other analysts ruled out the placebo hypothesis during the past century. A case in point is a 45-page study 'On the Efficacy of Psychoanalysis' (Bachrach et al. 1991), published in the official *Journal of the American Psychoanalytic Association*. Another is the account of analytic treatment process by Vaughan and Roose (1995).

Last, but not least, the repression etiology is evidentially ill founded, as we saw earlier and will see further in the next section. It is unavailing to the purported *etiologic* probativeness of free associations that they may lift repressions, since Freud failed to show that the latter are pathogenic. In sum, Freud's argument has forfeited its premises.

Freud's etiologic transference argument

Now let us consider Freud's argument for his cardinal thesis that *sexual* repressions in particular are the pathogens of all neuroses, an argument he deemed 'decisive'. Drawing on my earlier writings (Grünbaum, 1990, pp. 565–567; 1993, pp. 152–158), we shall now find that this argument is without merit.

According to Freud's theory of transference, the patient *transfers* onto his or her psychoanalyst feelings and thoughts that originally pertained to important figures in his or her earlier life. In this important sense, the fantasies woven around the psychoanalyst by the analysand, and quite generally the latter's conduct toward his or her doctor, are hypothesized to be *thematically recapitulatory* of childhood episodes. And by thus being recapitulatory, the patient's behavior during treatment can be said to exhibit a thematic kinship to such very early episodes. Therefore, when the analyst interprets these supposed re-enactments, the ensuing interpretations are called 'transference interpretations'.

Freud and his followers have traditionally drawn the following highly questionable causal inference: Precisely in virtue of being thematically recapitulated in the patient–doctor interaction, the hypothesized earlier scenario in the patient's life can cogently be held to have originally been a *pathogenic* factor in the patient's affliction. For example, in his case history of the 'Rat-Man', Freud (1909) infers that a certain emotional conflict had originally been the precipitating cause of the patient's inability to work, merely because this conflict had been thematically re-enacted in a fantasy the 'Rat-Man' had woven around Freud during treatment.

Thus, in the context of Freud's transference interpretations, the thematic re-enactment is claimed to show that the early scenario had originally been *pathogenic*. According to this etiologic conclusion, the patient's thematic re-enactment in the treatment setting is also asserted to be *pathogenically* recapitulatory by being pathogenic in the adult patient's here and now, rather than only thematically recapitulatory. Freud (1914b, p. 12) extols this dubious etiologic transference argument in his 'History of the Psycho-Analytic Movement', claiming that it furnishes the most unshakable proof for his sexual etiology of all the neuroses:

The fact of the emergence of the transference in its crudely sexual form, whether affectionate or hostile, in every treatment of a neurosis, although this is neither desired nor induced by either doctor or patient, has always seemed to me the most irrefragable proof [original German: 'unerschütterlichste Beweis'] that the source of the driving forces of neurosis lies in sexual life [sexual repressions]. This argument has never received anything approaching the degree of attention that it merits, for if it had, investigations in this field would leave no other conclusion open. As far as I am concerned, this argument has remained the decisive one, over and above the more specific findings of analytic work.

On the contrary, the patient's thematically recapitulatory behavior toward his doctor *does not show* that it is also *pathogenically* recapitulatory. How, for example, does the re-enactment, during treatment, of a patient's early conflict show at all that the original conflict had been pathogenic in the first place? Quite generally, how do transference phenomena focusing on the analyst show that a presumed current replica of a past event is *pathogenic* in the here and now?

Therefore, I submit, the purportedly 'irrefragable proof' of which Freud spoke deserves more attention *not* because its appreciation 'would leave no other conclusion open', as he would have it; instead, I contend that the 'Rat-Man' case and other such case histories show how baffling it is that Freud deemed the etiologic transference argument cogent *at all*, let alone unshakably so.

Marshall Edelson (1984, p. 150) has offered a rebuttal to my denial of the cogency of the etiologic transference argument:

in fact, in psychoanalysis the pathogen is not merely a remote event, or a series of such events, the effect of which lives on. The pathogen reappears in all its virulence, with increasing frankness and explicitness, in the transference – in a new edition, a new version, a re-emergence, a repetition of the past pathogenic events or factors.

And Edelson elaborates (p. 151):

The pathogen together with its pathological effects are [*sic*], therefore, under the investigator's eye, so to speak, in the psychoanalytic situation, and demonstrating the causal relation between them in that situation, by experimental or quasi-experimental methods, surely provides support, even if indirect, for the hypothesis that in the past the same kind of pathogenic factors were necessary to bring about the same kind of effects.

But how does the psychoanalyst demonstrate, within the confines of his or her clinical setting, that the supposed *current* replica of the remote, early event is presently the virulent *cause* of the patient's neurosis, let alone that the original pathogen is replicated at all in the transference? Having fallaciously identified a conflict as a pathogen because it reappears in the transference, many Freudians conclude that pathogens must reappear in the transference. And in this way, they beg the key question I have just asked. How, for example, did Freud show that the 'Rat-Man's' marriage conflict depicted in that patient's transference fantasy was the current cause of his *ongoing death obsessions*? Neither Edelson's book nor his (1986) paper offers a better answer. Thus, in the latter paper, he declares:

> The psychoanalyst claims that current mental representations of particular past events or fantasies are constitutive (i.e., *current* operative) causes of current behavior, and then goes on to claim that therefore past actual events or fantasies are etiological causes of the analysand's symptoms.

And Edelson (1986) concludes: 'Transference phenomena are . . . nonquestion-begging evidence for . . . inferences about causally efficacious psychological entities existing or occurring in the here and now' (p. 110).

In sum, despite Edelson's best efforts, the etiologic transference argument on which both Freud and he rely is illfounded: (1) They employ epistemically circular reasoning when inferring the occurrence of infantile episodes from the adult patient's reports, and then claiming that these early episodes are thematically recapitulated in the adult analysand's conduct toward the analyst; (2) they beg the *etiologic* question by inferring that, qua being thematically recapitulated, the infantile episodes had been pathogenic at the outset; (3) they reason that the adult patient's thematic re-enactment is *pathogenically* recapitulatory such that the current replica of the infantile episodes is pathogenic in the here and now.

Freud went on to build on the quicksand of his etiologic transference argument. It inspired two of his further fundamental tenets: first, the *investigative* thesis that the psychoanalytic dissection of the patient's behavior toward the analyst can reliably identify the *original pathogens* of his or her long-term neurosis; second, the cardinal therapeutic doctrine that the working through of the analysand's so-called 'transference neurosis' is the key to overcoming his or her perennial problems.

Free association as a method of dream interpretation

Yet as we learn from Freud's opening pages on his method of dream interpretation, he *extrapolated* the presumed causally probative role of free associations from being only a method of etiologic inquiry aimed at therapy, to serving likewise as an avenue for finding the purported *unconscious* causes of dreams (1900, pp. 100–101; see also p. 528). And in the same breath, he reports that when patients told him about their dreams while associating freely to their symptoms, he extrapolated his compromise model from neurotic symptoms to manifest dream contents. A year later, he carried out the same twofold extrapolation to include slips or bungled actions.

But what do free associations tell us about our dreams? Whatever the manifest content of dreams, they are *purportedly wish-fulfilling* in at least two logically distinct specific ways, as follows: For every dream *D*, there exists at least one normally unconscious infantile wish *W* such that (1) *W* is the motivational cause of *D*, and (2) the manifest content of *D* graphically displays, more or less disguisedly, the state of affairs desired by *W*. As Freud opined (1924c/1925, p. 44): 'When the latent dream-thoughts that are revealed by the analysis [via free association] of a dream are examined, one of them is found to stand out from among the rest . . . the isolated thought is found to be a wishful impulse'. But Freud manipulated the free associations to yield a distinguished wish motive (Glymour 1983).

Quite independently of Freud's abortive therapeutic argument for the causal probativeness of free association, he offered his analysis of his 1895 'Specimen Irma Dream' as a *non*therapeutic argument for the method of free association as a cogent means of identifying hypothesized hidden, forbidden wishes as the motives of our dreams. But in my detailed critique of that unjustly celebrated analysis (Grünbaum 1984, ch. 5), I have argued that Freud's account is, alas, no more than a piece of false advertising: (1) It does not deliver at all the promised vindication of the probativeness of free association, (2) it does nothing toward warranting his foolhardy dogma that *all* dreams are wish-fulfilling in his stated sense, (3) it does not even pretend that his alleged 'Specimen Dream' is evidence for his compromise model of manifest-dream content, and (4) the inveterate and continuing celebration of Freud's analysis of his Irma Dream in the psychoanalytic literature as the paragon of dream interpretation is completely unwarranted, because it is mere salesmanship.

Alas, Freud's 1895 neurobiological wish-fulfillment theory of dreaming was irremediably flawed from the outset (Grünbaum 2005). Furthermore, he astonishingly did not heed a patent epistemological consequence of having abandoned his 1895 *Project's* neurological energy model of *wish-driven* dreaming: by precisely that abandonment, he himself had *forfeited* his initial biological *rationale* for claiming that at least all 'normal' dreams are wish fulfilling. *A fortiori*, this forfeiture left him without any kind of energy-based warrant for then *universalizing* the doctrine of wish fulfillment on the psychological level to extend to *any* sort of dream. Yet, unencumbered by the total absence of any such warrant, the *universalized* doctrine, now formulated in psychological terms, rose like a Phoenix from the ashes of Freud's defunct energy model.

Once he had clearly *chained* himself gratuitously to the universal wish monopoly of dream generation, his interpretations of dreams were constrained to reconcile wish-contravening dreams with the decreed universality of wish fulfillment. Such reconciliation demanded imperiously that all other parts and details of his dream theory be obligingly *tailored* to the governing wish dogma so as to sustain it. Yet Freud artfully obscured this *dynamic* of theorizing, while begging the methodological question (1900, p. 135). Wish-contravening dreams include anxiety dreams, nightmares, and the so-called 'counter-wish dreams'

(1900, p. 157). As an example of the latter, Freud reports a trial attorney's dream that he had lost all his court cases (1900, p. 152).

Freud's initial 1900 statement of his dual wish fulfillment in dreams had been: '*Thus its content was the fulfilment of a wish and its motive was a wish*' (1900, p. 119). But the sense in which dreams are wish fulfilling *overall* is purportedly *threefold* rather than only two fold: One motivating cause is the universal *preconscious* wish to sleep, which purportedly provides a generic causal explanation of dreaming *as such* and, in turn, makes dreaming the guardian of sleep (1900, pp. 234, 680); another is the individualized *repressed* infantile wish, which is activated by the day's residue and explains the *particular* manifest *content* of a given dream; furthermore, as already noted, that manifest content of the dream graphically displays, more or less disguisedly, the state of affairs desired by the unconscious wish. The disguise is supposedly effected by the defensive operation of the 'dream-*distortion*' of the content of forbidden unconscious wishes.

But this theorized distortion of the hypothesized latent content must not be identified with the very familiar *phenomenological bizarreness* of the manifest dream content! That bizarreness stands in contrast to the stable configurations of ordinary waking experiences. By achieving a compromise with the *repressed* wishes, the postulated distortion makes 'plausible that even dreams with a distressing content are to be construed as wish fulfillments' (1900, p. 159). Accordingly, Freud concedes: 'The fact that dreams really have a secret meaning which represents the fulfillment of a wish must be proved afresh in each particular case by analysis' (1900, p. 146).

But in a 1993 book (Grünbaum 1993, ch. 10; and in Grünbaum 2005), I have argued that this dream theory of universal wish fulfillment should be presumed to be false at its core rather than just ill founded.

More conservatively, the psychoanalysts Jacob Arlow and Charles Brenner (1964) had claimed, for reasons of their own, that 'A dream is not simply the visually or auditorily hallucinated fulfillment of a childhood wish' (Arlow and Brenner 1988, p. 7). And they countenanced a range of dream motives *other than* wishes, such as anxiety, though ultimately still rooted in childhood (p. 8).

But this modification did not remedy the fundamental epistemological defect in the claim that the method of free association can reliably identify dream motives. Undaunted, Arlow and Brenner declare (1988, p. 8): 'The theory and technique of dream analysis [by free association] in no way differs from the way one would analyze . . . a neurotic symptom, . . . a parapraxis, . . . or any other object of [psycho]analytic scrutiny'. By the same token, these analysts insouciantly announce:

'Dreams are, in fact, compromise-formations like any others' (pp. 7–8). Yet this ontological conclusion is predicated on the ill-founded epistemological thesis that free associations reliably identify repressions to be the causes of symptoms, dreams, and slips.

Careful studies have shown that the so-called free associations are not free but are strongly influenced by the psychoanalyst's subtle promptings to the patient

(Grünbaum 1984, pp. 211–212). And recent memory research has shown further how patients and others can be induced to generate *pseudo*-memories, which are false but deemed veridical by the patients themselves (Goleman 1994).

As a corollary of the latter epistemological defects of the method of free association, it appears that such associations *cannot* reliably vouch for the contents of presumed past repressions that are lifted by then. Thus, the products of such associations cannot justify the following repeated claim of the later (post-1923) Freud: The mere painfulness or unpleasurableness of an experience is itself the prime motive for its repression; instead, its negativity must involve the conscious emergence of an instinctual desire recognized by the superego as illicit or dangerous (1938a/1940a, pp. 184–187; 1932/1933, pp. 57, 89, 91, 94; 1937a, p. 227).

But since Freud had also stressed the well-nigh universal tendency to *forget* negative experiences *per se*, his later view of the dynamics of repression disappointingly leaves dangling theoretically (1) the relation of forgetting to repression, and (2) why some forgettings, no less than repressions, supposedly cannot be undone without the use of the controlled method of free association. In James Strachey's *Standard Edition* (1901, p. 301), the general index lists two subcategories, among others, under 'Forgetting': (1) 'motivated by avoidance of unpleasure', and (2) 'motivated by repression'. But alas, Freud himself leaves us in a total quandary whether these two categories of Strachey's represent a distinction without a difference.

The explanatory *pseudo*-unification generated by Freud's compromise model of neuroses, dreams and slips

My indictment of the compromise model, if correct, spells an important lesson, I claim, for both philosophical ontology and the theory of scientific explanation. Advocates of psychoanalysis have proclaimed it to be an explanatory virtue of their theory that its compromise model gives a *unifying* account of such *prima facie* disparate domains of phenomena as neuroses, dreams, and slips, and indeed that the theory of repression also illuminates infantile sexuality and the four stages hypothesized in Freud's theory of psychosexual development. In fact, some philosophers of science, such as Michael Friedman, have hailed explanatory unification as one of the great achievements and desiderata of the scientific enterprise. Thus, one need only think of the beautiful way in which Newton's theory of mechanics and gravitation served all at once to explain the motions of a pendulum on earth and of binary stars above by putting both terrestrial and celestial mechanics under a single theoretical umbrella.

Yet, in other contexts, unification can be a vice rather than a virtue. Thales of Miletus, though rightly seeking a rationalistic, rather than mythopoeic, picture of the world, taught that everything is made of water. And other philosophical monists have enunciated their own unifying ontologies. But the Russian chemist

Dmitry Mendeleyev might have said to Thales across the millennia in the words of Hamlet: 'There are more things in heaven and earth, Horatio, than are dreamt of in your philosophy' (Shakespeare, *Hamlet*, Act I, Scene V).

As I have argued, the same moral applies to Freud: By invoking the alleged causal cogency of the method of free association as a warrant for his compromise model, he generated a pseudo-unification of neurotic behavior with dreaming and the bungling of actions. This dubious unification was effected by conceiving of the normal activities of dreaming and occasionally bungling actions as *mini*-neurotic symptoms, of a piece with *abnormal* mentation in neuroses and even psychoses. To emphasize this monistic psychopathologizing of normalcy, Freud pointedly entitled his magnum opus on slips *The Psychopathology of Everyday Life* (1901). To this I can only say in metaphorical theological language: 'Let no man put together what God has kept asunder', a gibe that was used by Wolfgang Pauli, I believe, against Einstein's unified field theory.

The 'hermeneutic' reconstruction of psychoanalysis

The French philosopher Paul Ricoeur (1970, p. 358), faced with quite different criticisms of psychoanalysis from philosophers of science during the 1950s and 1960s (von Eckardt 1985, pp. 356–364), hailed the *failure* of Freud's theory to qualify as an empirical science by the received standards as the basis for 'a counter-attack' against those who deplore this failure. In concert with the other so-called hermeneutic German philosophers Karl Jaspers and Jürgen Habermas, Ricoeur believed that victory can be snatched from the jaws of the *scientific failings* of Freud's theory by abjuring his scientific aspirations as misguided. Claiming that Freud himself had 'scientistically' misunderstood his own theoretical achievement, some hermeneuts misconstrue it as a semantic accomplishment by trading on the multiply ambiguous word 'meaning' (Grünbaum 1984, Introduction, Sections 3 and 4; 1990; 1993, ch. 4). In Freud's theory, an overt symptom manifests one or more underlying unconscious causes and gives evidence for its cause(s), so that the 'sense' or 'meaning' of the symptom is constituted by its latent motivational cause(s). But this notion of 'meaning' is different from the one appropriate to the context of *communication*, in which *linguistic* symbols *acquire semantic* meaning by being used deliberately to designate their referents. Clearly, the relation of being a manifestation, which the symptom bears to its cause, differs from the semantic relation of designation, which a linguistic symbol bears to its object.

The well-known academic psychoanalyst Marshall Edelson (1988, ch. 11, 'Meaning', pp. 246–249) is in full agreement with this account and elaborates it lucidly:

> For psychoanalysis, the *meaning* of a mental phenomenon is a set of unconscious psychological or intentional states (specific wishes or impulses, specific fears aroused by these wishes, and thoughts or images which might

remind the subject of these wishes and fears). The mental phenomenon substitutes for this set of states. That is, these states would have been present in consciousness, instead of the mental phenomenon requiring interpretation, had they not encountered, at the time of origin of the mental phenomenon or repeatedly since then, obstacles to their access to consciousness. If the mental phenomenon has been a relatively enduring structure, and these obstacles to consciousness are removed, the mental phenomenon disappears as these previously unconscious states achieve access to consciousness.

That the mental phenomenon substitutes for these states is a manifestation of a causal sequence (pp. 247–248). And drawing on Freud's compromise model of symptoms in which symptoms are held to provide substitutive outlets or gratifications, Edelson continues:

> Suppose the question is: 'Why does the analysand fear the snake so?' Suppose the answer to that question is: 'A snake stands for or symbolizes, a penis.' It is easy to see that by itself this is no answer at all; for one thing, it leads immediately to the question: 'Why does the analysand fear a penis so?' The question is about an inexplicable [unexplained] mental phenomenon (i.e., 'fearing the snake so') and its answer depends on an entire causal explanation . . . 'A snake stands for, or symbolizes, a penis' makes sense as an answer only if it is understood as shorthand for a causal explanation . . . Correspondingly, 'the child stands for, or symbolizes, the boss' is not a satisfactory answer (it does not even sound right) to the question, 'Why does this father beat his child?'

For my part, in this context I would wish to forestall a semantic misconstrual of the perniciously ambiguous term 'symbol' by saying: In virtue of the similarity of shape, the snake *causally* evokes the unconscious image of a feared penis; thereby the snake itself becomes a dreaded object.

Speaking of Freud's writings, Edelson (1988, p. 247) says illuminatingly:

> Certain passages (occasional rather than preponderant) allude, often metaphorically, to symbolizing activities in human life. I think it could be argued that these indicate an effort on Freud's part to clarify by analogy aspects of the subject matter he is studying, including in some instances aspects of the clinical activity of the psychoanalyst – while at the same time perhaps he paid too little attention to disanalogies – rather than indicate any abandonment on his part of the [*causally*] explanatory objectives he so clearly pursues. There is no more reason to suppose that just because Freud refers to language, symbols, representations, and symbolic activity (part of his subject matter), he has rejected, or should have rejected, canons of scientific method and reasoning, than to suppose that just because Chomsky studies language (his subject matter), his theory of linguistics cannot be a theory belonging to

natural science and that he cannot be seeking causal explanations in formulating it.

The 'hermeneutic' reconstruction of psychoanalysis slides illicitly from one of two familiar senses of 'meaning' encountered in ordinary discourse to another. When a pediatrician says that a child's spots on the skin '*mean* measles', the 'meaning' of the symptom is constituted by one of its *causes*, much as in the Freudian case. Yet, the analyst Anthony Storr (1986, p. 260), when speaking of Freud's 'making sense' of a patient's symptoms, conflates the fathoming of the *etiologic* 'sense' or 'meaning' of a symptom with the activity of making *semantic* sense of a text (Grünbaum 1986, p. 280), declaring astonishingly: 'Freud was a man of genius whose expertise lay in semantics.' And Ricoeur erroneously credits Freud's theory of repression with having provided, *malgré lui*, a veritable 'semantics of desire'.

In a book that appeared before mine (Grünbaum, 1990; 1993, ch. 4), Achim Stephan (1989, Section 6.7, 'Adolf Grünbaum', pp. 144–149) takes issue with some of my views. (Quotations from Stephan below are my English translations of his German text.) He does not endorse Ricoeur's 'semantics of desire' (p. 123). But he objects (p. 146, item [3]) to my claim that 'In Freud's theory, an overt symptom manifests one or more underlying unconscious causes and gives evidence for its cause(s), so that the "sense" or "meaning" of the symptom is constituted by its latent motivational cause(s).'

As Stephan recognizes (p. 27), Freud (1913, pp. 176–178) avowedly 'overstepped' common usage when he generalized the term 'language' to designate not only the verbal expression of thought but also gestures 'and every other method . . . by which mental activity can be expressed' (p. 176). And Freud declared that 'the interpretation of dreams [as a cognitive activity] is completely analogous to the decipherment of an ancient pictographic script such as Egyptian hieroglyphs' (p. 177). But surely this common challenge of *problem solving* does not license the assimilation of the *psychoanalytic* meaning of manifest dream content to the *semantic* meaning of spoken or written language (Grünbaum 1993, p. 115).

Stephan does countenance (p. 148) my emphasis on the distinction between the relation of manifestation, which the symptom bears to its cause, and the semantic relation of designation, which a linguistic symbol bears to its object. Yet his principal objection to my view of the psychoanalytic 'sense' of symptoms as being causal manifestations of unconscious ideation is that I assign 'exclusively nonsemantic significance' to them by *denying* that they also have 'semiotic' significance like linguistic symbols (pp. 148–149). He grants that Freud did not construe the sense or meaning of symptoms as one of semantic reference to their causes. Yet according to Stephan's own reconstruction of Freud's conception, 'he did assume that the manifest phenomena [symptoms] semantically stand for the same thing as the (repressed) ideas for which they substitute', i.e., 'they stand semantically for what the repressed (verbal) ideas stand (or rather would stand, if they were expressed verbally)' (p. 149).

Searle (1990, pp. 161–167) has noted illuminatingly (p. 175) that, unlike many mental states, language is not *intrinsically* 'intentional' in Brentano's directed sense; instead, the intentionality (aboutness) of language is *extrinsically imposed* on it by deliberately 'decreeing' it to function referentially. Searle (1990, pp. 5, 160, and 177) points out that the mental states of some animals and of 'pre-linguistic' very young children do have intrinsic intentionality but *no* linguistic referentiality.

I maintain that Stephan's fundamental hermeneuticist error was to slide illicitly from the intrinsic, nonsemantic intentionality of (many, but *not* all) mental states to the imposed, semantic sort possessed by language. Moreover, *some* of the neurotic symptoms of concern to psychoanalysts, such as diffuse depression and manic, undirected elation even *lack* Brentano intentionality.

Finally, the aboutness (contents) of Freud's repressed conative states is avowedly different from the intentionality (contents) of their psychic manifestations in symptoms. But Stephan erroneously insists that they are the same.

Yet some version of a hermeneutic reconstruction of the psychoanalytic enterprise has been embraced with alacrity by a considerable number of analysts no less than by professors in humanities departments of universities. Its psychoanalytic adherents see it as buying absolution for their theory and therapy from the criteria of validation mandatory for causal hypotheses in the empirical sciences, although psychoanalysis is replete with just such hypotheses. This form of escape from accountability also augurs ill for the future of psychoanalysis, because the methods of the hermeneuts have not spawned a single new important hypothesis. Instead, their reconstruction is a negativistic ideological battle cry whose disavowal of Freud's scientific aspirations presages the death of his legacy from sheer sterility, at least among those who demand the validation of theories by cogent evidence.

Post-Freudian psychoanalysis

But what have been the contemporary *post*-Freudian developments insofar as they still qualify as psychoanalytic in content rather than only in name? And have they advanced the debate by being on firmer epistemological ground than Freud's original major hypotheses (Grünbaum 1984, ch. 7)? Most recently, the noted clinical psychologist and philosopher of psychology Morris Eagle (1993) has given a comprehensive and insightful answer to this question on which we can draw.

Eagle (1993, p. 374) begins with a caveat:

> It is not at all clear that there is a uniform body of thought analogous to the main corpus of Freudian theory that can be called contemporary psychoanalytic theory. In the last forty or fifty years there have been three major theoretical developments in psychoanalysis: ego psychology, object relations

theory, and self-psychology. If contemporary psychoanalytic theory is any-thing, it is one of these three or some combination, integrative or otherwise, of the three.

Eagle makes no mention of Lacan's version of psychoanalysis, presumably because he does not take it seriously, since Lacanians have avowedly forsaken the need to validate their doctrines by familiar canons of evidence, not to mention Lacan's willful, irresponsible obscurity and notorious cruelty to patients (Green 1995–1996).

Previously we had occasion to note that Heinz Hartmann's ego psychology departed from Freud's instinctual anchorage of the cognitive functions. But more important, both Heinz Kohut's self-psychology and the object relations theory of Otto Kernberg and the British school more fundamentally reject Freud's compromise model of psychopathology. Indeed, self-psychology has repudiated virtually every one of Freud's major tenets (Eagle 1993, p. 388). Thus, Kohut supplants Freud's conflict model of psychopathology, which is based on the repression of internal sexual and aggressive wishes, by a psychology of self-defects and faulty function caused by hypothesized *environmental events* going back to the first two years of infancy. Relatedly, Kohut denies, contra Freud, that insight is curative, designating instead the analyst's empathic understanding as the operative therapeutic agent (Kohut 1984). Again, the object relations theorists deny that the etiology of pathology lies in Freudian (Oedipal) conflicts and traumas involving sex and aggression, claiming instead that the quality of maternal caring is the crucial factor.

Yet these two post-Freudian schools not only diverge from Freud but also disagree with each other. Thus, the orthodox psychoanalysts Arlow and Brenner speak ruefully of 'the differences among all these theories, so apparent to every observer' (1964, p. 9), hoping wistfully that refined honing of the psychoanalytic method of free association will yield a common body of data, which 'would in the end resolve the conflict among competing theories' (p. 11). But their hope is utopian, if only because of the severe probative limitations of the method of free association. How, for example, could a method of putting adults on the couch possibly have the epistemological resources to resolve the three-way clash among the Freudian and two post-Freudian schools in regard to the infantile *etiologies* of psychopathology? Otto Kernberg's (1993) account of the 'Convergences and Divergences in Contemporary Psychoanalytic Technique' does not solve that problem. And as other psychoanalysts themselves have documented, there are several clear signs that the future of the sundry clinical and theoretical enterprises that label themselves 'psychoanalytic' is now increasingly in jeopardy. For example, the pool of patients seeking (full-term) psychoanalytic treatment in the United States has been steadily shrinking, and academic psychoanalysts are becoming an endangered species in American medical schools (Reiser 1989). No wonder that the subtitle of the 1988 book on *Psychoanalysis* by the well-known analyst Marshall Edelson is *A Theory in Crisis* (Edelson 1988).

But what about the evidential merits of the two post-Freudian developments usually designated as '*contemporary* psychoanalysis'? Do they constitute an *advance* over Freud? The answer turns largely, though not entirely, on whether there is *better evidential support* for them than for Freud's classical edifice. But Eagle (1993, p. 404) argues that the verdict is clearly negative:

> the different variants of so-called contemporary psychoanalytic theory . . . are on no firmer epistemological ground than the central formulations and claims of Freudian theory . . . There is no evidence that contemporary psychoanalytic theories have remedied the epistemological and methodological difficulties that are associated with Freudian theory.

What are the future prospects of psychoanalysis?

Finally, what are the prospects for the future of psychoanalysis in the twenty-first century? In their 1988 paper on that topic, the psychoanalysts Arlow and Brenner (1988, p. 13) reached the following sanguine conclusion about both its past and its future:

> Of some things about the future of psychoanalysis we can be certain. Fortunately, they are the most important issues as well. Psychoanalysis will continue to furnish the most comprehensive and illuminating insight into the human psyche. It will continue to stimulate research and understanding in many areas of human endeavor. In addition to being the best kind of treatment for many cases, it will remain, as it has been, the fundamental base for almost all methods that try to alleviate human mental suffering by psychological means.

By contrast, a dismal verdict is offered by the distinguished American psychologist and psychoanalyst Paul E. Meehl (1995, p. 1021). Since one of my main arguments figures in it, let me mention that apropos of my critiques of Freud's theories of transference and of obsessional neurosis ('Rat-Man'), I had demonstrated the *fallaciousness* of inferring a *causal* connection between mental states from a mere 'meaning' or thematic connection between them. Meehl refers to the latter kind of shared thematic content as 'the existence of a theme':

> His [Grünbaum's] core objection, the epistemological difficulty of inferring a causal influence from the existence of a theme (assuming the latter can be statistically demonstrated), is the biggest single methodological problem that we [psychoanalysts] face. If that problem cannot be solved, we will have another century in which psychoanalysis can be accepted or rejected, mostly as a matter of personal taste. Should that happen, I predict it will be slowly but surely abandoned, both as a mode of helping and as a theory of the mind [reference omitted].

Returning to Arlow and Brenner, I hope I have shown that, in regard to the last hundred years, their rosy partisan account is very largely ill founded, if only because the lauded comprehensiveness of the core theory of repression is only a *pseudo*-unification, as I have argued. Among Arlow and Brenner's glowingly optimistic statements about the future, just one is plausible: The expectation of a continuing heuristic role for psychoanalysis. Such a function does *not* require the correctness of its current theories at all. As an example of the heuristic role, one need only think of the issues I raised apropos of Freud's dubious account of the relation of affect to forgetting and remembering. These issues range well beyond the concerns of psychoanalysis. As the Harvard psychoanalyst and schizophrenia researcher Philip Holzman sees it (Holzman, 1994, p. 190): 'This view of the heuristic role of psychoanalysis, even in the face of its poor science, is beginning to be appreciated only now.' Holzman (private communication) mentions three areas of inquiry as illustrations: (1) The plasticity and reconstructive role of memory as against photographic reproducibility of the past, (2) the general role of affect in cognition, and (3) the relevance of temperament (e.g., shyness) in character development, as currently investigated by Jerome Kagan at Harvard.

Freud's Permanent Revolution

Thomas Nagel

This paper appeared in the New York Review of Books, *May 12, 1994, as a review of* The Mind and its Depths, *by Richard Wollheim (1993) and* Freud and his Critics, *by Paul Robinson (1993). The Addendum is Nagel's response to Grünbaum's reply (NYRB, August 11, 1994). The review and addendum are reprinted in Nagel's collection of reviews,* Other Minds *(1995).*

Great intellectual revolutionaries change the way we think. They pose new questions and devise new methods of answering them – and we cannot unlearn those forms of thought simply by discovering errors of reasoning on the part of their creators, unless we persuade ourselves that the thoughts are identical with the errors. There is something strange about recent debates over the evidence on which Freud based his theories. His influence is not like that of a physicist who claims to have discovered a previously unobserved particle by an experiment that others now think to be flawed. Whatever may be the future of psychoanalysis as a distinctive form of therapy, Freud's influence seems to me no more likely to be expunged from modern consciousness than that of Hobbes, for example, or Descartes. Such thinkers have an effect much deeper than can be captured by a set of particular hypotheses, an effect that would not go away even if, in a wave of Europhobia, their writings should cease to be read.

I

The correct interpretation of Freud's influence, and the way we should evaluate it, is a common theme of the two books under review, and *The Mind and its Depths* provides in addition a leading example of that influence. It is a collection of essays on art, morality, and the mind written by Wollheim during the period when he also published *The Thread of Life*[1] and *Painting as an Art*,[2] books whose subjects overlap with the essays. In *The Mind and its Depths* we encounter one of the most psychoanalytic of contemporary thinkers. Wollheim has a strong sense of the reality and pervasive influence of the unconscious, and of the impact of infantile sexuality on the rest of mental life.

He holds that what Freud achieved was a vast expansion of psychological insight, rooted in commonsense psychology and employing some of its concepts, but going far beyond it. Psychological insights are not unusual, since we spend our lives trying to understand ourselves and each other, but the scope and imaginative character of Freud's methods of understanding create a special problem of interpretation and evaluation.

The problem is this. As Wollheim observes, commonsense explanations are a form of understanding 'from within'; even when they provide insights into the mind of another, they depend, in part, on self-understanding, since they interpret the other person as another self. To understand someone else's thought, feelings, or behavior requires that we make sense – even if only irrational sense – of his point of view, by using our own point of view as an imaginative resource. Imagination enables us to make internal sense of beliefs, emotions, and aims that we do not share – to see how they hang together so as to render the other's conduct intelligible. But Freud's extension of this form of insight to unconscious thoughts, motives, and fantasies, and into the minds of infants, threatens to deprive ordinary psychological concepts, like belief, wish, and desire, of their familiar empirical support in the common experience and understandings of everyday life.

Some, like Sartre, have felt there was an outright contradiction in the idea of a thought of which one is not aware, but Freud could deal with that objection. In metaphysical outlook he was a sophisticated materialist; he believed that even conscious mental processes were also physical events in the brain, though we know almost nothing about their physical character. If that is true, then it makes sense to ask whether there may not also be other brain processes that are analogous to the conscious ones in physical structure, that have recognizably psychological causes and effects, but that are not conscious. Their reality would be physical, even though we could know about them only through their psychological manifestations, just as we can at present, with very limited exceptions, refer to conscious brain processes only in psychological terms.[3] So the main problem about the unconscious is not metaphysical. The problem, rather, is whether the evidence supports such a vast extension, by analogy, of mental concepts to the unconscious, and the concomitant growth of psychological explanation.

* * *

Commonsense psychology allows us to identify the experiences or deliberations that have led to a belief, or the emotions expressed by a particular reaction, or the aims or values behind a course of conduct. Causal judgments of this kind are largely automatic; they fill our lives and our relations with others and are heavily supported by their usefulness, although they can also lead us astray. When we interpret other people in this way by making sense of their point of view, we are not merely imagining things, as when we see animals in the clouds or ascribe malice to a defective toaster. Rather we are trying to understand, within the limits of a nonscientific psychology, what really makes people tick, and we often hope to be confirmed by the person's own self-understanding.

Freud extended the range of such explanation to unheard-of lengths, to cover not only memory lapses and slips, but jokes, dreams, neurotic symptoms, and the substructure of erotic life and family ties – with forays into morality, politics, art, and religion. About some of these phenomena, no adequate psychological understanding was available at all; about others, he proposed to add a deeper level of understanding than that provided by conscious psychology. And he did it in many cases not by offering insights that others could easily evaluate from their own experience and observation, but by appealing to evidence gathered under the highly unusual conditions of psychoanalytic treatment, evidence that could be understood only by those familiar with the process.

Yet the entire system remained psychological in the sense Wollheim has specified. It sought to provide an understanding of human beings 'from within', so that we could put ourselves in their shoes and make sense of their symptoms and responses by attributing to them beliefs, desires, feelings, and perceptions – with the difference that these were aspects of their point of view of which they were not consciously aware. What reason is there to believe that such a vast extension of psychological interpretation is not merely a fantasy, like seeing animals in the clouds, rather than genuine knowledge?

It is a familiar fact that people can be unaware of their true motives, and that we often understand others better than they understand themselves. (Anyone knows this who has listened with embarrassment to a flagrant name-dropper making what he thinks is just amiable conversation.) But Freud carried this idea so far that he could not defend it just by appealing to common sense. He insisted on the scientific character of his findings and their support by clinical observation – meaning not controlled experiments, but the data that emerge in the analytic process. The analyst's sustained and unique interaction with the neurotic patient supplies him with much more extensive and systematic evidence for interpretation than is available to someone who merely observes the patient's symptoms – even someone who knows the patient well in the ordinary way.

Freud's confidence can best be understood, I think, as the belief that exposure in a great many cases to the various extremely detailed accounts of experience that emerge in analysis enabled him to see a deeper psychological coherence in phenomena that, taken in isolation, seem meaningless and inexplicable. No doubt such coherence can be misleading. One can imagine, for example, that a drug-induced mental disorder might produce elaborate patterns of thought and feeling that seem to point to a psychological, not a chemical, cause. In general, it is important to keep in mind the real possibility that a syndrome that makes psychological 'sense' may nevertheless have a purely physiological explanation. But that means only that psychoanalytic evidence, like most evidence, is not conclusive.

* * *

Richard Wollheim's most direct comments on this matter appear in an essay called 'Desire, Belief, and Professor Grünbaum's Freud'. It is a response to Adolf Grünbaum's *The Foundations of Psychoanalysis*,[4] a book that takes the scientific claims of psychoanalysis seriously but interprets them in a curiously external way, neglecting the distinctively inner character of psychological insight. Toward the end of the essay Wollheim remarks tellingly, 'If . . . psychoanalytic theory is an extension of commonsense psychology, perhaps we should begin by asking, How is commonsense psychology tested?' I take it the answer is that the evidence for commonsense psychology, instead of being the result of controlled experiments, is complex and widely dispersed. Wollheim charges Grünbaum with having an impoverished conception of how psychological explanation works, and with neglecting the essential role of psychological structure – that is, the need to use psychological categories of *some* kind – in both psychoanalytic and commonsense understanding.

> If what the patient says or does is to be brought to bear upon the hypothesis under consideration so that it, the hypothesis, can then be said to have been tested on the couch, the patient's material will in most circumstances have to be subsumed under categories deriving from psychoanalysis . . . In saying or doing what he does, the patient has to be identified as, say, presenting *anal material* on a massive scale; resorting to *phantasies of omnipotence*; *assaulting*, or *fragmenting*, or *idealizing*, the analyst's interpretation; *acting out*; and so on. In other words, the patient's material must be subsumed under transference categories: that is, categories which capture what the person is doing *vis-à-vis* the analytic situation as he phantasizes it.
>
> (Wolheim 1993, p. 108)

Each of these categories, or hypotheses explaining the patient's behavior, has to find its empirical support in countless other applications to other patients in other settings. In other words, psychoanalysis makes use of a complex network of interpretations, just as commonsense psychology does when it allows us to understand someone's reactions by referring to an interconnected network of desires, beliefs, emotions, memories, obsessions, inhibitions, values, and identifications. And Wollheim observes that even where Grünbaum proposes a more or less commonsense alternative to psychoanalytic explanation, namely, that the apparent clinical evidence for psychoanalysis is the result of suggestion by the analyst, he sees no need to make the dynamics of such suggestion psychologically comprehensible or to explain the mental processes through which it operates. The hypothesis of 'suggestion', after all, is an alternative *psychological* explanation and has to be evaluated by the same standards as the explanations it is called on to refute.

How do we know whether a psychological explanation is correct? Although statistical analysis is not needed to prove that someone put on a sweater because he felt cold, one could easily imagine an idiotic psychological experiment statistically confirming the likelihood of a causal link in such cases. But the more interesting the case, the harder it is to reproduce it. What experimental evidence, for example, would help us to answer the question why Mikhail Gorbachev began the dismantling of the Soviet empire? Anything we can say about this will have to depend on the application of general methods for the motivational interpretation of intentional conduct to the unique circumstances of the case.

Much of human mental life consists of complex events with multiple causes and background conditions that will never precisely recur. If we wish to understand real life, it is useless to demand repeatable experiments with strict controls. (The same problem arises with regard to historical explanation, since historical events are, if anything, even less reproducible.) That doesn't mean that explanation is impossible, only that it cannot be sought by the methods appropriate in particle physics, cancer research, or the study of reflexes. We may not be able to run controlled experiments, but we can still try to make internal sense of what people do, in light of their circumstances, by trying to see how it might appear justified from their point of view – a technique supported by its usefulness in countless other cases, none of them exactly the same.

Explanations that refer to unconscious mental processes should be evaluated by the same standard. There may be some psychoanalytic explanations so simple that they can be tested by experiment or statistical analysis, but most are certainly not like that – rather they are applications of psychological insight in highly specific circumstances, which go beyond the bounds of consciousness. When we come to a brilliant and circumstantially rich conjecture like Freud's attribution of the forgetting of the word in a Latin quotation to the subject's anxiety that his mistress might be pregnant,[5] statistical confirmation is completely impossible, and we simply have to decide whether this is an intuitively credible extension of a general structure of explanation that we find well supported elsewhere, and whether it is more plausible than the alternatives – including the alternative that there is no psychological explanation.

The same problem arises for more general proposals, like Freud's hypothesis that in cases of melancholia an object-loss (such as the departure of a lover) is transformed into an ego-loss (the sense that one is worthless or despicable) through identification of the ego with the object of love by which it has been abandoned; the self-hatred that results can be understood as abuse by the ego of the internalized object. There seems no way to evaluate such a proposal experimentally – yet it is an empirical hypothesis about a psychic process that certainly appears to shed light on what goes on in some cases of acute depression.[6]

For most of those who believe in the reality of repression and the unconscious, whether or not they have gone through psychoanalysis, the belief is based not on blind trust in the authority of analysts and their clinical observations but on the evident usefulness of a rudimentary Freudian outlook in understanding ourselves and other people, particularly erotic life, family dramas, and what Freud called the psychopathology of everyday life. Things that would otherwise surprise us do not; behavior or feelings that would otherwise seem simply irrational become nevertheless comprehensible. You feel miserable all day, and then discover that it is the forgotten anniversary of the death of someone who was important to you; you find yourself repeatedly becoming absurdly angry with certain women in your professional life, and come to realize that your anger is a throwback to a childhood struggle with your mother. In the end, if we are to believe that Freud was getting at the truth, we must be able in some degree to make use of his approach ourselves. Since controlled and reproducible experiments are impracticable here, the kind of internal understanding characteristic of psychoanalysis must rely on the dispersed but cumulative confirmation in life that supports more familiar psychological judgments.

The question is not whether Freud got it exactly right, or whether strong criticisms cannot be made of some of his case histories, but whether the types of explanation he introduced substantially amplify the understanding of ourselves and others that commonsense psychology provides. I believe that the pervasive Freudian transformation of our modern working conception of the self is evidence of the validity of his attempt to extend the psychological far beyond its conscious base. Common sense has in fact expanded to include parts of Freudian theory. This in turn makes it credible that more extensive and systematic insights of the same type can be developed by analysts who probe far more deeply and uncover far more material for interpretation. To many of us it certainly *feels* as if, much of the time, consciousness reveals only the surface of our minds and, for many, this feeling is confirmed by their dreams.

II

Grünbaum's view is quite distant from the basic Freudian outlook that is such a familiar feature of modern culture. Wollheim, by contrast, is at home in a rich undergrowth of psychoanalytic categories, some developed by Melanie Klein. He puts special and interesting emphasis on the phenomenology of the unconscious – that is, the subjective feelings and fantasies the unconscious includes, which he argues are essential to its explanatory power. For example, Wollheim puts forward the thesis of the 'bodily ego', according to which we conceive, when we are very young,

> of mental states on the model of corporeal entities, . . . of a thought as a piece of food in the mouth, or as faeces, and we conceive of accepting the thought as swallowing the piece of food, or of rejecting the thought as excreting faeces.
>
> (Wollheim 1993, p. 87)

Because they incorporate these fantasies, the Freudian mechanisms of defense are not abstract forces but have a highly specific subjective (though unconscious) character.

It is difficult for an amateur to evaluate such claims; even when the subject matter is more familiar, the difficulty remains. The psychoanalytic understanding of morality is an interesting example. The story of the formation of the superego, 'the internal version of the father in the Oedipal drama', has passed into popular psychology. But Wollheim resists this conception of morality, holding with Melanie Klein 'that the injunctions or fulminations of internal figures not lying at the core of the ego play at best an unreliable, at worst a deleterious, role in the moral life'. He thinks of the superego, in other words, as a threatening, punitive, and alien incorporated object, rather than as a better self with which the person comes to identify. Instead of basing moral development on the internalization of the disapproving father, Wollheim, following Klein, bases it on the reconciliation of much earlier feelings. After the first year of life the infant discovers that the object it loves and the object it hates are both its mother; the infant then struggles to repair, preserve, or revive the loved object it has injured in omnipotent fantasy. In time the infant will be led to integrate the good self and the bad self, the one that loves and the one that hates.

Wollheim describes the process, which is considerably more complicated than my brief sketch here, in an essay called 'The Good Self and the Bad Self', which compares Klein with the philosopher F.H. Bradley,[7] who also held that morality must offer a form of harmonious self-realization. Wollheim is a naturalist about morality, in the sense that he believes that to have a claim on us it must be rooted in our earliest and most basic feelings. He urges us to avoid 'the phantasy that morality marks the spot where human beings discard human nature'. This appears to mean that we should not try to understand morality as a radical transcendence of infantile needs and wishes, and of the mental structures established before the age of two. Unless morality is rooted in those very needs and wishes, it will be superficial.

I cannot evaluate the Kleinian theory of infantile development even if I am an instance of it, but apart from that, I do not see how a theory of this kind could by itself explain more than the very beginnings of the complex system of restraints on aggression and self-interest, acknowledgment of formal obligations and of the rights and claims of others, that make up fully developed morality. The same could be said of the more familiar Freudian superego theory. Even if it starts with a family drama, morality in the strict sense requires forms of thought that are much more impersonal than fear of, love for, or identification with particular external or internal 'objects', whether fathers or mothers. It aims to supply objective standards in the realm of conduct, which will allow us to justify ourselves to one another and to agree on what should be done.[8]

Wollheim's attitude toward morality is far more radical than Freud's and closer in spirit to Nietzsche's. His naturalism is applied in a startling way in an essay called 'Crime, Punishment, and "Pale Criminality"', which suggests that human beings have a disposition 'bound up with what is deepest in us, to do what is forbidden, and to do it for that reason'; and that if this is so, then the criminal justice system is based on a flawed understanding of human nature: what it forbids, it makes more attractive. Many social institutions, such as the criminal law, 'imply a particular psychology', Wollheim writes, and if that psychology is false about human beings, 'then the institution is at fault because instead of facilitating, it impedes, self knowledge'.

This, he says, raises a further question:

> How much security from criminal behavior are we entitled to expect? How much protection can we rightly claim from those with whom we share our psychology? If, not criminality, but the seeds of criminality, are, in some identifiable way which the science of mind can make clear, present in all of us, how far are we right to distance it from us? . . . How far, if the need arose, should we be prepared to sacrifice security for self-knowledge?
>
> (Wollheim 1993, p. 130)

But how is that need going to arise? Perhaps the human disposition to do what is forbidden causes some prohibitions to heighten the appeal of crime, but that only means that if we want security, we should take this into account in designing the criminal law. Where is the sacrifice of self-knowledge in this? I suspect that Wollheim is talking about something deeper than self-knowledge. He asks for a form of self-affirmation that is incompatible with rejecting anything at the core of the self; and this explains his distrust of conventional morality.

Art is different. Wollheim writes:

> It seems to me natural to think that art is more deeply rooted in human nature than morality, and I am surprised that philosophers make little of the fact that, though good art is more likeable than bad art, virtuous people do not enjoy this same advantage over those to whom we are drawn primarily for their charm, or their gaiety, or their sweetness of nature, or their outrageousness.
>
> (p. x)

A number of Wollheim's essays discuss artistic expression, perception, and style, and here too Wollheim is committed to psychological naturalism: 'The broad characteristics of art, including expressiveness, originate outside art.' Wollheim emphasizes the psychological importance of the phenomenon of 'projection', the infusion of our perceptions of the outer world with inner mental states, which he believes is at the heart of the aesthetic response. Art gives meaning to our lives by its expressiveness, which creates a fit between our deep inner feelings and our external perceptions, and makes us at home in the world. Here again, as with the analysis of morality, a question arises whether such a personal theory doesn't make aesthetic response too subjective and idiosyncratic – but that will depend both on how objective we take such responses to be and how universal are the mental structures responsible, according to this theory, for the projections called forth by art. Wollheim himself believes that there is a universal human nature that all art, 'or at any rate all great art', presupposes.

Both art and nature can be targets of projected feelings: both a real and a painted landscape can be seen as melancholy, for example. But with a work of art, Wollheim believes that the right response is determined by the artist's intention: the work has been created in order to evoke certain projections, and if the intention is fulfilled, that is what the spectator will see in it. Wollheim rejects the view 'that criticism is at liberty to project on to a work of art whatever it wishes'. He argues that the artist's own projective response to the work as he is creating it – his dual role as creator and spectator – has an essential part in the creative process: 'the central fact about art [is] that it is an intentional manifestation of mind'.

Painting as an Art contains many applications of this idea. For example, Wollheim attributes the uncanny effect of Caspar David Friedrich's great landscape, *The Large Enclosure near Dresden*, to the presence of an invisible 'spectator in the picture', whose viewpoint does not have a natural relation to the landscape. When we look at the picture we are led to identify with this disembodied spectator inside it; we find ourselves both standing before the picture and floating above the landscape, which extends under the invisible spectator, and we are drawn into the attitude of detached but absorbed contemplation of nature expressive of Friedrich's early nineteenth-century Pietism. (On the only occasion when I saw it, the picture induced a strange spiritual disorientation, as if I had lost my self and were viewing the world *sub specie aeternitatis*, so I found Wollheim's account convincing.)

How much background knowledge we need in order to see the work as it was intended to be seen by the artist is another question. To perceive the meaning of a work of art generally requires some prior knowledge beyond what is needed to find a natural landscape beautiful: even to perceive a work's formal and nonrepresentational properties requires that the work 'be perceived as part of an aesthetic tradition'. But if the work is successful, understanding it will consist not in a deliberate act of inference and interpretation but simply in perceiving it as it was intended to be perceived. The essence of aesthetic understanding is to be found in experience, not theory. It is not to be found in social or economic explanation or in symbolic decoding.

The appeal of Wollheim's position lies in its insistence that what is important about a work of art is directly perceptible in it. What is harder to accept is his claim that the goal of aesthetic perception is always to experience the projection intended by the artist. This implies that a work of art cannot mean more than the artist intended it to mean, or knew that it meant, and that historical and symbolic and formal interpretation cannot produce a perceptual understanding of the work that interprets it as more than a product of the artist's purposes. A view contrary to Wollheim's might even include the possibility that the meaning of a work may develop over time, as the background of interpretation changes. I am drawn to Wollheim's emphasis on aesthetic experience. However, his theory may go too far in reducing aesthetics to psychology. The dominant role it gives to both intention and projection means that the work of art is not a freestanding creation whose aesthetic characteristics transcend both those psychological facts. I doubt that even great artists always know in all respects what they're doing, even if it is no accident that their works produce the effects they do.

III

Wollheim's diverse and unusual writings on many different subjects exemplify the influence of psychoanalytic modes of thought beyond therapy, and such influence is emphasized by Paul Robinson (1993) in his forceful response to three recent commentators on Freud: Frank Sulloway, Jeffrey Masson, and Adolf Grünbaum.[9] *Freud and his Critics* contains interesting general reflections on the significance of recent reactions to Freud as well as a dissection of these three writers. Robinson argues persuasively that none of the three makes a good case for their most distinctive claims about Freud and, further, that they all miss the real significance of Freud's intellectual contribution.

Sulloway is a historian who presents himself as a reintepreter of Freud, not as one of his critics. But Robinson believes he diminishes the interest and originality of Freud's ideas by exaggerating their biological content at the expense of the psychological. Freud's conviction that the mind, being a function of the brain, is a product of biological development, and that its structure is subject to evolutionary influences should be evident to any reader of his writings, and Sulloway provides a very detailed account of the biological and neurological background to Freud's intellectual development. But to treat this as the essence of a Freudian understanding of the mind is to read Freud much too reductively. The mind may be a biological product, but biological concepts can provide us with only a superficial understanding of its content and workings. Sulloway magnifies the influence on Freud of the crackpot theories of his early confidant Wilhelm Fliess, even though they left their traces. It is true that Freud corresponded with Fliess about the effects on the mind of biological calendars, the sense of smell, and the evolution of upright posture. But it is not possible, Robinson argues, to replace psychological insight – an understanding 'from within' of the type that engaged Freud's real genius – with such hypotheses.

Robinson (1993) turns next to the egregious Masson, who accuses Freud of being a liar and a coward because he abandoned the claim that his early patients had been victims of real sexual abuse as children, and explained their symptoms instead by the theory of infantile sexuality and fantasy. Masson believes Freud thus missed the chance to be a great crusader against child molestation and that his theory became a means for blaming innocent victims. Robinson demonstrates that Masson's claims that the patients had in fact been sexually abused are simply unsupported assertions. And he adds: 'The most powerful objection to Masson's thesis of moral cowardice is that Freud abandoned the seduction theory only to embrace an idea that was even more offensive to the prejudices of his culture, the theory of infantile sexuality.' Freud always recognized the existence of child abuse. His doubts had to do with its extent. But the claim that some accusations of childhood seduction are the product of fantasy provokes extreme resistance, and not only from Masson. I believe this insistence on the innocence of childhood and the evil behavior of adults covers up deeper feelings, which then surface in an emotionally delicious blend of prurience and moral outrage. The recent popular obsession with child molestation owes a good deal to such feelings.[10] Robinson persuasively identifies Masson as a representative of the new puritanism that emerged in the 1980s as a reaction to the sexually expansive 1960s. Masson's view of sex as joyless and charged with aggression belongs to an antiliberal tendency that has been gaining strength recently. It fits well with the outlook of those who see in pornography only an instrument for the subjection of women. Freud is a natural target for such enemies of self-knowledge.

Robinson's criticism of Grünbaum takes issue with the importance he assigns to therapeutic success as the empirical ground on which Freud's theories must stand or fall. Freud at various times denied that effective therapy was the ultimate test of his theories.[11] The theory of repression is an explanatory one, and the evidence for it comes from a variety of sources. I agree with Robinson that by insight and imagination it is possible, and sometimes even easy, to extrapolate from the conscious and familiar, and to discover unconscious psychological explanations in complex individual cases where statistical verification is impossible.

Only particular examples can provide evidence for this claim – examples that leave no credible alternative. Though some may find Freud's famous case histories persuasive, I believe they are too complex and ambiguous to serve this purpose. It is not surprising that they have generated so much interpretive and historical controversy. The best evidence for skeptics is smaller in scale. Einstein once wrote, in a letter to Freud:

> Until recently I could only apprehend the speculative power of your train of thought, together with its enormous influence on the *Weltanschauung* of the present era, without being in a position to form a definite opinion about the amount of truth it contains. Not long ago, however, I had the opportunity of hearing about a few instances, not very important in themselves, which in my judgment exclude any other interpretation than that provided by the theory of repression.[12]

But how could Einstein tell? What is it about a concatenation of circumstances that 'exclude any other interpretation'?

Not knowing what Einstein's instances were, I can only describe an episode I witnessed myself. At a dinner party, an elderly man of independent means, who had spent his life as a private scholar without an academic position, challenged a psychiatrist who was present to explain why, whenever he listened to the news on the radio, he fell asleep just at the point when the stock market report came on. The psychiatrist, knowing these facts, replied that it probably expressed difficult feelings about his father. '*My father!*' said the man incredulously, 'My father has been dead for fifty years!' The conversation then went on to other things, but the next day, the man telephoned the psychiatrist to report that later in the evening the memory had come flooding back to him that when, in his youth, he had resisted going into the family business, his father had made him promise at least to listen to the stock market report on the radio every day.

Many people have been exposed to equally obvious examples – though most are not so cut and dried, and the material produced in psychoanalysis is much more complex and strange. Grünbaum is inhospitable to the use of psychological insight to extend familiar and basic forms of psychological explanation to radically unfamiliar situations. But this may be partly because he himself has a rather wooden psychological imagination. As Robinson points out, when Grünbaum tries to propose an alternative interpretation to Freud's for the same data, the interpretation falls flat. (And his idea of a slip of the tongue that might be caused by a concealed but conscious thought is 'the man who turns from the exciting view of a lady's exposed bosom muttering, "Excuse me, I have got to get a *breast* of *flesh* air!"')

Robinson concludes with an excellent statement of Freud's true intellectual legacy, which these critics fail to recognize:

> He is the major source of our modern inclination to look for meanings beneath the surface of behavior – to be always on the alert for the 'real' (and presumably hidden) significance of our actions. He also inspires our belief that the mysteries of the present will become more transparent if we can trace them to their origins in the past, perhaps even in the very earliest past . . . And, finally, he has created our heightened sensitivity to the erotic, above all to its presence in arenas . . . where previous generations had neglected to look for it.
>
> (Robinson 1993, pp. 270–271)

The book is flawed, however, by one serious confusion, which crops up occasionally, as in the following passage: 'One would simply never know from reading Sulloway, Masson, and Grünbaum that many of their contemporaries entertained profound doubts about science, objectivity, truth, and the possibility of achieving stable, irrefragable knowledge of the self and society.' Robinson describes all three writers as 'positivists', because of their innocent attachment to outmoded ideas of truth and objectivity, and he regards this attitude as itself a rejection of Freud's outlook:

> Modernism entailed a loss of confidence in the stability and transparency of the self. It also entailed the recognition that all human knowledge is subjective and indeterminate. Freud's theory of the unconscious, which denies that the self is aware even of its own ideas, was the most powerful articulation of this modernist sensibility.
>
> (Robinson 1993, p. 16)

Robinson is referring to the facile subjectivism that now blights many of the humanities and social sciences. According to this view, anyone who thinks that some questions have right and wrong answers, which can be confirmed or refuted by evidence and argument, is an epistemological caveman.

Robinson incorrectly attributes such a view to Freud. There is a vast difference between holding that we are not transparent to ourselves and must discover our real mental nature by difficult and indirect investigative methods, and holding that there is no such thing as truth or objectivity. The unconscious does not abolish objectivity, even if it makes it more difficult to achieve. In Robinson's sense, Freud was certainly a 'positivist' and a believer in the pursuit of truth by the correct assessment of evidence.

That does not imply that what we believe to be true is immune to revision in the light of later evidence or argument, nor does it imply that everything can be known. But it does imply that, even though like any science psychology relies on imagination to frame its hypotheses, its aim is to discover objective truths about the human mind, and that if all Freud succeeded in doing was to develop a new way of talking or seeing things, he failed. That is what he meant by his repeated insistence that what he was doing was science. Freud would have been delighted to tangle with Grünbaum and would have had no patience whatever with the attacks on objectivity that Robinson depressingly describes as 'the most visible intellectual current of the age'. It is no service to Freud to defend him by appealing to this slothful outlook, let alone to ascribe it to him.

ADDENDUM

Since my comments on Grünbaum occurred in a review of two books by other people, I am glad of this opportunity for a more direct exchange.

A fundamental problem in making progress with this dispute is that there is no agreement over what should be regarded as Freud's distinctive contribution, specifically for the purpose of assessing its validity, value, or degree of empirical support. Grünbaum identifies it with a set of general psychological principles; I identify it with a form of understanding, which manifests itself in countless individual interpretations and explanations. We both agree that psychoanalytic hypotheses are causal and require empirical confirmation, but we differ as to the kind of evidence that is most important. I don't deny the importance of possible future epidemiological and experimental tests of the sort that he thinks crucial. My central disagreement with Grünbaum is about whether there is now, in advance of all such experiments, substantial reason to believe in the unconscious and psychoanalytic explanations that refer to it – reasons of a kind that were also available to Freud.

I don't think the crucial question for evaluating Freud's legacy is whether he was right (to take Grünbaum's example) in proposing that repressed homo-sexuality is a necessary causal condition of paranoid delusions. Even apart from the likelihood that paranoid delusions often have nonpsychological causes, this universal generalization seems thoroughly implausible on its face, and no doubt Freud's writings are filled with general hypotheses that are just as false. But the core of his contribution lies elsewhere, in a form of insight that depends not on the application of specifically psychoanalytic laws but on the extension of the familiar forms of psychological explanation beyond their traditional, rational domain.

I make a point of the continuity between psychoanalytic and commonsense explanations because I believe that psychoanalysis can borrow empirical evidence for its most important general foundations from the ubiquitous confirmation of the system of ordinary psychological explanation in everyday life. (Here I follow not only Richard Wollheim but two other philosophers, Donald Davidson and James Hopkins, who develop this point of view much more thoroughly than I can do here.)[13] Commonsense psychology depends not just on causal generalizations of the kind Grünbaum cites (that insults anger people, that good tidings create joy, etc.); a list of such laws wouldn't take you very far in understanding people. Much more important is the general scheme by which we try to make sense of others as more or less rational beings – each with a complex system of beliefs, assumptions, preferences, desires, values, aims, and dispositions to make inferences – and interpret their conduct as purposive and intentional in the light of these conditions.

The fundamental causal principle of commonsense psychology is that, in most cases, you can discover causally relevant conditions (conditions that make a *difference* in precisely Grünbaum's sense) for a human action or thought or emotion by fitting it into a rationally coherent interpretation of the whole person as an intentional subject of this type – by seeing how from the person's point of view it is in some way *justified*. Interpretation reveals causation because that's the kind of system a human being is. And this principle is so well supported in endless simple cases, in which it can be confirmed by the possibilities of prediction and control, that we are fully warranted in applying the same principle to identify psychological causes in unique and unrepeatable cases: by trying to make intentional and purposive sense of them.

That's what I mean by intuitive plausibility, and it necessarily applies in the first instance to specific explanations, rather than to general principles. I believe the essence of Freud's method was to extend the reach of this explanatory system to areas of human behavior and feeling where it had previously not seemed that sense could be found. In this way he increased our understanding of the influence of the mind, but confirmation goes from the particular to the general: the general theory of repression and psychosexual development has to be supported by its individual instances, rather than the reverse.

I don't have the sort of experience that would enable me to form a judgment on the conflicts between different post-Freudian theories at the level of general principles. But the general Freudian method of extending the familiar interpretive scheme of psychological explanation to the unconscious in particular cases, the method on which all such theories depend for evidence, is something that all of us should be able to confirm from our own experience: it is simply a matter of making sense of irrational or unintentional or involuntary conduct, when it fits into the same type of pattern so familiar from ordinary psychology, with some of the blanks filled in by thoughts or wishes of which the subject is not aware.

The case of the stock market sleeper, standing for countless others, was supposed to illustrate the point; Grünbaum's reaction to it shows how far apart we are. First, he says that Freud was wrong to think that there is a tendency to forget painful experiences. I entirely agree that this is not a universal tendency; the opposite is true for me. But the point is irrelevant, because no generalization of this kind enters into the grounds for the explanation, which depends only on the particulars of the case. Next, Grünbaum says I don't allow for 'the psychiatrist's rash creation of a mind-set in the gentleman, when he told him, without *any* additional information, that his falling asleep during the stock market news probably expressed difficult feelings about his father'. Grünbaum seems to have missed the significance of the crucial background evidence, known to the psychiatrist, of the man's ambivalence toward his inherited wealth, as shown by his unusual life as a private scholar on the periphery of the academy. That is what prompted the interpretation, since in light of the background, the otherwise puzzling symptom *makes expressive sense*. The recovered memory, vividly evoked by the interpretive suggestion, falls into place like another piece cut from the same jigsaw puzzle and strongly reinforces the 'sense' of the symptom – though this is obviously just the beginning of the story: we don't know what blend of defiance, fear, love, and guilt characterized the man's actual feelings about his father.

But Grünbaum won't have any of this. His reference to 'creation of a mind-set' implies, I take it, that the memory was probably false and planted by the suggestion of the psychiatrist. To prefer this alternative to one that makes sense of the symptom reveals, I think, both Grünbaum's deep-seated allergy to the admission of unconscious motives and his readiness to call on suggestion as an all-purpose alternative explanation with the slimmest excuse. I don't know whether the symptom ceased after this episode, but no doubt if it had, Grünbaum would have attributed that to suggestion too.

In appealing to the pervasive influence of Freudian ideas on modern self-consciousness, I meant that we all employ these forms of understanding constantly, that experience continually presents us with circumstances where they are appropriate. Evidently this is not true of Grünbaum; perhaps he regards it all as so much vulgarization. Let me try to answer his final question, however.[14] Religious superstitions, ethnic canards, witchcraft, and slavery are very different examples of entrenched error, but I'll focus on witchcraft, which is often brought up in these debates. Neither of us believes in witchcraft, but the interesting question is, 'Why?' Would Grünbaum appeal to controlled experiments establishing that curses issued by fully certified witches have no statistical effect on the death rate of their victims? I wouldn't be interested in such data even if they existed; my reason for dismissing witchcraft, even though countless people have believed and still believe in it, is that we know on much more general grounds that the world doesn't work that way. There are no supernatural forces that can be invoked by sticking pins in a doll. This simply follows from a general knowledge of physics and biology.

But psychoanalysis is not a theory of supernatural forces. It is an extension of psychological explanation to further phenomena *within* the domain of its original application, that is, the lives of human beings with minds. This is not in any way incompatible with the rest of our scientific understanding of how things work. It is part of our idea of the natural order that people's behavior is influenced by their mental condition; that the influence should be larger and more various than we originally thought should not surprise us.[15]

A final comment on therapeutic efficacy, which is indirectly relevant to the issue of confirmation. I have had no first-hand experience of psychoanalysis or psychotherapy, but I know many people who have. While I don't know whether psychoanalysis is more or less effective in eliminating unwanted symptoms than medication or behavior therapy, for example, I am quite sure that it has a different *kind* of effect on patients from more 'external' forms of treatment. My observation is that psychoanalysis can confer a valuable form of self-knowledge that is deep though essentially perceptual and not theoretical, and that this self-understanding, whether or not it cures neuroses directly, can be *used* by those who have it to anticipate, identify, and manage forms of irrationality that would otherwise victimize or even disable them. It also permits a subtler response to neurotic irrationality in others, through the enhancement of psychological imagination. For this reason I believe it will survive the development of simpler symptomatic cures, even though, because of its cost in time and money, the traditional form will always be an option for only a small minority.

The Scientistic Self-Misunderstanding of Metapsychology

On the Logic of General Interpretation

Jürgen Habermas

This paper is Chapter 11 of Jürgen Habermas' Knowledge and Human Interests *(1971).*

In his 'Autobiographical Study', Freud confesses that even in his early years his scientific interest was directed 'at human relations rather than natural objects'. Neither then nor later did he experience a predilection for the position and activity of a doctor. Yet as a student he first found 'calm and full gratification' in physiology. In Ernst Brücke's laboratory he worked for six years on problems of the histology of the nervous system.[1] This dichotomy in his interest may have contributed to Freud's founding what is in fact a new *science of man* while always considering it a *natural science*. Moreover, it was from neurophysiology, where he had learned to treat questions of human relevance according to medical and natural-scientific methods, that Freud borrowed the models that served him in theory formation. Freud never doubted that psychology is a natural science.[2] Psychic processes can be made the objects of research in the same way as observable natural events.[3] Conceptual constructions do not have a different role in psychology from that in a natural science. The physicist, for example, does not provide information about the essence of electricity, but instead uses 'electricity' as a theoretical concept, just as the psychologist uses 'instinct'.[4] However, only psychoanalysis made psychology into a science:

> The hypothesis we have adopted of a psychical apparatus extended in space, expediently put together, developed by the exigencies of life, which gives rise to the phenomena of consciousness only at one particular point – and under certain conditions – this hypothesis has put us in a position to establish

psychology on foundations similar to those of any other science, such, for instance, as physics.[5]

Freud does not evade the consequences of this identification of psychoanalysis with the natural sciences. He considers it possible in principle that some day the therapeutic employment of psychoanalysis will be replaced by the pharmacological employment of biochemistry. The self-understanding of psychoanalysis as a natural science suggests the model of the technical utilization of scientific information. If analysis only *seems* to appear as an interpretation of texts and *actually* leads to making possible technical control of the psychic apparatus, then there is nothing unusual about the idea that psychological influence could at some point be replaced with greater effect by somatic techniques of treatment:

> The future may teach us to exercise a direct influence, by means of particular chemical substances, on the amounts of energy and their distribution in the mental apparatus . . . But for the moment we have nothing better at our disposal than the technique of psycho-analysis.[6]

This passage reveals that a technological understanding of analysis accords only with a theory that has cut itself loose from the categorial framework of self-reflection and replaced a structural model suitable for self-formative processes with an *energy-distribution model*. As long as the theory derives its meaning in relation to the reconstruction of a lost fragment of life history and, therefore, to self-reflection, its application is necessarily *practical*. It effects the reorganization of the action-orienting self-understanding of socialized individuals, which is structured in ordinary language. In this role, however, psychoanalysis can never be replaced by technologies derived from other theories of the empirical sciences in the rigorous sense. For psychopharmacology only brings about alterations of consciousness to the extent that it controls functions of the human organism as objectified natural processes. In contrast, the experience of reflection induced by enlightenment is precisely the act through which the subject frees itself from a state in which it had become an object for itself. This specific activity must be accomplished by the subject itself. There can be no substitute for it, including a technology, unless technology is to serve to unburden the subject of its own achievements.

Starting from models of the pathlike flow of energy between neurons, current in contemporary neurophysiology, Freud in his early years outlined a psychology from which he then immediately distanced himself.[7] At that time Freud hoped to be able to provide psychology with an *immediate* foundation as a natural science, namely as a special part of the physiology of the brain, which was itself patterned after mechanics. This psychology was to represent 'psychical processes as quantitatively determined states of specifiable material particles'.[8] Categories such as tension, discharge, stimulation, and inhibition were applied to the distribution of energy in the nervous system and the paths of conduction connecting neurons, conceived of in accordance with the mechanics of solids. Freud abandoned this physicalist program in favor of a psychological approach in the narrower sense. This approach, in turn, retains the neurophysiological language of the original but makes its basic predicates accessible to a tacit *mentalist reinterpretation*. Energy becomes instinctual energy, about whose physical substratum no statements can be made. The inhibition and discharge of energy supplies and the mechanism of their distribution are supposed to operate after the pattern of a spatially extended system, whose localization, however, is henceforth eliminated:

> What is presented to us in these words is the idea of *psychical locality*. I shall entirely disregard the fact that the mental apparatus with which we are here concerned is also known to us in the form of an anatomical preparation, and shall carefully avoid the temptation to determine psychical locality in any anatomical fashion. I shall remain upon psychological ground, and I propose simply to follow the suggestion that we should picture the instrument which carries out our mental functions as resembling a compound microscope or a photographic apparatus, or something of the kind. On that basis, psychical locality will correspond to a point inside the apparatus at which one of the preliminary stages of an image comes into being. In the microscope and tele-scope, as we know, these occur in part at ideal points, regions in which no tangible component of the apparatus is situated. I see no necessity to apologize for the imperfections of this or of any similar imagery. Analogies of this kind are only intended to assist us in our attempt to make the complications of mental functioning intelligible by dissecting the function and assigning its different constituents to different component parts of the apparatus.[9]

> Accordingly, we will picture the mental apparatus as a compound instrument, to the components of which we will give the name of 'agencies', or (for the sake of greater clarity) 'systems'. It is to be anticipated, in the next place, that these systems may perhaps stand in a regular spatial relation to one another, in the same kind of way in which the various systems of lenses in a telescope are arranged behind one another. Strictly speaking, there is no need for the hypothesis that the psychical systems are actually arranged in a *spatial* order. It would be sufficient if a fixed order were established by the fact that in a given psychical process the excitation passes through the systems in a particular *temporal* sequence.[10]

Freud sets up several elementary correlations between subjective experiences on the one hand and energy currents, conceived of as objective, on the other.[11] Pain (*Unlust*) results from the accumulation of stimulation, with the intensity of the stimulation proportional to an energy quantum. Inversely, pleasure originates in the discharge of dammed-up energy, in other words through a decrease of stimulation. The motions of the apparatus are regulated by the tendency to avoid the accumulation of stimulation. This correlation of mentalistic expressions (such as impulse, stimulation, pain, pleasure, wish) and physical processes (such as energy quanta, energy tension and discharge, and, as a system property, the tendency toward the efflux of energy) suffices to sever the categories of the conscious and the unconscious, which were primarily derived from communication between physician and patient, from the frame of reference of self-reflection and transfer them to the energy-distribution model:

> The first wishing seems to have been a hallucinatory cathecting of the memory of satisfaction. Such hallucinations, however, if they were not to be maintained to the point of exhaustion, proved to be inadequate to bring about the cessation of the need or, accordingly, the pleasure attaching to satisfaction. A second activity – or, as we put it, the activity of a second system – became necessary, which would not allow the mnemic cathexis to proceed as far as perception and from there to bind the psychical forces; instead, it diverted the excitation arising from the need along a roundabout path which ultimately, by means of voluntary movement, altered the external world in such a way that it became possible to arrive at a real perception of the object of satisfaction. We have already outlined our schematic picture of the psychical apparatus up to this point; the two systems are the germ of what, in the fully developed apparatus, we have described as the *Ucs.* and *Pcs.*[12]

In 1895, together with Breuer, Freud had published *Studies on Hysteria*, where pathological phenomena were already explained according to the model developed later. Under hypnosis Breuer's patient had revealed that her symptoms were connected with past scenes of her life history in which she had to suppress strong stimuli. These affects could be interpreted as displaceable quantities of energy for which the normal paths of discharge were closed off and which therefore had to be used abnormally. Considered psychologically, the symptom comes into being through the damming up of an affect. In the model this can also be represented as a result of the conversion of a quantity of energy that is impeded in flowing out. The therapeutic procedure practiced by Breuer was supposed to have the aim of providing

> that the quota of affect used for maintaining the symptom, which had got on to the wrong lines and had, as it were, become strangulated there, should be directed on to the normal path along which it could obtain discharge (or *abreaction*).[13]

Freud soon recognized the disadvantages of hypnosis and introduced instead the technique of free association. The 'basic rule of analysis' formulates the conditions of a reserve free from repression in which the 'serious situation' (*Ernstsituation*), that is the pressure of social sanctions, can be suspended as credibly as possible for the duration of the communication between doctor and patient.

The transition from the old to the new technique is essential. It results not only from considerations of therapeutic utility but from insight into a principle: that for the patient's remembering to be therapeutically successful, it must lead to the *conscious* appropriation of a suppressed fragment of life history. Because the hypnotic release of the unconscious only manipulates processes of consciousness and does not entrust them *to the subject itself*, it cannot definitively penetrate the barrier to memory. Freud rejected Breuer's technique because analysis is not a *steered natural process* but rather, on the level of intersubjectivity in ordinary language between doctor and patient, *a movement of self-reflection*. Freud elaborated this especially in the abovementioned paper on 'Remembering, Repeating, and Working-Through'. And yet, at the end of the same paper, he still conceives this movement of self-reflection, induced under conditions of the basic rule of analysis, according to the old model of Breuer – that is, of remembering as abreacting:

> This working-through of the resistances may in practice turn out to be an arduous task for the subject of the analysis and a trial of patience for the analyst. Nevertheless it is a part of the work which effects the greatest changes in the patient and which distinguishes analytic treatment from any kind of treatment by suggestion. From a theoretical point of view one may correlate it with the 'abreacting' of the quotas of affect strangulated by repression – an abreaction without which hypnotic treatment remained ineffective.[14]

Because Freud was caught from the very beginning in a scientistic self-understanding, he succumbed to an objectivism that regresses immediately from the level of self-reflection to contemporary positivism in the manner of Mach and that therefore takes on a particularly crude form. Independently of the evolution of his work, the way in which Freud went astray methodologically can be reconstructed approximately as follows. The basic categories of the new discipline, the conceptual constructions, the assumptions about the functional structures of the psychic apparatus and about mechanisms of both the genesis of symptoms and the dissolution of pathological compulsions – this metapsychological framework was first derived from experiences of the analytic situation and the interpretation of dreams. The meaning of this observation bears on methodology and not only the psychology of research. For these metapsychological categories and connections were not only *discovered* under determinate conditions of specifically sheltered communication, they cannot even be *explicated* independently of this context. The conditions of this communication are thus the conditions of the possibility of analytic knowledge for both partners, doctor and patient, likewise. Perhaps Freud was thinking of this implication when he wrote that the claim to fame of analytic work was that 'in its execution research and treatment coincide'.[15] We have shown on the basis of the structural model that, with regard to the logic of science, the categorial framework of psychoanalysis is tied to the presuppositions of the interpretation of muted and distorted texts by means of which their authors deceive themselves. If this is so, however, then psychoanalytic theory formation is embedded in the context of self-reflection.

An alternative is the attempt to reformulate psychoanalytic assumptions in the categorial framework of a strict empirical science. Some have been newly formulated in the framework of behavioristically oriented learning psychology and then subjected to the usual procedures of verification. More sophisticated is the attempt to take the personality model developed by ego psychology but rooted in instinct theory and reformulate it as a self-regulating system in terms of modern functionalism. In both cases the new theoretical framework makes possible the operationalization of concepts; in both cases it requires verification of the derived hypotheses under experimental conditions. Freud surely assumed tacitly that his metapsychology, which severs the structural model from the basis of communication between doctor and patient and instead attaches it to the energy-distribution model by means of definitions, represented an empirically rigorous scientific formulation of this sort.

However, his relation to metapsychology, of which he occasionally spoke as a 'witch' in order to resist its terribly speculative character, was not free of ambivalence.[16] This ambivalence may imply a mild doubt of the status of this science, which he nevertheless defended so emphatically. Freud erred in not realizing that psychology, insofar as it understands itself as a strict empirical science, cannot content itself with a model that keeps to a physicalistic use of language without seriously leading to operationalizable assumptions. The energy-distribution model only creates the semblance that psychoanalytic statements are about measurable transformations of energy. Not a single statement about quantitative relations derived from the conception of instinctual economics has ever been tested experimentally. The model of the psychic apparatus is so constructed that metapsychological statements imply the observability of the events they are about. But these events are never observed – nor *can* they be observed.

It may be that Freud did not become aware of the methodological import of this limitation because he considered the analytic situation of dialogue quasi-experimental in character and therefore viewed the clinical basis of experience as a sufficient substitute for experimental verification. He countered the reproach that psychoanalysis did not admit of experimental verification by referring to astronomy, which also does not experiment with its heavenly bodies but is limited to their observation.[17] The real difference between astronomical observation and analytic dialogue, however, is that in the former the quasi-experimental selection of initial conditions permits the controlled observation of predicted events, while in the latter the level of control of the results of instrumental action[18] is completely missing and replaced by the level of the intersubjectivity of mutual understanding about the meaning of incomprehensible symbols. Despite his assertion, Freud unswervingly retained analytic dialogue as the sole empirical basis not only for the development of metapsychology but for the validity of psychoanalytic theory as well, and this betrays consciousness of the real status of the science. Freud surely surmised that the consistent realization of the program of a 'natural-scientific' or even rigorously behavioristic psychology would have had to sacrifice the *one intention* to which psychoanalysis owes its existence: the intention of enlightenment, according to which ego should develop out of id. But he did not abandon this program, he did not comprehend metapsychology as the only thing it can be in the system of reference of self-reflection: a *general interpretation of self-formative processes.*

It would be reasonable to reserve the name metapsychology for the fundamental assumptions about the pathological connection between ordinary language and interaction that can be set forth in a structural model based on the theory of language. Here we are dealing not with an empirical theory but a metatheory or, better, *metahermeneutics*, which explicates the conditions of the possibility of psychoanalytic knowledge. Metapsychology unfolds *the logic of interpretation in the analytic situation of dialogue.* In this respect it is on the same level as the methodology of the natural and cultural sciences. It, too, reflects on the transcendental framework of analytic knowledge as an objective structure of organized processes of inquiry, which here include processes of self-knowledge. However, in contrast to the logic of the natural and cultural sciences, methodology cannot exist detached from material content at the level of self-reflection. For here the structure of the cognitive situation is identical with the object of knowledge. To comprehend the transference situation as the condition of possible knowledge means at the same time comprehending a pathological situation. Because of this material content, the theoretical propositions that we should like to allocate to metapsychology are not recognized as metatheoretical propositions. This is why they are scarcely distinguished from empirically substantive interpretations of deviant self-formative processes themselves. Yet there remains a distinction on the methodological level. For like theories in the empirical sciences, no matter how different their empirical basis, general interpretations are directly accessible to empirical corroboration. In contrast, basic metahermeneutical assumptions about communicative action, language deformation, and behavioral pathology derive from subsequent reflection on the conditions of possible psychoanalytic knowledge. They can be confirmed or rejected only indirectly, with regard to the outcome of, so to speak, an entire category of processes of inquiry.

At the level of its self-reflection, the methodology of the natural sciences takes cognizance of a specific connection between language and instrumental action, comprehends it as an objective structure, and defines its transcendental role. The same holds for the methodology of the cultural sciences with regard to the connection between language and interaction. Metapsychology deals with just as fundamental a connection: the connection between *language deformation* and *behavioral pathology.* In so doing, it presupposes a theory of ordinary language having two tasks: first, to account for the intersubjective validity of symbols and the linguistic mediation of interactions on the basis of reciprocal recognition; second, to render comprehensible socialization – that is, initiation into the grammar of language games – as a process of individuation. Since, according to this theory, the structure of language determines likewise both language and conduct, motives of action are also comprehended as linguistically interpreted needs. Thus motivations are not impulses that operate from behind subjectivity but subjectively guiding, symbolically mediated, and reciprocally interrelated intentions.

It is the task of metapsychology to demonstrate this normal case as the limiting case of a motivational structure that depends simultaneously on publicly communicated and repressed and privatized need interpretations. Split-off symbols and defended-against motives unfold their force over the heads of subjects, compelling substitute-gratifications and symbolizations. In this way they distort the text of everyday language games and make themselves noticeable as disturbances of habitual interactions: as compulsion, lies, and the inability to correspond to expectations that have been made socially obligatory. In contrast to conscious motivations, the unconscious ones hereby acquire the driving, instinctual character of something that uncontrollably compels consciousness from outside it. Impulse potential, whether incorporated in social systems of collective self-preservation or suppressed instead of absorbed, clearly reveals libidinal and aggressive tendencies. This is why an instinct theory is necessary. But the latter must preserve itself from false objectivism. Even the concept of instinct that is applied to animal behavior is derived privately from the preunderstanding of a linguistically interpreted, albeit reduced human world: in short, from situations of hunger, love, and hate. The concept of instinct, when transferred back from animals to men, is still rooted in meaning structures of the life-world, no matter how elementary they may be. They are twisted and diverted intentions that have turned from conscious motives into causes and subjected communicative action to the causality of 'natural' conditions. This is the causality of fate, and not of nature, because it prevails through the symbolic means of the mind. Only for this reason can it be compelled by the power of reflection.

The work of Alfred Lorenzer, which conceives the analysis of processes of instinctual dynamics as linguistic analysis in the sense of depth hermeneutics,[19] has rendered us capable of grasping more precisely the crucial mechanisms of linguistic pathology, the deformation of internal structures of language and action, and their analytic elimination. Linguistic analysis takes symptoms and deciphers unconscious motives present in them just as a meaning suppressed by censorship can be reconstructed from corrupt passages and gaps in a text. In so doing, it transcends the dimension of the subjectively intended meaning of intentional action. It steps back from language as a means of communication and penetrates the symbolic level in which subjects *deceive themselves* about themselves through language and simultaneously give themselves away in it. As soon as language is excluded from public communication by repression, it reacts with a complementary compulsion, to which consciousness and communicative action bend as to the force of a second nature. Analysis attends to causal connections that come into being in this way. The terms of this relation are usually traumatic experiences of a childhood scene on the one hand and falsifications of reality and abnormal modes of behavior, both perpetuated owing to the repetition compulsion, on the other. The original defensive process takes place in a childhood conflict situation as flight from a superior partner. It removes from public communication the linguistic interpretation of the motive of action that is being defended against. In this way the grammatical structure of public language remains intact, but portions of its semantic content are privatized. Symptom formation is a substitute for a symbol whose function has been altered. The split-off symbol has not simply lost all connection with public language. But this grammatical connection has as it were gone underground. It derives its force from confusing the logic of the public usage of language by means of semantically false identifications. At the level of the public text, the suppressed symbol is objectively understandable through rules *resulting* from contingent circumstances of the individual's life history, but not connected with it according to intersubjectively *recognized* rules. That is why the symptomatic concealment of meaning and corresponding disturbance of interaction cannot at first be understood either by others or by the subject himself. They can only become understandable at the level of an intersubjectivity that must be created between the subject as ego and the subject as id. This occurs as physician and patient together reflectively break through the barrier to communication. This is facilitated by the transference situation; for the analyst does not participate in the patient's unconscious actions. The repeated conflict returns upon the patient and, with the interpretive assistance of the analyst, can be recognized in its compulsiveness, brought into connection with repetitive scenes outside the analysis, and ultimately be traced back to the scene in which it originated. This reconstruction undoes false identifications of common linguistic expressions with their meanings in private language and renders comprehensible the hidden grammatical connection between the split-off symbol and the symptomatically distorted public text. The essentially *grammatical* connection between linguistic symbols appears as a *causal* connection between empirical events and rigidified personality traits.[20] Self-reflection dissolves this connection, bringing about the disappearance of the deformation of private language as well as the symptomatic substitute-gratification of repressed motives of action, which have now become accessible to conscious control.

The model of the three mental agencies, id, ego, and super-ego, permits a systematic presentation of the structure of language deformation and behavioral pathology. Metahermeneutic statements can be organized in terms of it. They elucidate the methodological framework in which empirically substantive interpretations of self-formative processes can be developed. These general interpretations, however, must be distinguished from the metapsychological framework. They are interpretations of early childhood development (the origins of basic motivational patterns and the parallel formation of ego functions) and serve as narrative forms that must be used in each case as an interpretive scheme for an individual's life history in order to find the original scene of his unmastered conflict. The learning mechanisms described by Freud (object choice, identification with an ideal, introjection of abandoned love objects) make understandable the dynamics of the genesis of ego structures at the level of symbolic interaction. The defense mechanisms intervene in this process when and where social norms, incorporated in the expectations of primary reference persons, confront the infantile ego with an unbearable force, requiring it to take flight from itself and objectivate itself in the id. The child's development is defined by problems whose solution determines whether and to what extent further socialization is burdened with the weight of unsolved conflicts and restricted ego functions, creating the predisposition to an accumulation of disillusionments, compulsions, and denials (as well as failure) – or whether the socialization process makes possible a relative development of ego identity.

Freud's general interpretations contain assumptions about interaction patterns of the child and his primary reference persons, about corresponding conflicts and forms of conflict mastery, and about the personality structures that result at the end of the process of early childhood socialization, with their potential for subsequent life history. These personality structures even make possible conditional predictions. Since learning processes take place in the course of communicative action, theory can take the form of a narrative that depicts the psychodynamic development of the child as a course of action: with typical role assignments, successively appearing basic conflicts, recurrent patterns of interaction, dangers, crises, solutions, triumphs, and defeats. On the other hand, conflicts are comprehended metapsychologically from the viewpoint of defense, as are personality structures in terms of the relations between ego, id, and superego. Consequently this history is represented schematically as a self-formative process that goes through various stages of selfobjectivation and that has its telos in the self-consciousness of a reflectively appropriated life history.

Only the metapsychology that is presupposed allows the *systematic generalization* of what otherwise would remain pure *history*. It provides a set of categories and basic assumptions that apply to the connections between language deformation and behavioral pathology in general. The general interpretations developed in this framework are the result of numerous and repeated clinical experiences. They have been derived according to the elastic procedure of hermeneutic anticipations (*Vorgriffe*),[21] with their circular corroboration. But these experiences were already subject to the *general anticipation of the schema of disturbed self-formative processes*. In addition, an interpretation, once it claims the status of 'generality', is removed from the hermeneutic procedure of continually correcting one's pre-understanding on the basis of the text. In contrast to the hermeneutic anticipation of the philologist, general interpretation is 'fixed' and, like a general theory, must prove itself through predictions deduced from it. If psychoanalysis offers a narrative background against which interrupted self-formative processes can be filled out and become a complete history, the predictions that have been obtained with its help serve the reconstruction of the past. But they, too, are hypotheses that can prove wrong.

A general interpretation defines self-formative processes as lawlike successions of states of a system: Each succession varies in accordance with its initial conditions. Therefore the relevant variables of developmental history can be analyzed in their dependence on the system as a whole. However, the objective-intentional structure of life history, which is accessible only through self-reflection, is not functionalistic in the normal sense of this term. The elementary events are processes in a drama, they do not appear within the instrumentalist viewpoint of the purposive-rational organization of means or of adaptive behavior. The functional structure is interpreted in accordance with a dramatic model. That is, the elementary processes appear as parts of a structure of interactions through which a 'meaning' is realized. We cannot equate this meaning with ends that are realized through means, on the model of the craftsman. What is at issue is not a category of meaning that is taken from the behavioral system of instrumental action, such as the maintenance of the state of a system under changing external conditions. It is a question, rather, of a meaning that, even if it is not intended as such, takes form in the course of communicative action and articulates itself reflectively as the experience of life history. This is the way in which 'meaning' discloses itself in the course of a drama. But in our own self-formative process, we are at once both actor and critic. In the final instance, the meaning of the process itself must be capable of becoming part of our consciousness in a critical manner, entangled as we are in the drama of life history. The subject must be able to relate his own history and have comprehended the inhibitions that blocked the path of self-reflection. For the final state of a self-formative process is attained only if the subject remembers its identifications and alienations, the objectivations forced upon it and the reflections it arrived at, as the path upon which it constituted itself.

Only the *metapsychologically founded and systematically generalized history* of infantile development with its typical developmental variants puts the physician in the position of so combining the fragmentary information obtained in analytic dialogue that he can reconstruct the gaps of memory and hypothetically anticipate the experience of reflection of which the patient is at first incapable. He makes interpretive suggestions for a story that the patient cannot tell. Yet they can be verified in fact only if the patient adopts them and tells his own story with their aid. The interpretation of the case is corroborated only by the successful continuation of an interrupted self-formative process.

General interpretations occupy a singular position between the inquiring subject and the object domain being investigated. Whereas in other areas theories contain statements about an object domain to which they remain external as statements, the validity of general interpretations depends directly on statements about the object domain being applied by the 'objects', that is the persons concerned, to *themselves*. Information in the empirical sciences usually has meaning only for participants in the process of inquiry and, subsequently, for those who use this information. In both cases, the validity of information is measured only by the standards of cogency and empirical accuracy. This information represents cognitions that have been tested on objects through application to reality; but it is valid only for subjects. To the contrary, analytic insights possess validity for the analyst only after they have been accepted as knowledge by the analysand himself. For the empirical accuracy of general interpretations depends not on controlled observation and subsequent communication among investigators but rather on the accomplishment of self-reflection and subsequent communication between the investigator and his 'object'.

It may be objected that, just as with general theories, the empirical validity of general interpretations is determined by repeated applications to real initial conditions and that, once demonstrated, it is binding for all subjects who have any access to knowledge. Although correct in its way, this formulation conceals the specific difference between general theories and general interpretations. In the case of testing theories through observation (that is in the behavioral system of instrumental action), the application of assumptions to reality is a matter for the inquiring subject. In the case of testing general interpretations through self-reflection (that is in the framework of communication between physician and patient), this application becomes *self-application* by the object of inquiry, who participates in the process of inquiry. The process of inquiry can lead to valid information only via a transformation in the patient's self-inquiry. When valid, theories hold for all who can adopt the position of the inquiring subject. When valid, general interpretations hold for the inquiring subject and all who can adopt its position only to the degree that those who are made the object of individual interpretations *know and recognize themselves* in these interpretations. The subject cannot obtain knowledge of the object unless it becomes knowledge for the object – and unless the latter thereby emancipates itself by becoming a subject.

This is not as odd as it may sound. Every accurate interpretation, including those in the cultural sciences, is possible only in a language *common* to the interpreter and his object, owing to the fact that interpretation restores an intersubjectivity of mutual understanding that had been disturbed. Therefore it must hold likewise for both subject and object. But this function of thought has consequences for general interpretations of self-formative processes that do not occur in the case of interpretations in the cultural sciences. For general interpretations share with general theories the additional claim of allowing causal explanations and conditional predictions. In distinction from the strict empirical sciences, however, psychoanalysis cannot make good this claim on the basis of a methodologically clear separation of the object domain from the level of theoretical statements. This has implications (1) for the construction of the language of interpretation, (2) for the conditions of empirical verification, and (3) for the logic of explanation itself.

Like all interpretations, (1) general interpretations also remain rooted in the dimension of ordinary language. Although they are systematically generalized narratives, they remain historical. Historical representation makes use of narrative statements. They are narrative because they represent events as elements of histories.[22] We explain an event narratively if we show how a subject is involved in a history. In every history, individual names appear, because a history is always concerned with changes in the state of a subject or of a group of subjects who consider themselves as belonging together. The unity of the history is provided by the identity of the horizon of expectations that can be ascribed to them. The narrative tells of the influence of subjectively experienced events that change the state of the subject or group of subjects by intervening in a life-world and attaining significance for acting subjects. In such histories, the subjects must be able to understand both themselves and their world. The historical significance of events always refers implicitly to the meaning structure of a life history unified by ego identity or of a collective history defined by group identity. That is why narrative representation is tied to ordinary language. For only the peculiar reflexivity of ordinary language makes possible communicating what is individual in inevitably general expressions.[23]

By representing an individuated temporal structure, every history is a particular history. Every historical representation implies the claim of *uniqueness*. A *general* interpretation, on the contrary, must break this spell of the historical without departing from the level of narrative representation. It has the form of a narrative, because it is to aid subjects in reconstructing their own life history in narrative form. But it can serve as the background of *many* such narrations only because it does not hold merely for an individual case. It is a *systematically generalized history*, because it provides a scheme for many histories with foreseeable alternative courses. Yet, at the same time, each of these histories must then be able to appear with the claim of being the autobiographical narrative of something individuated. How is such a generalization possible? In every history, no matter how contingent, there is something general, for someone else can find something exemplary in it. Histories are understood as examples in direct proportion to the typicality of their content. Here the concept of type designates a quality of translatability: a history or story is typical in a given situation and for a specific public, if the 'action' can be easily taken out of its context and transferred to other life situations that are just as individuated. We can apply the 'typical' case to our own. It is we ourselves who undertake the application, abstract the comparable from the differences, and concretize the derived model under the specific life circumstances of our own case.

So the physician, too, proceeds when reconstructing the life history of a patient on the basis of given material. So the patient proceeds himself when, on the basis of the scheme offered him, he recounts his life history even in its previously forgotten phases. Both physician and patient orient themselves not toward an *example* but, indeed, toward a *scheme*. In a general interpretation, the individual features of an example are missing; the step of abstraction has already been taken. Physician and patient have only to take the further step of application. What characterizes systematic generalization, therefore, is that in hermeneutic experiences, which are relatively a priori to application, the abstraction from many typical histories with regard to many individual cases has already taken place. A general interpretation contains no names of individuals but only anonymous roles. It contains no contingent circumstances, but recurring configurations and patterns of action. It contains no idiomatic use of language, but only a standardized vocabulary. It does not represent a typical process, but describes in type-concepts the scheme of an action with conditional variants. This is how Freud presents the

Oedipal conflict and its solutions: by means of structural concepts such as ego, id, and super-ego (derived from the experience of analytic dialogue); by means of roles, persons, and patterns of interaction (arising from the structure of the family); and by means of mechanisms of action and communication (such as object-choice, identification, and internalization). The terminological use of ordinary language is not just an attribute of an accidental stage in the development of psychoanalysis. Rather, all attempts to provide metapsychology with a more rigorous form have failed, because the conditions of the application of general interpretations exclude the formalization of ordinary language. For the terms used in it serve the structuring of narratives. It is their presence in the patient's ordinary language which the analyst and the patient make use of in completing an analytic narrative scheme by making it into a history. By putting individual names in the place of anonymous roles and filling out interaction patterns as experienced scenes, they develop ad hoc a new language, in which the language of general interpretation is brought into accord with the patient's own language.

This step reveals application to be a translation. This remains concealed as long as, owing to the common social background of bourgeois origins and college education, the terminological ordinary language of the theory meets the patient's language halfway. The problem of translation becomes explicit as such when the linguistic distance increases on account of social distance. Freud is aware of this. This is shown in his discussion of the possibility that in the future psychoanalysis might be propagated on a mass basis:

> We shall then be faced by the task of adapting our technique to the new conditions. I have no doubt that the validity of our psychological assumptions will make its impression on the uneducated too, but we shall need to look for the simplest and most easily intelligible ways of expressing our theoretical doctrines.[24]

The problems of application that arise with theories in the empirical sciences only seem to be analogous. In the application of lawlike hypotheses to initial conditions, it is true that the singular events expressed in existential statements ('this stone') have to be brought into relation to the universal expressions of theoretical statements. But this subsumption is unproblematic, since the singular events only come into consideration insofar as they satisfy the criteria of general predicates ('this stone' is considered, for example, as 'mass'). Thus it suffices to establish whether the singular event corresponds to the operational definition through which the theoretical expression is determined. This operational application necessarily proceeds within the framework of instrumental action. Consequently it does not suffice for the application of the theoretical expressions of general interpretations. The material to which the latter are applied consists not of singular events but of symbolic expressions of a fragmentary life history, that is of components of a structure that is individuated in a specific way. In this case it depends on the hermeneutic understanding of the person providing the material whether an element of his life history is adequately interpreted by a suggested theoretical expression. This hermeneutic application necessarily proceeds in the framework of communication in ordinary language. It does not do the same job as operational application. In the latter case, the deciding factor is whether given empirical conditions may count as a case for the application of the theory, leaving untouched the theoretical deductions as such. In contrast, hermeneutic application is concerned with *completing* the narrative background of a general interpretation by creating a narrative, that is the narrative presentation of an individual history. The conditions of application define a *realization* of the interpretation, which was precluded on the level of general interpretation itself. Although theoretical deductions are mediated by communication with the physician, they must be made by the patient himself.

This is the context of (2) the methodological peculiarity that general interpretations do not obey the same criteria of refutation as general theories. If a conditional prediction deduced from a lawlike hypothesis and initial conditions is falsified, then the hypothesis may be considered refuted. A general interpretation can be tested analogously if we derive a construction from one of its implications and the communications of a patient. We can give this construction the form of a conditional prediction. If it is correct, the patient will be moved to produce certain memories, reflect on a specific portion of forgotten life history, and overcome disturbances of both communication and behavior. But here the method of falsification is not the same as for general theories. For if the patient rejects a construction, the interpretation from which it has been derived cannot yet be considered refuted at all. For psychoanalytic assumptions refer to conditions in which the very experience in which they must corroborate themselves is suspended: the experience of reflection is the only criterion for the corroboration or failure of hypotheses. If it does not come about, there is still an alternative: either the interpretation is false (that is, the theory or its application to a given case) or, to the contrary, the resistances, which have been correctly diagnosed, are too strong. The criterion in virtue of which false constructions fail does not coincide with either controlled observation or communicative experience. The interpretation of a case is corroborated only by the successful *continuation of a self-formative process*, that is by the completion of self-reflection, and not in any unmistakable way by what the patient says or how he *behaves*. Here success and failure cannot be intersubjectively established, as is possible in the framework of instrumental action or that of communicative action, each in its way. Even the disappearance of symptoms does not allow a compelling conclusion. For they may have been replaced by other symptoms that at first are inaccessible to observation or the experience of interaction. For the symptom, too, is bound in principle to the meaning that it has *for* the subject engaged in defense. It is incorporated in the structure of self-objectivation and self-reflection and has no falsifying or verifying power independent of it. Freud is conscious of this methodological difficulty. He knows that the 'no' of the analysand rejecting a suggested construction is ambiguous:

In some rare cases it turns out to be the expression of a legitimate dissent. Far more frequently it expresses a resistance which may have been evoked by the subject-matter of the construction that has been put forward but which may just as easily have arisen from some other factor in the complex analytic situation. Thus, a patient's 'No' is no evidence of the correctness of a construction, though it is perfectly compatible with it. Since every such construction is an incomplete one, since it covers only a small fragment of the forgotten events, we are free to suppose that the patient is not in fact disputing what has been said to him but is basing his contradiction upon the part that has not yet been uncovered. As a rule he will not give his assent until he has learnt the whole truth – which often covers a very great deal of ground. So that the only safe interpretation of his 'No' is that it points to incompleteness; there can be no doubt that the construction has not told him everything.

It appears, therefore, that the direct utterances of the patient after he has been offered a construction afford very little evidence upon the question whether we have been right or wrong. It is of all the greater interest that there are indirect forms of confirmation which are in every respect trustworthy.[25]

Freud is thinking of the confirming associations of the dreamer, who brings up previously forgotten text fragments or produces new dreams. On the other hand, doubt then arises whether the dreams have not been influenced by suggestion on the part of the physician:

If a dream brings up situations that can be interpreted as referring to scenes from the dreamer's past, it seems especially important to ask whether the physician's influence can also play a part in such contents of the dream as these. And this question is most urgent of all in the case of what are called 'corroborative' dreams, dreams which, as it were, 'tag along behind' the analysis. With some patients these are the only dreams that one obtains. Such patients reproduce the forgotten experiences of their childhood only after one has constructed them from their symptoms, associations and other signs and has propounded these constructions to them. Then follow the corroborative dreams, concerning which, however, the doubt arises whether they may not be entirely without evidential value, since they may have been imagined in compliance with the physician's words instead of having been brought to light from the dreamer's unconscious. This ambiguous position cannot be escaped in the analysis, since with these patients unless one interprets, constructs and propounds, one never obtains access to what is repressed in them.[26]

Freud is convinced that the physician's suggestion finds its limit in the mechanism of dream formation, which cannot be influenced. Still, the analytic situation attributes a special significance not only to the patient's 'No' but to his 'Yes' as well. For even the patient's confirmations cannot be taken at face value. Some critics charge that the analyst merely induces a modification of a previous interpretation of life history by talking the patient into a new terminology.[27] Freud counters that the patient's confirmation does not have a different implication for the verification of a construction than for its denial:

> It is true that we do not accept the 'No' of a person under analysis at its face value; but neither do we allow his 'Yes' to pass. There is no justification for accusing us of invariably twisting his remarks into a confirmation. In reality things are not so simple and we do not make it so easy for ourselves to come to a conclusion.
>
> A plain 'Yes' from a patient is by no means unambiguous. It can indeed signify that he recognizes the correctness of the construction that has been presented to him; but it can also be meaningless, or can even deserve to be described as 'hypocritical', since it may be convenient for his resistance to make use of an assent in such circumstances in order to prolong the conceal-ment of a truth that has not been discovered. The 'Yes' has no value unless it is followed by indirect confirmations, unless the patient, immediately after his 'Yes', produces new memories which complete and extend the construction. Only in such an event do we consider that the 'Yes' has dealt completely with the subject under discussion.[28]

Even indirect confirmation by association only has a relative value when considered in isolation. Freud is right in insisting that only the further course of analysis can decide a construction's usefulness or lack of it. Only the context of the self-formative process as a whole has confirming and falsifying power.[29]

As with the other forms of knowledge, the testing of hypotheses in the case of general interpretations can follow only those rules that are appropriate to the test situation. Only they guarantee the rigorous objectivity of validity. Whoever demands, to the contrary, that general interpretations be treated like the philo-logical interpretation of texts or like general theories and subjected to externally imposed standards, whether of a functioning language game or of controlled observation, places himself from the very beginning outside the dimension of self-reflection, which is the only context in which psychoanalytic statements can have meaning.

A final peculiarity of the logic of general interpretations results (3) from the combination of hermeneutic understanding with causal explanation: understand-ing itself obtains explanatory power. The fact that, with regard to symptoms, constructions can assume the form of explanatory hypotheses, shows their affinity with the causal-analytic method. At the same time, the fact that a construction is itself an interpretation and that the standard of verification is the patient's act of recollection and agreement demonstrates its difference from the causal-analytic procedure and a certain kinship with the hermeneutic-interpretive method. Freud takes up this question in a medical form by inquiring whether psychoanalysis may seriously be called a causal therapy. His answer is conflicting; the question itself seems to be wrongly posed:

> In so far as analytic therapy does not make it its first task to remove the symptoms, it is behaving like a causal therapy. In another respect, you may say, it is not. For we long ago traced the causal chain back through the repressions to the instinctual dispositions, their relative intensities in the constitution and the deviations in the course of their development. Supposing, now, that it was possible, by some chemical means, perhaps, to interfere in this mechanism, to increase or diminish the quantity of libido present at a given time or to strengthen one instinct at the cost of another – this then would be a causal therapy in the true sense of the word, for which our analysis would have carried out the indispensable preliminary work of reconnaissance. At present, as you know, there is no question of any such method of influencing libidinal processes; with our psychical therapy we attack at a different point in the combination – not exactly at what we know are the roots of the phenomena, but nevertheless far enough away from the symptoms, at a point which has been made accessible to us by some very remarkable circumstances.[30]

The comparison of psychoanalysis with biochemical analysis shows that its hypotheses do not extend to causal connections between observable empirical events. For if they did, then scientific information would put us in a position, as in biochemistry, to manipulatively transform a given situation. Psychoanalysis does not grant us a power of technical control over the sick psyche comparable to that of biochemistry over a sick organism. And yet it achieves more than a mere treatment of symptoms, because it certainly does grasp causal connections, although not at the level of physical events – at a point 'which has been made accessible to us by some very remarkable circumstances'. This is precisely the point where language and behavior are pathologically deformed by the causality of split-off symbols and repressed motives. Following Hegel we can call this the causality of fate, in contrast to the causality of nature. For the causal connection between the original scene, defense, and symptom is not anchored in the invariance of nature according to natural laws but only in the spontaneously generated invariance of life history, represented by the repetition compulsion, which can nevertheless be dissolved by the power of reflection.

The hypotheses we derive from general interpretations do not, like general theories, refer to nature, but rather to the sphere that has become second nature through self-objectivation: the 'unconscious'. This term designates the class of all motivational compulsions that have become independent of their context, that proceed from need dispositions that are not sanctioned by society, and that are demonstrable in the causal connection between the situation of original denial on the one hand and abnormal modes of speech and behavior on the other. The importance of causal motivations of action having this origin is a measure of the disturbance and deviance of the self-formative process. In technical control over nature we get nature to work for us through our knowledge of causal connections. Analytic insight, however, affects the causality of the unconscious as such. Psychoanalytic therapy is not based, like somatic medicine, which is 'causal' in the narrower sense, on making use of known causal connections. Rather, it owes its efficacy to overcoming causal connections themselves. Metapsychology does, indeed, contain assumptions about the mechanisms of defense, the splitting-off of symbols, the suppression of motives, and about the complementary mode of operation of self-reflection: assumptions that thus 'explain' the origin and elimi- nation of the causality of fate. The analogue to the lawlike hypotheses of general theories would thus be these metapsychological basic assumptions about linguistic structure and action. But they are elaborated on the metatheoretical level and therefore do not have the status of normal lawlike hypotheses.

The concept of a causality of the unconscious also renders comprehensible the therapeutic effect of 'analysis', a word in which critique as knowledge and critique as transformation are not accidentally combined. The immediate practical consequences of critique are obtained by causal analysis only because the *empirical* structure that it penetrates is at the same time an *intentional* structure that can be reconstructed and understood according to grammatical rules. We can at first view a construction offered to the patient by the physician as an explanatory hypothesis derived from a general interpretation and supplementary conditions. For the assumed causal connection exists between a past conflict situation and compulsively repeated reactions in the present (symptoms). Substantively, how- ever, the hypothesis refers to a meaning structure determined by the conflict, the defense against the wish that sets off the conflict, the splitting-off of the wish symbol, the substitute gratification of the censored wish, symptom formation, and secondary defense. A causal connection is formulated hypothetically as a hermeneutically understandable meaning structure. This formulation satisfies simultaneously the conditions of a causal hypothesis and of an interpretation (with regard to a text distorted by symptoms). Depth-hermeneutic understanding takes over the function of explanation. It proves its explanatory power in self-reflection, in which an objectivation that is both understood and explained is also overcome. This is the critical accomplishment of what Hegel had called comprehending (*Begreifen*).

In its logical form, however, explanatory understanding differs in one decisive way from explanation rigorously formulated in terms of the empirical sciences. Both of them have recourse to causal statements that can be derived from universal propositions by means of supplementary conditions: that is, from derivative interpretations (conditional variants) or lawlike hypotheses. Now the content of theoretical propositions remains unaffected by operational application to reality. In this case we can base explanations on context-free laws. In the case of hermeneutic application, however, theoretical propositions are translated into the narrative presentation of an individual history in such a way that a causal statement does not come into being without this context. General interpretations can abstractly assert their claim to universal validity because their derivatives are additionally determined by context. Narrative explanations differ from strictly deductive ones in that the events or states of which they assert a causal relation is further defined by their application. Therefore general interpretations do not make possible context-free explanations.[31]

Systems theory and the metapsychology

Cordelia Schmidt-Hellerau (2001) puts forward her reading of the metapsychology as a genuine mental-physical synthesis as Freud intended. Using an 'information and systems theory' approach, she presents it as bridging the levels of psychology and physiology through the patterns they jointly manifest. This would make the metapsychology a theory which is at once 'protoneurophysiological' and 'proto-psychological'.

Impressive as her model is, it does not seem to offer the conceptual resolution she seeks. Information theory and systems theory are founded in mathematics; they can be applied to biological or artificial systems alike precisely because they conceive the mind not in personal terms, but as an input-output machine (a computer). This makes them more sophisticated versions of Newton's 'clock-work universe', drawing on the analogy of the mind with the most sophisticated technology available in just the same way. Schmidt-Hellerau's model is a modern rendition of the 'spatial-but-not-material' thinking of Freud's metapsychology, with striking correspondences to current neurophysiological theory (pp. 265–283). However, in assimilating mental conceptions to physical conceptions, she falls short of laying out a common ground for physical and mental explanations. This general point is also discussed by Nagel (1998).

The impossibility of psychophysical laws

The relation of mental and physical events and explanations is a principal theme of the philosopher Donald Davidson. In his *Essays on Actions and Events* (1970, 2001) he sustains and develops the distinction between explanation in terms of reasons and explanation in terms of cause. His analysis of what these different accounts of 'human' phenomena entail explains their incompatibility. Yet reasons are a subset of causes, he argues, because causality is the vehicle of explanation: what else could the 'because' of reason explanations mean? 'Cause is the cement of the universe; the concept of cause is what holds together our picture of the universe, a picture that would otherwise disintegrate into a diptych of the mental and the physical' (2001, p. xv).

Davidson's (1970) study of 'Mental Events' lays out why psychophysical laws are an impossibility. He sees this as a matter of vocabulary. Whether or not an event is explainable in terms of 'law' depends on how it is described; and how it is described is what makes an event mental or physical in the first place. Like Freud and Nagel, Davidson holds that 'mental events are identical with physical events' (2001, p. 209), and that 'at least some mental events interact causally with physical events' (p. 208). This establishes that the issue at stake is not that they are made of different 'stuff'. Mental events are no more immaterial than the bang of an explosion; they are physical events under a different description. Nevertheless, they cannot be reduced to physical events, because they can never be fully expressed in non-mental vocabulary.

Davidson explains:

> Suppose we try to say, not using any mental concepts, what it is for a man to believe there is life on Mars . . . [No] matter how we patch and fit the non-mental conditions, we always find the need for an additional condition that is mental in character.
>
> (Davidson 2001, p. 217)

There is simply no way of defining a mental event such as a belief, a value or an emotion in purely physical terms; it always leaves something out. Thus Davidson drives a wedge between ontological identity (identicalness) and conceptual identity. He is implying that while psychophysical phenomena may exist, they cannot be expressed as such, because of the different linguistic and causal organizations of the mental and physical schemes. The incommensurability of physical and mental descriptions means that we can never know in advance if a particular description, whether mental or physical, necessarily corresponds to an identifiable description of the other kind: 'we can pick out each mental event using the physical vocabulary alone, but no purely physical predicate, no matter how complex, has, as a matter of law, the same extension [refers to the same things] as a mental predicate' (p. 215). They constitute not just different vocabularies but different languages.

These languages have different structural characteristics and foundational premises. The language of the physical is nomological, or based on universal law and linear cause and effect; the language of the mental is teleological, or based on purposive action or response by a thinking and feeling individual. These different causal orders make physically- or mentally-described events explicable as physical or mental events.

> It is a feature of physical reality that physical changes can be explained by laws that connect it with other changes and conditions physically conceived. It is a feature of the mental that the attribution of mental phenomena must be responsible to the background of reasons, beliefs, and intentions of the individual.
>
> (Davidson 2001, p. 222)

Davidson is saying that since physical units are interchangeable, all physical explanations are instances of general explanations. But since each individual's 'propositional network' of 'reasons, beliefs and intentions' is in continual flux and change, mental explanations are one-offs. Mental events cannot take up a place in nomological (law-based) explanations any more than physical concepts can figure in propositional networks. 'There are no strict psychophysical laws because of the disparate commitments of the mental and physical schemes . . . nomological slack between the mental and the physical is essential as long as we conceive of man as a rational animal' (pp. 222–223); and unless we so conceive him, we cannot 'explain' him as a person, but only as a 'system'. There is thus no possible principle by which a mentally described event could be lined up with its physically-described counterpart. If they did line up, this would be purely coincidental: 'If by some absurdly remote chance we were to stumble on a nonstochastic [nonrandom] true psychophysical generalization, we would have no reason to believe it more than roughly true' (p. 216).

Davidson's account establishes the ground of difference between the mental and physical dimensions. This challenges Freud's unitary conception of the psychical and renders Grünbaum's physicalistic criterion inapplicable to the practical explanations of psychoanalysis and 'commonsense psychology'. Gardner's work takes up the discordance between Davidson's rationalistic 'mind' and Freud's psychoanalytic 'psyche' by showing that in psychoanalysis, the concept of intentionality is extended beyond rationality. This provides the beginnings of a bridge between the two.

Glossary

Abreaction The discharge of psychical 'energy'.

Antireductionism The principle that mental concepts cannot be reduced to physical concepts.

Apparatus of the soul Term used by Freud as a direct alternative to 'psychic apparatus'.

A priori Philosophical term usually applied to knowledge which can be assumed in advance of experience or investigation. In contrast to a *posteriori*: to be discovered through experience.

Basic assumption of psychoanalysis The assumption that there must be a way of theorizing the processes which connect physical processes in the brain and nervous system with conscious experience.

Categorial Pertaining to categories. NB not 'categorical'.

Cathexis Psychoanalytic term for the investing (*Besetzung*) of energy in a psychical structure.

Clinical theory Psychoanalytic theory that can be expressed in the language of experience.

Cognitive interest Habermas' term for one of the standpoints from which knowledge is sought. He identifies technical, practical and emancipatory cognitive interests, corresponding to the categories of empirical, hermeneutic and critical science.

Commonsense psychology The practical, pre-theoretical knowledge people draw on to understand themselves and others in everyday life.

Conative Purposive.

Conscious-preconscious Psychoanalytic term for the psychical system in which mental phenomena are either conscious or readily available to consciousness.

Critical science Habermas' term for a theoretical system which reflects on normally accepted premises.

Descriptive metaphysics Description and analysis of metaphysical structures.

Drive See instinct.

Dual aspect theory Nagel's term for a unitary conception of reality based on a single category with mental and physical aspects.

Ego Translation of Freud's term, *das Ich* (the 'I'), denoting the 'psychical agency' which mediates between the pressures of the id, the super-ego and the external world. The overriding aim of the ego is self-preservation.

Eliminative materialism Philosophical approach which holds that only the material conception of reality is valid, and that mental concepts should therefore be expressed in physical terms.

Emancipatory Directed toward freeing oneself from conceptual or material constraints.

Empirical science Body of theory validated by sensory 'experience', generally measurable data drawn from observation and experiment.

Empirical-analytic sciences Habermas' term for the empirical sciences.

Endo-psychic From within the psyche.

Epiphenomenon An offshoot or by-product.

Epistemology Philosophical term for the theoretical study of knowledge.

Explananda What is to be explained.

Extension Philosophical term meaning the range of things a concept refers to.

Freudian slip A slip of the tongue arising from a repressed wish or thought.

Fundamental hypotheses of psychoanalysis First hypothesis: the spatial conception of the psyche. Second hypothesis: the essentially unconscious nature of psychical processes.

General interpretations Habermas' term for the general clinical concepts and theories which he treats as the true foundations or 'metapsychology' of psychoanalysis.

God's-eye view Philosophical expression for a fully impersonal viewpoint which is only theoretically available. Cf. Nagel's 'view from nowhere'.

Hallucination Perception without an external cause. In psychoanalysis, this includes not only the hallucinations of psychosis, but also those which arise in the pre-propositional unconscious system, in which reality testing is absent or minimal. Dreams and unconscious wishes are examples of this normal kind of hallucination.

Hermeneutic To do with interpretation.

Hermeneutic science Organized body of interpretational theory.

Historical-hermeneutic science Habermas' term for a theoretical system based on understanding reality through a template of sharable meanings by interpreting symbolic structures. This often involves a historical component.

Humanities The category of cultural theory, as opposed to empirical science.

Hypothetico-deductive model Model of explanation used in empirical science, in which conclusions are deduced logically from a given hypothesis. The hypothetico-deductive formula is *Law + Conditions → Event to be explained*.

Id Translation of Freud's term, *das Es* (the 'it'), denoting the psychical agency which forms the biological ground of psychical life and contains the instinctual energy. The id is directed solely towards pressing for gratification of the drives or instincts.

Instinct English translation of Freud's term *Trieb*, more accurately translated as 'drive'. Freud divides the drives or instincts into two groups. The original division is between the ego instincts (directed towards the preservation of the individual) and the sexual instincts (directed towards the preservation of the species). The later division is between Eros (the life instincts) and Thanatos (the death instincts).

Instrumental reasoning 'Means-end' reasoning.

Intentionality Philosophical term referring to the mental characteristic of being 'about' something, or directed towards something.

Interpretation The elucidation of meaning.

Introjection Psychoanalytic term denoting the opposite of projection: relocating, in phantasy, an object or psychological structure from outside to inside the psyche.

Mentalistic Described in experiential terms, as though the phenomenon in question were mental.

Metahermeneutics The hermeneutic equivalent of metaphysics: the 'first principles' of hermeneutics.

Metaphysics The picture or conception of reality from which a theoretical investigation starts.

Metapsychology Freud's term for the psychological equivalent of metaphysics: the 'first principles' of psychology. This term denotes the deepest level of psychoanalytic theory, intended to supply the principles and models by which the clinical theory can be explained. The upper level consists of specific models and theories. The lower level consists of the two 'fundamental hypotheses' and the 'basic assumption' of psychoanalysis.

Motivational state Sebastian Gardner's term for the prototypical psychical process: an instinctual urge to which meaning has been added, transforming a purely physical instinct into an unconscious wish 'for' something.

Nomological Based on the concept of universal law.

Normative To do with rules, tests and standards.

Object In psychoanalytic terms, not a 'thing' but the target or focus of the drive (instinct) or desire of the subject. This is typically a person or an aspect (or part) of a person.

Objective knowledge In the empirical-scientific sense, knowledge of something which exists independently of any point of view. In the hermeneutic sense, knowledge of something which is held in common by a number of human beings, and therefore does not depend on any single point of view.

Object Relations theory Branch of psychoanalysis centred on the subject's relational structures and needs, rather than on drive or instinct theory.

Ontology Philosophical term denoting the nature of being; for example, physical or mental ontology.

Paradigm change Term introduced by Thomas Kuhn to describe the introduction of a new theoretical template into a scientific field, bringing in a new 'paradigm', or way of understanding the phenomena concerned.

Particulars Philosophical term for phenomena which are separately identifiable.

Phantasy Psychoanalytic term for the primary content of unconscious mental processes; the essentially unconscious, often wish-fulfilling story-lines which underlie and influence conscious experience and thought.

Philosophy of psychoanalysis Study of the first principles or presuppositions on which psychoanalysis is based.

Physical To do with matter. Validated through the principles of physics, the overarching science of the physical.

Physicalistic Described in material terms, as though the phenomenon in question were physical.

Physical reduction Reducing mental terms and explanations to physical terms and explanations.

Pleasure principle Freud's term for the motivational principle of the psychical domain, or 'unconscious' system (*Ucs.*).

Pleasure–unpleasure The qualitative continuum Freud ascribes to psychic functioning. He assumed, but could not demonstrate, that there must be a systematic correspondence to a 'quantitative' continuum resulting from the accumulation and discharge of psychic 'energy'.

Positivism System of knowledge introduced by Auguste Comte, built around the belief that only empirical methodology gives real or 'positive' knowledge.

Pre-conscious Mental states or processes which are not currently conscious, but which can easily become conscious. The psychoanalytic abbreviation for the conscious-preconscious psychical system is *Pcs.*

Predicate The part of a sentence which says something about the subject.

Principle of full determination (determinism) The principle that every event or state has a necessary cause.

Projection In psychoanalysis, the attribution of one's own mental states to others.

Propositional psychology The field of processes and states that contain a proposition, or proposal.

Pseudo-science A body of theory which appears to be empirical-scientific in nature, but which in fact fails to meet the criteria of empirical science.

Psyche Psychoanalytic term for the locus of subjectivity.

Psychical Literally, this term refers to phenomena conceived in non-physical terms. In psychoanalysis, this is understood as Freud's 'third area' of reality, the point at which the mental and the physical meet; the essence of the mental.

Psychic apparatus Freud's term for the complex psychical system he envisaged.

Psychoanalysis Any psychological theory and therapy based on Freud's concept of the unconscious.

Quasi-manifestability Gardner's term for the way in which normally unconscious phantasy can be glimpsed in consciousness.

Rational Based on reason, as the common standard used to justify responses, thoughts and decisions. Philosophically speaking, the rational is more than the cognitive: it encompasses emotions as well as beliefs.

Realism   The belief that reality exists independently of any perception of it.

Reality principle   Freud's term for the motivational principle of the rational domain, or conscious-preconscious system (*Pcs.*).

Repression   Psychoanalytic concept for the banishing of unwelcome experience into the unconscious. This concept is represented at both the clinical and metapsychological levels.

Resistance   Psychoanalytic concept denoting the subject's unwillingness to allow unconscious material into consciousness.

Retrodiction   The opposite of prediction. Drawing conclusions about the causes or antecedents of a phenomenon from the circumstances in which the phenomenon occurs.

Revisionary metaphysics   Work directed towards the revising or modifying of a metaphysical scheme.

Science   An organized body of knowledge. Colloquially, 'empirical science' only.

Scientific realism   The belief that science can give a true picture of a reality which exists independently of its being perceived.

Scientism   The belief that knowledge gained through the methodology of empirical science is superior to any other kind.

Self-reflection   Means of obtaining knowledge by introspection and reflection.

Semantic   Meaning-based.

Super-ego   Translation of Freud's term 'das Über-Ich' (the 'over-I'), denoting the psychical agency which holds the critical function (derived from internalizing perceived parental demands) and exerts a moral pressure on the ego.

Supersede   Be the exact equivalent of, though expressed in different terms.

Teleological   Towards a purpose or end (*telos*). Intentional causality is teleological, or purposive, whereas physical determinism is nomological, or law-based.

Theoretical foundations   The principles on which a theoretical system is based.

Topography   The spatial conception of phenomena. In psychoanalysis, the conception of the psyche in terms of levels and structures.

Transcendental   In philosophy: transcending, or going beyond, sense-experience.

Transference   Psychoanalytic term to denote the transferring of the unconscious dynamics of early relationships into the therapeutic relationship, recreating the emotional atmosphere.

Unconscious   Literally, not conscious. In psychoanalysis, a level of experience which affects conscious experience but is inaccessible to consciousness, and operates according to different principles. The psychoanalytic abbreviation for the unconscious psychical system is *Ucs.* (often referred to as 'the' unconscious).

Wish Psychoanalytic term for the most primitive mental state, consisting of an unconscious motivation to seek a particular form of instinctual satisfaction. This means that by definition, the psychoanalytic 'wish' includes some image or sense of 'wish fulfilment'.

Notes

1 Introduction

1 Details of the exchange are given at the beginning of the Bibliography.
2 'The Freud Wars' is both a specific and a general term, referring to the general wave of criticism directed towards psychoanalysis in the 1990s as well as this particular dispute. See Forrester (1997).
3 Crews' (1995) book includes NYRB reviews, selected responses, Crews' counter-responses, and an 'Afterword: Confessions of a Freud Basher'.
4 'With a friend like Professor Grünbaum does psychoanalysis need any enemies?' (Grünbaum et al. 1986, p. 228)
5 Nagel mentions that all his reviews are written 'on request' (Nagel 1995, p. 3).
6 It may partly derive from the more rationalistic post-Freudian tradition of American Ego Psychology. If the reviews had been published in the *London Review of Books*, for example, the view might well have prevailed that psychoanalysis is only as good as the linguistic or philosophical grounds brought to it.
7 This is the title of Habermas' first psychoanalytic chapter. The second is 'The Scientist Self-Misunderstanding of Metapsychology' and the third is 'Psychoanalysis and Social Theory'. They make up Chapters 10, 11 and 12 of *Knowledge and Human Interests* (Habermas 1971).
8 Freud was particularly influenced by Jean-Martin Charcot (known as the 'Napoleon of the neuroses') and his Salpêtrière school of hypnotism; Hippolyte Bernheim and his divergent Nancy school of suggestion; the psychopathologist Pierre Janet; and Josef Breuer, Freud's early mentor. See Ellenberger (1970) and Freud (1924c, S.E. 20) for further details.
9 'Triebe', misleadingly translated as 'instincts'; Freud reserves the term 'Instinkt' for animal instincts. See Freud S.E. 1, pp. xxiv–xxvi for translator's discussion.
10 It is termed 'conscious-preconscious' since it includes not just what is immediately in consciousness, but what can enter into consciousness without hindrance.
11 The instinctual (or drive) level is represented by the id, the moral or cultural level by the super-ego, and the level of reality-orientation and decision-making by the ego.
12 There are thus both clinical and metapsychological theories of repression.

2 The Foundations of Psychoanalysis

1 Grünbaum also examines and rejects Paul Ricoeur's hermeneutic account. See Grünbaum (1984, ch. 3) and (2002, p. 131 above).
2 The inductivist method was developed in the seventeenth century by the scientific pioneer Francis Bacon, and adapted for the human sciences in the nineteenth century by the philosopher John Stuart Mill (1843).

3 Valerii Leibin quotes no fewer than ten different ways in which Freud defines psychoanalysis (Grünbaum et al. 1986, p. 246).

4 Freud does, however, distinguish between psychological and physiological levels of explanation, and relinquishes physical reduction as a goal. See the following passages, and also Freud (1900, S.E. 5, pp. 536 and 611; 1915a, S.E. 14, p. 168; and of course the 'basic assumption' of psychoanalysis, 1938a, S.E. 23, p.144).

5 Neurath's boat might be a better analogy: 'We are like sailors who have to rebuild their ship on the open sea, without ever being able to dismantle it in dry-dock and reconstruct it from the best components' (quoted in Honderich 1995, p. 96).

6 Problems arise in distinguishing a 'refutation' from a 'puzzle'. All investigations throw up negative results, but these are usually treated as challenges to develop the theory further rather than as reasons to reject it. See Lakatos' (1973) critique of falsificationism in his witty 'Lectures on Scientific Method'.

7 Popper terms this the 'Oedipus effect', since 'the causal chain leading to Oedipus' parricide was started by the oracle's prediction of this event' (Popper 1962, p. 38, fn 3).

8 Grünbaum explains: 'The central causal and explanatory significance enjoyed by unconscious ideation in the entire clinical theory rests, I submit, on two cardinal inferences drawn by Breuer and Freud' (1984, p. 177). He is speaking of the inferences, drawn from observation, that repression is a necessary antecedent in the kind of neuroses which are amenable to psychoanalytic intervention, and consequently that the lifting of repression through insight is necessary to its cure. 'The dramatic improvements observed after treatment were produced by none other than the cathartic lifting of the pertinent repressions' (ibid.). Since repressed psychical aims are unconscious, Grünbaum takes the lifting of repression as evidence of unconscious motivation.

9 See, for example, Sachs (1989) for discussion.

10 Grünbaum makes this explicit: 'whenever empirical indicators can warrant the absence of a certain theoretical pathogen P as well as a differential diagnosis of the presence of a certain theoretical neurosis N, then an etiologic hypothesis of the strong form "P is causally necessary for N" is clearly empirically falsifiable . . . by any victim of N who had not been subjected to P' (1984, p. 109).

11 Grünbaum manages to pick apart the causal links, empirical and argumentative, at every stage. He shows that Freud can provide no non-inductive evidence that repression causes neurosis, that the lifting of repression cures neurosis, or that the insight attained through the psychoanalytic method is sufficiently uncontaminated by the effects of suggestion to enable psychoanalytic theory to be underwritten by clinical data. Since these hypotheses rely wholly on inductive reasoning and methods, they must be vulnerable to refutation by induction; and he points out that Freud himself supplies the refuting evidence (Grünbaum et al. 1986, p. 222). He concludes that with no alternative trial in sight, psychoanalytic knowledge and the method by which it is reached cannot count as scientifically valid. Grünbaum's findings are not in dispute (but see Arthur Caplan, in ibid., p. 228), but the suppositions and conclusions that go with them are.

12 Though if a magnet were around, the 'circular array' would be accompanied by further physical signs.

13 Quantum physics is usually cited at this point as a theoretical system for which determinism is an inadequate foundation; but it is precisely this that makes it so disruptive to normal scientific assumptions. In practical living and basic scientific applications, physical determination remains a necessary presupposition.

14 Patricia Churchland (1986) and Paul Churchland (1984/1988) are leading advocates of this approach, which they urge should replace all other practical and philosophical accounts of the mind. For an interesting debate between Paul Churchland and Alasdair MacIntyre, who takes the other view, see Churchland (1998a, 1998b) and MacIntyre (1998). See also Sorell (1991, ch. 6).

15 Appendix 2 gives a summary of Donald Davidson's detailed analysis of this incompatibility.
16 Or rather: phenomena conceived physicalistically are reducible to mathematical formulation, but phenomena conceived mentalistically are not. No actual physical (or mental) substance is required.
17 It could also be that it is wrong, and that human beings (and probably some animals) acquire a degree of causal power which sets their actions apart from other natural phenomena.
18 Beck (1998, ch. 1) sets out this 'self-stultification' argument in 'Can a Human Machine Think?'
19 The Freudian original is less dogmatic than Grünbaum's version (Freud 1915c, S.E. 14, pp. 265–266).
20 See also his discussion of the meanings of 'meaning' in Grünbaum (2002, pp. 131–134 above).
21 This is one of the areas discussed in detail in David Sachs' 'Critical Notice of *The Foundations of Psychoanalysis*' (1989).
22 Grünbaum's routine objection is the possibility of contamination by suggestion; but as Sachs (1989) and others point out, this would equally apply to his 'obvious' examples and to 'commonsense' explanations in general.
23 Thus it would not be anti-psychoanalytic if other people, other times and other cultures should come up with modified or different subjective signs of the same unconscious processes.

3 'Freud's Permanent Revolution'

1 This theme is central to Nagel's philosophical position. He develops it independently of psychoanalysis in *The View from Nowhere* (1986).
2 Nagel sees this as the natural response of 'every creature with the impulse and capacity to transcend its particular point of view and to conceive of the world as a whole' (Nagel 1986, p. 3).
3 This objection would also apply, of course, to Grünbaum's own criterion of 'commonsense credibility' (see p. 31 above).
4 In a postscript added in 1969 Kuhn does, however, specify general 'values' which tend to mark out a scientific 'crisis' from a 'puzzle', and may help guide the choice between alternative paradigms. The most important is that 'predictions . . . should be accurate', and preferably quantitative (measurable) rather than qualitative. Theoretical features such as the potential for 'puzzle-formulation and solution', simplicity and coherence are also included, with 'plausibility' treated as consistency with other current theories (Kuhn 1996, p. 185).
5 One wonders, uncomfortably, just how far a psychoanalytic outlook would have spread into the public sphere without its exploitation for social control. Western governments and business interests apparently took up basic psychoanalytic ideas through the development of 'public relations' from wartime propaganda by Freud's wife's American nephew, Edward Bernays, in the 1920s (BBC2, 2002).
6 Nagel is taking the essence of psychoanalysis as the practical assumption of unconscious motivation. Grünbaum is identifying it with a range of causal propositions such as his causal concept of repression. In his *Critique of Psychoanalysis* he adds: 'How does the strength of the cultural influence of . . . religious beliefs and practices compare to that of Freud's teachings?' (p. 227 above). But this is not to compare like with like: Grünbaum is failing to differentiate between mentalistic and physicalistic concepts. Concepts which are taken to be practical, such as the recognition in consciousness of something which a clinical psychoanalytic concept describes best, can only be validated subjectively. Concepts which are taken to be substantive, including

the concrete existence of God or the devil, have traditionally been subjected to a different form of validation by empirical science.

7 'What else could it be?' he asks (Freud 1938b, S.E. 23, p. 282).

8 He is explicit that 'no new sources of knowledge or methods of research have come into being' (Freud 1932, S.E. 22, p. 159, also quoted in Grünbaum 1984, p. 2).

9 It was this, after all, that undermined Grünbaum's physicalistic treatment of psychoanalytic phenomena.

10 Freud is referring to conscious mental processes, but his point is applicable to all mental processes, conscious and unconscious. See Nagel (1974, p. 20) for discussion of this passage.

4 Self-Reflection as Science

1 Positivism was first brought in as an all-embracing system of knowledge by Auguste Comte, in the nineteenth century. The details of his system have been largely relinquished, but its overriding faith in normal empirical methodology is commonplace in empirical science, leading Habermas to ally positivism with scientism: 'Positivism stands and falls with the principle of scientism, that is, that the meaning of knowledge is defined by what the sciences do' (Habermas 1971, p. 67).

2 Quoted in McCarthy (1984, p. 58) in a concise exposition of Habermas' domains of knowledge.

3 Grünbaum is making this point when he remonstrates to Popper that 'even a circular array of iron filings does not deductively guarantee the presence of a magnet' (quoted on p. 25 above).

4 See Chapters 10 ('Self-Reflection as Science') and 11 ('The Scientistic Self-Misunderstanding of Metapsychology'); the latter is reprinted in Part II.

5 Habermas (1971) retranslates 'speech' as 'language' in this quote.

6 This use of 'game' does not imply manipulation or 'bad faith', but solely the framework of meaning taken on by all communicators.

7 This applies not only to obvious symbols such as words and signs, but also to quite basic physical gestures. Nodding and shaking one's head, the 'thumbs-up' sign, and even Stevie Smith's 'not waving but drowning' all mean different things depending on the context.

8 In his earlier theory, Freud defines these as the sexual instincts, in the service of the preservation of the species, and the ego-instincts such as hunger and aggression, directed towards the preservation of the individual (see Freud 1914c, S.E. 14). He introduces the later pairing of Eros, or the life instincts, and the death instincts in 'Beyond the Pleasure Principle' (1920, S.E. 18).

9 This seems to be the root of Grünbaum's misunderstanding of Habermas' reading of psychoanalysis. Grünbaum is taking repression itself, rather than the disturbing circumstance, to be the putative 'cause' of neurosis. This leads him to ridicule what he then sees as Habermas' confused attempt to invent a redundant concept of 'psychological' causal power. See Grünbaum (1984, p. 11).

10 This is a term introduced by the philosopher Georg Hegel, whose influence on Habermas' communicational reading of psychoanalysis is considerable. The 'causality of fate' is instigated when a personal phenomenon is banished, in imagination, to the realm of the impersonal. In psychoanalytic terms, part of the 'I' is treated as an 'it', and experienced as an external causal impact. This dissociation can be overcome only by recognizing that the repudiated symbolic structure is after all part of the subject, or 'I', reintegrating it into the individual's avowed subjectivity and its shared ground in intersubjectivity. The harmony of symbol, behaviour and emotional expression is restored through recognition, rather than through a technical procedure as in the

'causality of nature'. See Bernstein (1995) for a full discussion of this perspective in Habermas' work.

11 Christopher Nichols (1972) does so explicitly. He argues that the concept of the id is derived from Georg Groddeck's biological theory, and as such lies outside the sphere of self-reflection. Jonathan Lear (1990) makes the same point about the death instinct. The situation is complicated by Habermas' mentalistic interpretation of all psychoanalytic concepts, including these. Nevertheless, their use in psychoanalytic theory is based on clinical rather than biological considerations, leaving his main point intact.

12 Or a quasi-optical instrument, such as a microscope or telescope, the other analogy Freud introduces in *The Interpretation of Dreams* and refers to intermittently thereafter. See Freud (1900, S.E. 5, p. 536), quoted in Habermas (1971, p. 156 above).

13 These methods of treatment might include empirical psychological approaches such as cognitive approaches to psychotherapy, in which the aim is indeed the relief of symptoms over and above the gaining of insight.

14 See Habermas (1971, pp. 228–236). Strictly speaking, as Nichols (1972) points out, the id as genetic heritage must remain untouched by psychoanalysis or anything short of evolution. What Freud must mean in this careless phrase is what Habermas consistently takes as the 'id': the repressed ego, which according to Freud 'merges into' but is not the id. See diagrams and commentaries (Freud 1923, S.E. 19, p. 24; 1932, S.E. 22, p. 78).

15 We have seen that these tests could function only as secondary forms of evaluation, but Freud might still have thought that they might be better than nothing.

16 He reconceives the drives, for example, as 'twisted and diverted intentions that have turned from conscious motives into causes and subjected communicative action to the [seeming] causality of natural conditions' (1971, p. 161 above). He is saying that the Freudian drives or instincts are more readily conceived along psychological than biological lines: they only appear to exert an external causal force on behaviour and experience, in a further instance of the 'causality of fate'.

17 This too could be questioned (see 'Conclusions', pp. 103–104 above), but again it does not affect the main thrust of Habermas' argument.

18 This is partly what Kuhn is getting at, in saying that different paradigms offer different interpretations of the same 'reality'.

19 As has happened, for example, in accounts of the self and its travails which take religious interpretations of experience as concrete realities.

20 Habermas is referring to Freud's divisions of mental representations into primitive 'thing-presentations', which are mainly visual in nature, and symbolic 'word-presentations', which are predominantly aural. See Freud (1915a, S.E. 14, pp. 201–204).

21 Habermas is drawing on Alfred Lorenzer's linguistic theory of 'instinctual dynamics' (Lorenzer 1970a, 1970b).

5 The apparatus of the soul

1 See Laplanche (1976, 1992) for discussion.

2 The principle is not one of the three metapsychological principles, but the principle on which they themselves must rest.

3 In an earlier paper, Freud (1912b, S.E. 12, p. 261) describes how previously hypnotized subjects routinely perform actions which were suggested to them while they were under hypnosis. Since they have no memory of this suggestion, they produce a secondary rationalization for performing the action while unaware of the 'real' reason.

4 Freud was fond of quoting Charcot's adage, 'theory is good, but it doesn't stop things from existing' (e.g. Freud 1893a, S.E. 3, p. 13).

5 He is proposing a third conceptual domain of unitary structures and processes with subjective and organic 'sides', inhabiting their own region and operating under their own principles. Thus he did not regard psychical elements 'as localized in organic elements of the nervous system but rather . . . between them . . . Everything that can be an object of our internal perception is virtual, like the image produced in a telescope by the passage of light rays' (Freud 1900, S.E. 5, p. 611). 'Psycho-analysis . . . has led to a knowledge of characteristics of the unconscious psychical . . . and it has discovered some of the laws which govern it' (1938b, S.E. 23, p. 286).

6 As he advises 'physicians' under challenge to shrug their shoulders (Freud 1900, S.E. 5, p. 612).

7 Those who can think outside the dominant Western metaphysic, in which this division is at its most stark, may have more flexibility at their disposal. This aspiration is reflected in the work of authors such as Fritjof Capra (1982). His Eastern-influenced scientific thinking tends to be rather ungrounded, but points towards a direction for further enquiry.

8 This remains the case even with modern developments in neuropsychology. Freud puts it: 'Everything that lies between [the brain and experience of consciousness] is unknown to us, and the data do not include any direct relation between these two terminal points of our knowledge'. Nothing that is open to observation can tell us how physical processes come to appear as mental phenomena; for '[if] it existed, it would at the most afford an exact localization of the processes of consciousness and would give us no help towards understanding them' (1938a, S.E. 23, pp. 144–145).

9 Freud's later education took place at the conjunction of two opposing streams of thought, represented by different teachers closely associated with them. In the associationist psychological philosophy of Johann Herbart, priority is given to what is recorded in the mind over anything that might exist outside it. Herbart (1776–1841) worked in the wake of Kant, attempting to discern a mathematical basis for psychology; it could then be placed before rather than after the natural sciences in the hierarchy of knowledge. He uses a number of 'Freudian' terms and concepts, including repression, 'free' and 'bound' mental representations, and the pervasiveness of mental conflict (see Leader 2000, ch. 1; Leary 1980). At the same time, the 'biophysical' programme of Hermann von Helmholtz and his colleagues in the '1847 group' aimed to eliminate the conceptual hiatus between physics and the life sciences by rigorous physical reduction. The group vowed (in 1847) to prove that organic processes could be reduced to inorganic processes, and ultimately to atomic motion. When this proved too elusive a goal, Helmholtz (1821–1894) sought to unify different modes of explanation by identifying the processes of perception and thought on which explanatory validity must rest (see Cranefield 1966; Galaty 1974). Since one of Freud's teachers was a member of the group, and Herbartian influence was widespread at the time, it is not surprising that his ideas bear the imprint of these opposing currents.

10 *Vorstellungen*, often translated as 'ideas', but sometimes (and more accurately) as 'representations' or 'presentations'. The associationist conception of mental processes is a mental version of atomism. It recurs in many contexts, from John Locke in the seventeenth century to current neuroscience.

11 Accepting this does not commit us to Freud's stated metapsychological forms of organization; just to some that belong specifically to this level.

12 The inconsistency is sometimes because Freud does not make the context of his thought explicit and therefore treats the registration of reality as reality itself. At other times, he appears to revert to a standard materialist view, as in his unqualified definition of 'reality' as 'what exists outside us and independently of us' (1932, S.E. 22, p. 170). This demonstrates the fluidity of thought which defies all attempts to pin Freud's psychoanalysis down to any single theoretical categorization; but it would still

be more consistent, and more satisfactory for psychoanalysis, if this were qualified as 'what *we take to* exist outside us and independently of us'.

13 Again, Freud's stated metapsychological principles could be varied without detracting from the main picture.

14 Kant had concluded that space and time must go back to the way in which the mind works, rather than to the world outside the mind. With this in mind, Freud posits space but not time as a 'necessary [form] of thought' (1920, S.E. 18, p. 28), or rather of mentation as basic mental (or psychical) activity. Since unconscious mental processes do not appear to carry any reference to time, are not ordered sequentially and are not altered by time, Freud concludes that time is not a feature of unconscious mental processes, although it is a necessary feature of conscious or rational thinking. Thus in his view, 'spaceless' mental processes are a contradiction in terms, but 'timeless' mental processes are not. However, this seems dubious: as Werner Prall (personal communication, June 22, 2004) points out, the psychoanalytic concept of the wish contains the concept of the future within it.

15 A window as the 'mirror of nature' that Richard Rorty (1980) is at pains to refute. Rorty is named as one of Nagel's prime targets in his fulminations against relativism (1995, p. 9).

16 Explananda are the things psychoanalysis (or philosophy) explains.

17 See Gordon and Mayo (2004), particularly the editors' introduction and the chapter by Barbara Latham, for accounts of a psychoanalytic approach which seems closest to expressing this ideal.

18 Gardner adds that 'to show this would require a more intimate engagement with psychoanalysis than its critics have frequently accorded it.' He has been discussing the views of Popper and Grünbaum.

19 Some philosophical views consider that there is no such 'raw sensation' component, but only interpretations.

20 These desires are not to be confused with the psychoanalytic sense of unconscious desire.

21 'Intentionality' is a philosophical term which denotes both purposiveness and 'about-ness'. Intentional accounts of the mind present mental states as carrying direction and as being 'about' something. See Crane (2001, ch. 1) for a clear and helpful introductory account.

22 It is one of the mental quirks that disappear in the philosophical 'cleaning-up' process of bringing mental phenomena into the propositional frame.

23 The personal psychological network, or 'set', is termed the 'propositional network'; the 'beliefs, desires and intentions' which make it up are known as 'propositional attitudes' (Gardner 1993, p. 250).

24 Gardner argues against various such philosophical views, including Sartre's verdict of conscious self-manipulation ('bad faith'), Dennett's assumption of the mental equivalent of faulty wiring, and Davidson's contorted account of a 'mental cause that is not a reason' but is nevertheless rationally explicable.

25 It is also the detritus into which they regress: 'the state that was a propositional desire endures as a wish' (Gardner 1993, p. 123).

26 These wishes are not to be confused with the generalized wishes of ordinary conscious psychology.

27 Hallucination is the psychoanalytic term for this normal mode of primitive psychical functioning.

28 For example, an unconscious wish to see ourselves in a certain way can lead us to believe that this is who we are; equally, an inclination towards a certain interpretation of events can mean that this is what we think is happening.

29 'Anna Fweud, stwawbewwies, wild stwawbewwies, omblet, pudden!' She had gone to bed without food because of a stomach upset.

30 'On the day after his birthday sacrifice he awoke with a cheerful piece of news, which could only have originated from a dream: "Hermann eaten all the chewwies!"'

31 Phantasy was not discovered by psychoanalysis, of course. Authors from Shakespeare to Dostoevsky bring their characters to life through invoking the shadow of phantasy in their actions and choices. Phantasy makes them real in a way that their propositional thinking never could. Tragedy, similarly, consists of the enactment of ubiquitous phantasies, with spectators experiencing the clash of personal involvement and impersonal inexorability (Hegel's 'causality of fate'). Freud points this out in relation to the Oedipus myth. The possibility of control is also apparent in 'lucid dreaming', where, with practice, it is possible to know that one is dreaming, and to alter the course of events to a limited extent.

32 While, strictly speaking, 'psychoanalytic theory is . . . logically neutral between philosophical theories of the person or the self' (p. 206), Gardner points out that it inclines nevertheless towards a concept of the person which reflects the biological basis of the wish, and the general 'intertwining of the mental and the physical' (ibid.). This enquiry goes one step further, to say that that at every level of psychoanalysis, the mental and the physical are not 'intertwined', but at one.

33 Much of Gardner's study is taken up with countering 'partitive' views of the psychoanalytic psyche, from Sartre's to Donald Davidson's. Psychoanalysis postulates mental systems, or agencies, which sometimes seem to act in dislocation from each other. But these, Gardner explains, are no more a threat to the unity of personhood than analogous expressions in everyday life or literary evocation. Psychoanalytic explanations do not require us to suspend our idea of ourselves as persons: we cannot make use of them without it.

34 'Instinct' or intuition may seem to offer sufficient justification for one's own purposes, especially our less examined purposes, but neither provides sufficient justification for why others should accept these views. General or theoretical enquiries or systems have to be justified by 'reasons', underpinned by the rules of logic as the shared foundation of rational thought.

35 The 'individuals' of his title.

36 Part of the qualifying characteristic of a 'material body' is a degree of endurance over time. He includes fields and rivers, for example (p. 46), but not 'shafts of light or volumes of coloured gas' (p. 40). An entire chapter (ch. 2, 'Sounds') is given over to working out why sounds cannot form the basis of a conceptual framework that human beings could make use of.

37 The 'pure ego' was, as Strawson notes, the rock on which the eighteenth century Scottish philosopher, David Hume, ran aground. Instead of a constant centre of consciousness, he found only 'a bundle of perceptions' to hand. This led Kant to accord the subject of experience 'a purely formal unity' as a presupposition of experience, rather than a component of experience. Wittgenstein then went on to suggest 'firstly that there is no such thing, and then that it is not a part of the world, but its limit' (Strawson 1959, p. 103).

38 'Predicate' is a grammatical term which is the counterpart of 'subject'. It refers to something that is said of a subject. For example, in 'the house is green', 'the house' is the subject, and 'is green' is the predicate.

39 Descartes, for example, saw animals as machines without souls. Conversely, the general view today is that with the possible exception of the most primitive creatures, animals are more like persons than inanimate objects.

40 They also constitute the primary reference point for more abstract intentionality and more sophisticated communicational structures. Strawson's project does not require him to go into detail on this point; but it is difficult to see how language and conceptual thought could develop other than through gestures, which effectively make use of the recognizability of intentionality for expressive and communicational purposes.

41   Thus the environmental condition of personhood is, if anything, more transparent than the biological. We do not know, at least in a practical sense, the physiological conditions for the capacity to wish; and in any case, this can only develop by treating the individual as though it were already there. This makes it reasonable to treat as 'persons' all human organisms in which the ability to wish might develop, continue in abeyance or conceivably remain: the unborn, the comatose and the newly dead.

42   Such knowledge is not formulated, of course. The assumption of universal animacy is seen in non-industrialized societies, including pre-industrial Europe, as well as in individuals. It may be demonstrable through empirical studies of early childhood in the tradition of Piaget (Piaget and Inhelder 1969), and survives, perhaps, in our liking for magic and machinery, for nature and for inanimate objects which are special to us. This continues into adulthood, and is not completely explicable as interest and affection transferred from their original, external or internal human 'objects'.

43   This could be thought of as both a new slant on the same conceptual scheme, and an archaic configuration pressing on our normal ways of thinking in the same way that phantasy bears upon propositional rationality.

44   Most paradoxes fall into one of these two categories of contradiction or tautology. Nagel describes how there are some questions that we know in advance can be answered, even if we do not know the answer. The chemical composition of gold may elude us, or that of a newly discovered metal may be as yet unknown; but our ordinary pre-scientific concept of substance contains a 'blank space to be filled in by the discovery of the real, and essential chemical composition' (Nagel 1998, p. 344). There are other questions which we know in advance cannot be answered, because the terms they employ preclude it: 'we do not need a scientific investigation to be certain that the number 379 does not have parents' (ibid., p. 339). Neither situation applies to the question of how physical phenomena can also 'be' subjective experience.

45   Nagel makes direct use only of Strawson's later works, but includes *Individuals* as an example of a 'version' of dual aspect theory, as well as Davidson's 'Mental Events' (see Appendix 1). See Nagel (1986, p. 30, fn.).

6   Conclusions

1   To recoil the better to jump.

2   It has something in common with Roy Bhaskar's empirically-slanted 'critical natural-ism' (Archer et al. 1998), as well as Habermas' hermeneutically-inclined 'critical science'. It also recalls the seventeenth-century rationalist approach to external knowledge; see Kerz-Rühling (1996) for a rationalist view of psychoanalysis which takes up Grünbaum's critique.

3   This sense of reflection is wider than rationality, and includes experience.

4   Psychoanalysis now appears a less fixed and more 'critical' subject than even Habermas or Gardner seems happy to conclude. Both appear to allot psychoanalytic theory as it is given precedence over reflection. However, on each of their accounts, there is a loss of reflective potential to the extent that its concepts are taught or learned, rather than recognized. This is not to say that psychoanalytic practice must be confined to the 'lowest common denominator'; just that its interpretations should be individually rather than generally inspired, and should arise from the intersubjective therapeutic setting rather than straight from the theoretical preconceptions of the therapist. Psychotherapists as well as patients can only make therapeutic use of theory that they have assimilated and modified as personal knowledge. Although psychoanalysis reflects Freud's scientific knowledge, it does not stand or fall by it.

5   Of course, people will also make therapeutic use of personal knowledge from outside psychoanalysis.

6   See again Gordon and Mayo (2004).

7 There is also the rapidly changing nature of neuroscience and other relevant disciplines
   to contend with. However definite their conclusions seem in 2005, they are likely to
   look very different in 2055.

Nagel: Freud's Permanent Revolution and Addendum

1 Cambridge University Press and Harvard University Press, 1984.
2 Thames & Hudson and Princeton University Press, 1987.
3 This theme appears at various points in Freud's writings, including the 'Project for a
   Scientific Psychology' (1895), 'The Unconscious' (1915a), and 'An Outline of
   Psycho-Analysis' (1938a).
4 University of California Press, 1984. Grünbaum argues that Freud rests his case for
   the theory of repression on the superior therapeutic effectiveness of psychoanalysis
   in treating neuroses, and that such evidence is not available. His reading of Freud,
   and of the evidence, clinical and extraclinical, has been extensively criticized, notably
   by David Sachs, 'In Fairness to Freud' (1989), and by various commentators in
   Behavioral and Brain Sciences 9 (Grünbaum 1986). More recently Grünbaum has
   published *Validation in the Clinical Theory of Psychoanalysis* (International
   Universities Press, 1993), a further discussion of these issues, which includes both new
   material and versions of previously published essays, some predating *The Foundations
   of Psychoanalysis*.
5 *The Psychopathology of Everyday Life* (1901), Chapter 2.
6 See 'Mourning and Melancholia' (1915d/1917). Freud emphasizes that his proposal
   applies only to some cases of melancholia, and that others appear to be somatic in
   origin.
7 Bradley is the subject of Wollheim's first book, *F.H. Bradley* (Penguin, 1959).
8 A collection of essays on Wollheim's work contains two valuable discussions of this
   question by Marcia Cavell and Samuel Scheffler. Both of them argue that a more
   objective and less 'self'-centered conception of morality may be consistent with a
   psychoanalytic theory of moral development. See Jim Hopkins and Anthony Savile
   (eds) *Psychoanalysis, Mind and Art: Perspectives on Richard Wollheim* (Blackwell,
   1992). Scheffler develops his ideas on the subject further in *Human Morality* (Oxford
   University Press, 1992), and Cavell sets out her position in *The Psychoanalytic Mind:
   From Freud to Philosophy* (Harvard University Press, 1993), which includes a
   plausible critique of Freud's theory of morality.
9 In addition to Grünbaum's (1984) book, Robinson (1993) discusses Sulloway's *Freud,
   Biologist of the Mind* (Basic Books, 1979) and Masson's *The Assault on Truth:
   Freud's Suppression of the Seduction Theory* (Farrar, Straus & Giroux, 1984), drawing
   also on some of the responses these works have attracted.
10 It has resulted in some dreadful persecutions of the innocent. For example *The New
   York Times* of November 21, 1993 (p. 29) reported the acquittal of a Sunday school
   teacher charged with lurid rapes and tortures on the basis of testimony elicited from his
   pupils, who were three or four years old at the time.
11 For example in his 1916–1917 *Introductory Lectures on Psycho-Analysis* (*Standard
   Edition* vol. 16, p. 255).
12 Quoted in Ernest Jones, *The Life and Work of Sigmund Freud* (Basic Books, 1957),
   vol. 3, p. 203.
13 See Hopkins's 'Introduction: Philosophy and Psychoanalysis', in R. Wollheim and
   J. Hopkins (eds) *Philosophical Essays on Freud* (Cambridge University Press, 1982),
   Davidson's 'Paradoxes of Irrationality' in the same volume, and Hopkins's
   'Epistemology and Depth Psychology: Critical Notes on *The Foundations of
   Psychoanalysis*', in S. Clark and C. Wright (eds) *Mind, Psychoanalysis, and Science*
   (Blackwell, 1988).

14 Grünbaum had asked, 'If pervasive cultural influence were evidence of validity, then religious superstitions and ethnic canards or stereotypes, which are far more prevalent than Freud's ideas, as well as earlier witchcraft and slavery ought to possess a high degree of validity. Does Nagel apply his cultural criterion to them as well? If not, why not?'

15 Incidentally, the extended reach of the mind is also revealed in a completely different way – by the recent discovery that physiological processes ordinarily completely involuntary, like heartbeat and blood pressure, can be brought under conscious, voluntary control with the right kind of training.

Habermas: The Scientistic Self-Misunderstanding of Metapsychology

1 'An Autobiographical Study', *Standard Edition*, vol. 20, p. 20.
2 'What else can it be?' ('Some Elementary Lessons in Psycho-Analysis', S.E. 23, p. 282).
3 *New Introductory Lectures*, S.E. 22, p. 159.
4 'Some Elementary Lessons', S.E. 23, p. 282.
5 'An Outline of Psycho-Analysis', S.E. 23, p. 196.
6 Ibid., S.E. 23, p. 182.
7 The three parts that Freud sent to Fliess in October 1895 were first published in 1950 as an appendix to the collection of letters *Aus den Anfängen der Psychoanalyse*, translated as *Origins of Psychoanalysis* (New York: Basic Books). See Ernest Jones, *The Life and Work of Sigmund Freud* (New York: Basic Books, 1953), vol. 1, pp. 379 ff.
8 See Jones, ibid., p. 385.
9 *The Interpretation of Dreams*, S.E. 5, p. 536.
10 Ibid., S.E. 5, p. 537.
11 Ibid., S.E. 5, p. 598.
12 Ibid., S.E. 5, pp. 598f.
13 'An Autobiographical Study', S.E. 20, p. 22.
14 'Remembering, Repeating, and Working-Through', S.E. 12, pp. 155f.
15 'Recommendations to Physicians Practising Psychoanalysis', S.E. 12, p. 114.
16 'Analysis Terminable and Interminable', S.E. 23, p. 225.
17 *New Introductory Lectures*, S.E. 22, p. 22.
18 Or quasi-action: selection is a substitute for the actual manipulation of the initial conditions.
19 Alfred Lorenzer, *Kritik des psychoanalytischen Symbolbegriffs* and *Sprachzerstörung und –Rekonstruktion* (both published in Frankfurt am Main in 1970 by Suhrkamp Verlag).
20 Alasdair MacIntyre's separation of motive and cause in *The Unconscious* (London: Routledge & Kegan Paul, 1958) makes this relationship unrecognizable.
21 Translator's note: *Vorgriff*, here translated as 'anticipation', means an interpretive concept or model that pre-structures that to which it is applied.
22 See Arthur Danto, *Analytical Philosophy of History* (Cambridge: Cambridge University Press, 1965), pp. 143ff. Translator's note: The German *Geschichte*, like the French *histoire*, means both 'history' and 'story'.
23 See Habermas (1971, ch. 8).
24 'Lines of Advance in Psycho-Analytic Therapy', S.E. 17, p. 167.
25 'Constructions in Analysis', S.E. 23, p. 262.
26 'Remarks on the Theory and Practice of Dream-Interpretation', S.E. 19, p. 115.
27 See MacIntyre (1958, pp. 112 ff).
28 'Constructions in Analysis', S.E. 23, p. 262.

29 'In short, we conduct ourselves on the model of a familiar figure in one of Nestroy's farces – the manservant who has a single answer on his lips to every question or objection: "It will all become clear in the course of future developments".' (Ibid., S.E. 23, p. 265.)

30 *Introductory Lectures on Psycho-Analysis*, S.E. 16, p. 436.

31 See Danto (1965, chs X, XI, pp. 201ff).

Bibliography

The New York Review of Books exchange

1993	November 18	Crews, F., 'The Unknown Freud'.
1994	February 3	Letters include responses from J. Schimek, one of Crews' sources, dissociating himself from what he considers the reckless use made of his work; J. Hopkins, a philosopher with a special interest in psychoanalysis, disputing the interpretations of published material on which Crews bases his main claims; and H. Blum and B. Pacella of the Sigmund Freud Archives, deploring Crews' offensive tone and inaccurate use of source material.
	April 21	Further letters.
	May 12	Nagel, T., 'Freud's Permanent Revolution'.
	August 11	Letters, including Grünbaum's response to Nagel and Nagel's 'Addendum' answering Grünbaum.
	November 17	Crews, F., 'The Revenge of the Repressed, Part I', attacking the 'recovered memory movement' as a current example of the damage wreaked by what he considers the unsubstantiated hypothesis of repression.
	December 1	'The Revenge of the Repressed, Part II'.
1995	January–April	Further correspondence, with some discussion of Nagel's review.

References

Archer, M., Bhaskar, R., Collier, A., Lawson, T. and Norrie, A. (eds) (1998) *Critical Realism: Essential Readings*. London and New York: Routledge.

Arlow, J. and Brenner, C. (1964) *Psychoanalytic Concepts and the Structural Theory*. New York: International Universities Press.

—— (1988) 'The Future of Psychoanalysis', *Psychoanalytic Quarterly* 57, pp. 1–14.

Assoun, P. (1995) *Freud, la Philosophie, et les Philosophes*. Paris: Presses Universitaires de France.

Bachrach, H., Galatzer-Levy, R., Skolnikoff, A. and Waldron, S. (1991) 'On the Efficacy of Psychoanalysis', *Journal of the American Psychoanalytic Association* 39, pp. 871–916.

Basch, M. (1994) 'Psychoanalysis, Science and Epistemology', *Bulletin of the [Chicago] Institute for Psychoanalysis* 4, no. 2, p. 1; pp. 8–9.

BBC (2002) *Century of the Self* (series of BBC 2 television programmes), March.

Beck, L.W. (1998) *The Actor and the Spectator*. Bristol: Thoemmes. First published 1975 New Haven, Conn. and London: Yale University Press.

Bernstein, J.M. (1995) *Recovering Ethical Life: Jürgen Habermas and the Future of Critical Theory*. London: Routledge.

Borch-Jacobsen, M. (1996) *Remembering Anna O.: 100 Years of Psychoanalytic Mystification*. New York: Routledge.

Brenner, C. (1982) *The Mind in Conflict*. New York: International Universities Press.

Brentano, B. (1995) *Psychology from an Empirical Standpoint*. New York: Routledge & Kegan Paul.

Breuer, J. and Freud, S. (1893) 'On the Psychical Mechanism of Hysterical Phenomena: Preliminary Communication', *Standard Edition of the Complete Psychological Works of Sigmund Freud, Volume 2*, pp. 1–17. London: Hogarth Press.

—— (1893–1895) *Studies on Hysteria, Standard Edition 2*.

Bröder, A. (1995) *Unbewusstes semantisches Priming laborinduzierter Sprechfehler*. Bonn: University of Bonn. '*Diplomarbeit*' in psychology.

Bröder, A. and Bredenkamp, J. (1996) 'SLIP-Technik, Prozessdissoziationsmodell und multinomiale Modellierrung: Neue Werkzeuge zum experimentellen Nachweis "Freudscher versprecher"?', *Zeitschrift für experimentelle Psychologie* 43, pp. 175–202.

Capra, F. (1982) *The Turning Point: Science, Society and the Rising Culture*. New York: Simon & Schuster; London: Wildwood House.

Carrier, M. and Mittelstrass, J. (1991) *Mind, Brain, Behavior: The Mind–Body Problem and the Philosophy of Psychology*. New York: Walter de Gruyter.

Cavell, M. (1993) *The Psychoanalytic Mind: From Freud to Philosophy*. Cambridge, Mass. and London: Harvard University Press.

Churchland, Patricia (1986) *Neurophilosophy: Toward a Unified Science of the Mind-Brain*. Cambridge, Mass. and London: MIT Press.

Churchland, Paul (1984/1988) *Matter and Consciousness*. Cambridge, Mass. and London: MIT Press.

—— (1998a) 'Précis of *The Engine of Reason*', *Philosophy and Phenomenological Research* 58, no. 4, pp. 859–863.

—— (1998b) 'Replies', *Philosophy and Phenomenological Research* 58, no. 4, pp. 893–904.

Clark, S. and Wright, C. (eds) (1988) *Mind, Psychoanalysis, and Science*. Oxford: Blackwell.

Cleckley, H. (1988) *The Mask of Sanity*, 5th edn. Augusta, Ga.: Emily S. Cleckley.

Cohen, R.S. and Laudan, L. (eds) (1983) *Physics, Philosophy, and Psychoanalysis: Essays in Honor of Adolf Grünbaum*. Dordrecht: Reidel.

Crane, T. (2001) *Elements of Mind*. Oxford: Oxford University Press.

Cranefield, P. (1966) 'The Philosophical and Cultural Interests of the Biophysics Movement of 1847', *Journal of the History of Medicine and Allied Sciences* 21, pp. 1–7.

Crews, F. (1993) 'The Unknown Freud', *New York Review of Books* 40, no. 19, pp. 55–66.

—— (1994a) 'The Revenge of the Repressed', *New York Review of Books* 41, no. 19, pp. 54–60.

—— (1994b) 'The Revenge of the Repressed: Part II', *New York Review of Books* 41, no. 20, pp. 49–58.

—— (1995) *The Memory Wars: Freud's Legacy in Dispute*. New York: New York Review of Books.

Danto, A. (1965) *Analytical Philosophy of History*. Cambridge: Cambridge University Press.

Davidson, D. (1970) 'Mental Events', in *Essays on Actions and Events*, pp. 207–225. Oxford: Clarendon Press.

—— (1982) 'Paradoxes of Irrationality', in R. Wollheim and J. Hopkins (eds) *Philosophical Essays on Freud*. Cambridge and New York: Cambridge University Press.

—— (2001) *Essays on Actions and Events*, 2nd edn. Oxford: Clarendon Press.

Eagle, M. (1987) 'The Psychoanalytic and the Cognitive Unconscious', in R. Stern (ed.) *Theories of the Unconscious and Theories of the Self*, pp. 155–189. Hillsdale, NJ: Analytic Press.

—— (1993) 'The Dynamics of Theory Change in Psychoanalysis', in J. Earman, A. Janis, G. Massey and N. Rescher (eds) *Philosophical Problems of the Internal and External Worlds: Essays on the Philosophy of Adolf Grünbaum*, Chapter 15. Pittsburgh, Pa.: University of Pittsburgh Press.

Earman, J., Janis, A., Massey, G. and Rescher N. (eds) (1993) *Philosophical Problems of the Internal and External Worlds: Essays on the Philosophy of Adolf Grünbaum*. Pittsburgh, Pa.: University of Pittsburgh Press.

Edelson, M. (1984) *Hypothesis and Evidence in Psychoanalysis*. Chicago: University of Chicago Press.

—— (1986) 'Causal Explanation in Science and in Psychoanalysis', *Psychoanalytic Study of the Child* 41, pp. 89–127.

—— (1988) *Psychoanalysis: A Theory in Crisis*. Chicago: University of Chicago Press.

Ellenberger, H. (1970) *The Discovery of the Unconscious*. New York: Basic Books; London: Fontana (1994).

Erwin, E. (ed.) (2002) *The Freud Encyclopaedia: Theory, Therapy and Culture*. New York and London: Routledge.

Fenichel, O. (1945) *The Psychoanalytic Theory of Neurosis*. New York: Norton.

Forrester, J. (1997) *Dispatches from the Freud Wars*. Cambridge, Mass. and London: Harvard University Press.

Freud, S. (1893a) 'Charcot', *Standard Edition of the Complete Psychological Works of Sigmund Freud Volume 3*, pp. 11–23. London: Hogarth.

—— (1893b) 'On the Psychical Mechanism of Hysterical Phenomena', *Standard Edition 3*, pp. 27–39.

—— (1895/1950) 'Project for a Scientific Psychology', *Standard Edition 1*, pp. 295–397, and *Origins of Psychoanalysis*. New York: Basic Books.

—— (1896) 'Heredity and the Aetiology of the Neuroses', *Standard Edition 3*, pp. 143–156.

—— (1900) *The Interpretation of Dreams*, *Standard Edition 4*, pp. 1–338, and *5*, pp. 339–627.

—— (1901) *The Psychopathology of Everyday Life*, *Standard Edition 6*, pp. 1–279.

—— (1905a) 'Three Essays on the Theory of Sexuality', *Standard Edition 7*, pp. 130–243.

—— (1905b) 'Fragment of an Analysis of a Case of Hysteria', *Standard Edition 7*, pp. 249–254.

—— (1909) 'Notes Upon a Case of Obsessional Neurosis', *Standard Edition 10*, pp. 155–318.

—— (1910) '"Wild" Psycho-Analysis', *Standard Edition 11*, pp. 219–230.

—— (1911) 'Formulations on the Two Principles of Mental Functioning', *Standard Edition 11*, pp. 218–226.

—— (1912a) 'Recommendations to Physicians Practising Psychoanalysis', *Standard Edition 12*, pp. 109–120.

—— (1912b) 'A Note on the Unconscious in Psychoanalysis', *Standard Edition 12*, pp. 260–266.

—— (1913) 'The Claims of Psycho-Analysis to Scientific Interest', *Standard Edition 13*, pp. 165–190.

—— (1914a) 'Remembering, Repeating and Working Through', *Standard Edition 12*, pp. 145–156.

—— (1914b) 'On the History of the Psycho-Analytic Movement', *Standard Edition 14*, pp. 7–66.

—— (1914c) 'On Narcissism: An Introduction', *Standard Edition 14*, pp. 73–102.

—— (1915a) 'The Unconscious', *Standard Edition 14*, pp. 166–215.

—— (1915b) 'Repression', *Standard Edition 14*, pp. 146–158.

—— (1915c) 'A Case of Paranoia Running Counter to the Psycho-Analytic Theory of the Disease', *Standard Edition 14*, pp. 263–272.

—— (1915d/1917) 'Mourning and Melancholia', *Standard Edition 14*, pp. 243–258.

—— (1916–1917) *Introductory Lectures on Psycho-Analysis, Standard Edition 15*, pp. 1–239, and *16*.

—— (1918/1919) 'Lines of Advance in Psycho-Analytic Therapy', *Standard Edition 17*, pp. 157–168.

—— (1920) 'Beyond the Pleasure Principle', *Standard Edition 18*, pp. 7–64.

—— (1922a/1923) 'Two Encyclopaedia Articles', *Standard Edition 18*, pp. 235–259.

—— (1922b/1923) 'Remarks on the Theory and Practice of Dream-Interpretation', *Standard Edition 19*, pp. 109–122.

—— (1923) 'The Ego and the Id', *Standard Edition 19*, pp. 12–66.

—— (1924a) 'The Economic Problem of Masochism', *Standard Edition 19*, pp. 159–170.

—— (1924b) 'A Short Account of Psychoanalysis', *Standard Edition 19*, pp. 191–209.

—— (1924c/1925) 'An Autobiographical Study', *Standard Edition 20*, pp. 7–74.

—— (1926) 'The Question of Lay Analysis', *Standard Edition 20*, pp. 183–250.

—— (1932/1933) *New Introductory Lectures on Psychoanalysis, Standard Edition 22*, pp. 5–185.

—— (1937a) 'Analysis Terminable and Interminable', *Standard Edition 23*, pp. 209–253.

—— (1937b) 'Constructions in Analysis', *Standard Edition 23*, pp. 255–270.

—— (1938a/1940a) 'An Outline of Psycho-Analysis', *Standard Edition 23*, pp. 144–207.

—— (1938b/1940b) 'Some Elementary Lessons in Psycho-Analysis', *Standard Edition 23*, pp. 279–286.

—— (1938c/1941) 'Findings, Ideas, Problems', *Standard Edition 23*, pp. 299–300.

Fromkin, V. (ed.) (1980) *Errors in Linguistic Performance: Slips of the Tongue, Ear, Pen, and Hand*. New York and London: Academic Press.

Galaty, D. (1974) 'The Philosophical Basis of Mid-Nineteenth Century German Reductionism', *Journal of the History of Medicine and Allied Sciences* 29, pp. 295–316.

Gardner, S. (1993) *Irrationality and the Philosophy of Psychoanalysis*. Cambridge: Cambridge University Press.

Gay, P. (1987) *A Godless Jew: Freud, Atheism, and the Making of Psychoanalysis*. New Haven, Conn.: Yale University Press.

Geerardyn, F. (1997) *Freud's Project: On the Roots of Psychoanalysis*, trans. P. Vandendaele. London: Rebus. First published 1993 as *Freuds psychologie van het oordeel, Over het begin van de psychoanalyse*. Ghent: Idesça.

Glymour, C. (1983) 'The Theory of your Dreams', in R.S. Cohen and L. Laudan (eds) *Physics, Philosophy, and Psychoanalysis: Essays in Honor of Adolf Grünbaum*, pp. 57–71. Dordrecht: Reidel.

Goleman, D. (1994), 'Miscoding is Seen as the Root of False Memories', *New York Times*, May 31, pp. C1 and C8.

Gomez, L. (1997) *An Introduction to Object Relations*. London: Free Association Books; New York: New York University Press.

Gordon, P. and Mayo, R. (eds) (2004) *Between Psychotherapy and Philosophy*. London and Philadelphia, Pa.: Whurr.

Green, A. (1995–1996) 'Against Lacanism', *Journal of European Psychoanalysis* 2, pp. 169–185.

Grünbaum, A. (1973) *Philosophical Problems of Space and Time*, 2nd edn. Dordrecht: Reidel.

—— (1984) *The Foundations of Psychoanalysis: A Philosophical Critique*. Berkeley, Calif.: University of California Press.

—— (1986) Is Freud's Theory Well-founded?' *Behavioral and Brain Sciences* 9, pp. 266–281.

—— (1990) '"Meaning" Connections and Causal Connections in the Human Sciences: The Poverty of Hermeneutic Philosophy', *Journal of the American Psychoanalytic Association* 38, pp. 559–577.

—— (1993) *Validation in the Clinical Theory of Psychoanalysis: A Study in the Philosophy of Psychoanalysis*. Madison, Conn.: International Universities Press.

—— (1994) Letter to the Editor, *New York Review of Books* 41, no. 14, August 11, pp. 54–55. Contra Thomas Nagel's 'Freud's Permanent Revolution'.

—— (1997) 'Is the Concept of "Psychic Reality" a Theoretical Advance?' *Psychoanalysis and Contemporary Thought* 20, no. 2, pp. 83–105.

—— (2005) 'Critique of Freud's Neurobiological and Psychoanalytic Dream Theories', in A. Grünbaum, *Philosophy of Science in Action*, Vol. 2, Part 2. New York: Oxford University Press.

Grünbaum, A. with others (1986) 'Précis of *The Foundations of Psychoanalysis: A Philosophical Critique*', *Behavioral and Brain Sciences* 9, pp. 217–228, and 'Open Peer Commentary', pp. 228–284.

Habermas, J. (1971) *Knowledge and Human Interests*, trans. J.J. Shapiro. London: Heinemann. First published 1968 as *Erkenntnis und Interesse*. Frankfurt am Main: Suhrkamp Verlag.

—— (1973) *Theory and Practice*, trans. J. Viertel. Boston, Mass.: Beacon Press. First published 1968 as *Theorie und Praxis*. Neuwied/Berlin: Luchterhand. Expanded edition (1971), Frankfurt am Main: Suhrkamp Verlag.

Harman, G. (1965) 'Inference to the Best Explanation', *Philosophical Review* 74, pp. 88–95.

Holzman, P. (1994) 'Hilgard on Psychoanalysis as Science', *Psychological Science* 5, no. 4, pp. 190–191.

Hon, G. and Rackover, S.S. (eds) (2001) *Explanation: Theoretical Approaches and Applications*. Dordrecht: Kluwer.

Honderich, T. (1995) *The Oxford Companion to Philosophy*. Oxford and New York: Oxford University Press.

Hopkins, J. (1978) '"Mental States, Natural Kinds and Psychophysical Laws", Colin McGinn and James Hopkins, II – James Hopkins', in *Proceedings of the Aristotelian Society Supplement* 42, pp. 221–236.

—— (1982) 'Introduction: Philosophy and Psychoanalysis', in R. Wollheim and I. Hopkins (eds) *Philosophical Essays on Freud*. Cambridge and New York: Cambridge University Press.

—— (1988) 'Epistemology and Depth Psychology: Critical Notes on *The Foundations of Psychoanalysis*', in S. Clark and C. Wright (eds) *Mind, Psychoanalysis, and Science*. Oxford: Blackwell.

Hopkins, J. and Savile, A. (eds) (1992) *Psychoanalysis, Mind and Art: Perspectives on Richard Wollheim*. Oxford: Blackwell.

Isaacs, S. (1943) 'The Nature and Function of Phantasy', *International Journal of Psycho-Analysis* 29, pp. 73–97.

Jones, E. (1953/1957) *The Life and Work of Sigmund Freud*. New York: Basic Books; London: Hogarth.

Kernberg, O. (1993) 'Convergences and Divergences in Contemporary Psychoanalytic Technique', *International Journal of Psychoanalysis* 74, pp. 659–673.

Kerz-Rühling, I. (1996) 'The Validation of Psychoanalytical Hypotheses in Clinical Practice', *International Journal of Psycho-Analysis* 77, pp. 275–290.

Kohut, H. (1984) *How Does Analysis Cure?* Chicago: University of Chicago Press.

Kuhn, T. (1996) *The Structure of Scientific Revolutions*, 3rd edn. Chicago: University of Chicago Press. First published 1962.

Lakatos, I. (1973) 'Lectures on Scientific Method', in I. Lakatos and P. Feyerabend (1999) *For and Against Method*, ed. M. Motterlini, pp. 19–109. Chicago and London: University of Chicago Press.

Laplanche, J. (1976) *Life and Death in Psychoanalysis*, trans. Jeffrey Mehlman. Baltimore and London: Johns Hopkins University Press. First published 1970 as *Vie et mort en psychanalyse*. Paris: Flammarion.

—— (1992) 'Interpretation between Determinism and Hermeneutics', trans. P. Slotkin, *International Journal of Psycho-Analysis* 73, pp. 429–445. First given as a lecture to the Paris Psychoanalytical Society on January 15, 1991.

Laplanche, J. and Pontalis, J-B. (1973) *The Language of Psychoanalysis*, trans. Donald Nicholson-Smith. London: Hogarth Press. First published 1967 as *Vocabulaire de la psychanalyse*. Paris: Presses Universitaires de France.

Leader, D. (2000) *Freud's Footnotes*. London: Faber & Faber.

Lear, J. (1990) *Love and its Place in Nature: A Philosophical Interpretation of Freudian Psychoanalysis*. New York: Farrar, Straus & Giroux.

Leary, D. (1980) 'The Historical Foundation of Herbart's Mathematization of Psychology', *Journal of the History of the Behavioral Sciences* 16, pp. 150–163.

Leibniz, G. (c. 1705/1981) *New Essays on Human Understanding*, trans. P. Remnant and J. Bennett. Cambridge: Cambridge University Press.

Lorenzer, A. (1970a) *Kritik des psychoanalytischen Symbolbegriffs*. Frankfurt am Main: Suhrkamp Verlag.

—— (1970b) *Sprachzerstörung und -Rekonstruktion*. Frankfurt am Main: Suhrkamp Verlag.

McCarthy, T. (1984) *The Critical Theory of Jürgen Habermas*. Cambridge: Polity Press. First published 1978. Cambridge, Mass.: Massachusetts Institute of Technology Press.

MacIntyre, A. (1958) *The Unconscious*: *A Conceptual Analysis*. London: Routledge & Kegan Paul; New York: Humanities Press.
—— (1981) *After Virtue*. London: Duckworth.
—— (1998) 'What Can Moral Philosophers Learn from the Study of the Brain?' *Philosophy and Phenomenological Research* 58, no. 4, pp. 865–869.
Masson, J. (1984) *The Assault on Truth: Freud's Suppression of the Seduction Theory*. New York: Farrar, Straus & Giroux; London: Faber & Faber.
Meehl, P. (1995) 'Commentary: Psychoanalysis as Science', *Journal of the American Psychoanalytic Association* 43, no. 4, pp. 1015–1021.
Mill, J.S. (1843) 'A System of Logic', *Collected Works of John Stuart Mill*, vols. 7–8, ed. J. Robson (1961–1991). Toronto: University of Toronto; London: Routledge & Kegan Paul (1973–1974).
Motley, M. (1980) 'Verification of "Freudian Slips" and Semantic Prearticulatory Editing via Laboratory-induced Spoonerisms', in V. Fromkin (ed.) *Errors in Linguistic Performance: Slips of the Tongue, Ear, Pen, and Hand*, pp. 133–147. New York and London: Academic Press.
Nagel, T. (1974) 'Freud's Anthropomorphism', in *Other Minds*, pp. 13–25
—— (1986) *The View from Nowhere*. New York: Oxford University Press.
—— (1994a) 'Freud's Permanent Revolution', *New York Review of Books* 41, no. 9, pp. 34–38, and in *Other Minds* (1995), pp. 26–40.
—— (1994b) 'Addendum', *New York Review of Books* 41, no. 14, pp. 55–56, and in *Other Minds* (1995), pp. 41–44.
—— (1995) *Other Minds: Critical Essays 1969–1994* (collection of reviews, including 'Freud's Anthropomorphism' (1974), 'Freud's Permanent Revolution' and his 'Addendum' answering Grünbaum's response). New York: Oxford University Press.
—— (1998) 'Conceiving the Impossible and the Mind–Body Problem', *Philosophy* 73, no. 285, pp. 337–352. First given in London on February 18, 1998 as annual lecture for the Royal Institute of Philosophy.
Nichols, C. (1972) 'Science or Reflection: Habermas on Freud', *Philosophy of the Social Sciences* 2, no. 3, pp. 261–270.
Piaget, J. and Inhelder, B. (1969) *The Psychology of the Child*, trans. H. Weaver. London: Routledge & Kegan Paul. First published 1966 as *La Psychologie de l'enfant*. Paris: Presses Universitaires de France.
Popper, K. (1962) *Conjectures and Refutations*. London: Routledge & Kegan Paul.
Reiser, M. (1989) 'The Future of Psychoanalysis in Academic Psychiatry: Plain Talk', *Psychoanalytic Quarterly* 58, pp. 158–209.
Reppen, J. (ed.) (1985), *Beyond Freud: A Study of Modern Psychoanalytic Theorists*. Hillsdale, NJ: Analytic Press.
Ricoeur, P. (1970) *Freud and Philosophy*. New Haven, Conn. and London: Yale University Press.
Robinson, P. (1993) *Freud and his Critics*. Berkeley, Calif.: University of California Press.
Rorty, R. (1980) *Philosophy and the Mirror of Nature*. Oxford: Blackwell.
Sachs, D. (1989) 'In Fairness to Freud: A Critical Notice of *The Foundations of Psychoanalysis*, by Adolf Grünbaum', *The Philosophical Review* 98, no. 3, pp. 349–378.
Salmon, W. (1971) *Statistical Explanation and Statistical Relevance*. Pittsburgh, Pa.: University of Pittsburgh Press.
—— (2001) 'Explanation and Confirmation: A Bayesian Critique of Inference to the Best

Explanation', in G. Hon and S.S. Rackover (eds) *Explanation: Theoretical Approaches and Applications*. Dordrecht: Kluwer.

Sartre, J.P. (1958) *Being and Nothingness*, trans. H. Barnes. London: Methuen. First published 1943 as *L'Etre et le néant*. Paris: Librairie Gallimard.

Schapiro, M. (1968) 'The Apples of Cézanne', *Art News Annual* 34, pp. 34–53.

Scheffler, S. (1992) *Human Morality*. Oxford: Oxford University Press.

Schmidt-Hellerau, C. (2001) *Life Drive and Death Drive: Libido and Lethe*, trans. P. Slotkin. New York: Other Press. First published 1995 as *Lebenstrieb and Todestrieb, Libido und Lethe*. Stuttgart: Verlag Internationale Psychoanalyse.

Schüttauff, K., Bredenkamp, J. and Specht, E.K. (1997) 'Induzierte "Freudsche Versprecher" und zwangsneurotischer Konflikt', *Sprache und Kognition*, 16, pp. 3–13.

Searle, J. (1990) *Intentionality*. New York: Cambridge University Press.

Shevrin, H., Williams, W.J., Marshall, R.E., Hertel, R.K., Bond, J.A. and Brakel, L.A. (1992) 'Event-related Potential Indicators of the Dynamic Unconscious', *Consciousness and Cognition* 1, pp. 340–366.

Solms, M. and Saling, M. (trans. and eds) (1990) *A Moment of Transition: Two Neuroscientific Articles by Sigmund Freud*. New York: Karnac.

Solomon, D. (1994) 'Meyer Schapiro', *New York Times Magazine*, August 14, pp. 22–25.

Sorell, T. (1991) *Scientism: Philosophy and the Infatuation with Science*. London: Routledge.

Stephan, A. (1989) *Sinn als Bedeutung: Bedeutungstheoretische Untersuchungen zur Psychoanalyse Sigmund Freuds*. Berlin: Walter de Gruyter.

Stern, R. (ed.) (1987) *Theories of the Unconscious and Theories of the Self*. Hillsdale, NJ: Analytic Press.

Storr, A. (1986) 'Human Understanding and Scientific Validation', *Behavioral and Brain Sciences* 9, pp. 259–260.

Strawson, P. (1959) *Individuals*. London: Methuen.

Sulloway, F. (1979) *Freud, Biologist of the Mind*. New York: Basic Books; London: Burnett Books.

Taylor, R. (1979) 'Persons and Bodies', *American Philosophical Quarterly* 16, no. 1, pp. 67–72.

Thomä, H. and Kächele, H. (1987) *Psychoanalytic Practice*. Berlin: Springer-Verlag.

Vaughan, S. and Roose, S. (1995) 'The Analytic Process: Clinical and Research Definitions', *International Journal of Psycho-Analysis* 76, pp. 343–356.

von Eckardt, B. (1985) 'Adolf Grünbaum and Psychoanalytic Epistemology', in J. Reppen (ed.) *Beyond Freud: A Study of Modern Psychoanalytic Theorists*, pp. 353–403. Hillsdale, NJ: Analytic Press.

Walker, F. (1962) *The Man Verdi*. New York: Knopf.

Wollheim, R. (1959) *F.H. Bradley*. Harmondsworth and Baltimore, Md: Penguin.

—— (1984) *The Thread of Life*. Cambridge: Cambridge University Press; Cambridge, Mass.: Harvard University Press.

—— (1987) *Painting as an Art*. London: Thames & Hudson; Princeton, NJ: Princeton University Press.

—— (1993) *The Mind and its Depths*. Cambridge, Mass. and London: Harvard University Press.

Wollheim, R. and Hopkins, J. (eds) (1982) *Philosophical Essays on Freud*. Cambridge and New York: Cambridge University Press.

Zentner, M. (1995) *Die Flucht ins Vergessen: Die Anfänge der Psychoanalyse Freuds bei Schopenhauer*. Darmstadt, Germany: Wissenschaftliche Buchgessellschaft.

Index

Page numbers in **bold** indicate glossary definitions.